THE
BIBLE
AS A
WHOLE

Stephen H. Travis

 The Bible Reading Fellowship

Published by
Bible Reading Fellowship
Peter's Way, Sandy Lane West
Oxford OX4 5HG
ISBN 0 7459 3524 9
Albatross Books Pty Ltd
PO Box 320, Sutherland
NSW 2232, Australia
ISBN 0 7324 0952 7

First edition 1994
This edition 1996
10 9 8 7 6 5 4 3 2 1 0

Acknowledgments
Scripture quotations are taken from:

Holy Bible, New International Version,
copyright © 1973, 1978, 1984 by International
Bible Society. Used by permission of Hodder
and Stoughton Limited.

Revised English Bible copyright © 1989 by
permission of Oxford and Cambridge University
Presses.

A catalogue record for this book is available
from the British Library

Printed and bound in Finland

CONTENTS

About the author

Stephen Travis is vice-principal of St John's College, Nottingham, where he teaches the New Testament. He has written several books designed to relate the message of the Bible to life today, including *Getting to Know the New Testament* (Mowbray), *Introducing the Bible* (Lion) and *I Believe in the Second Coming of Jesus* (Hodder & Stoughton).

GETTING STARTED

How to use this book

What is the Bible? Not, as I once thought, a black book full of small print and obscure religious language. It is a whole collection of books which tell how God has made himself known to the human race and what is involved in responding to his love.

It deals with the big questions I really want to ask—What is the meaning of life? How can I know God? Is death the end? Can I make any sense of suffering? What makes a happy and stable society? How can I help to build a world that is safe for my children to grow up in?

It tackles such questions in a whole variety of ways. Among the books of the Bible there is history, songs, letters, humour, prophecy, love poems, laws, proverbs, reflections on the mysteries of life, parables, visions, prayers and much more. All of it, in one way or another, is 'inspired by God and is useful for teaching the truth, rebuking error, correcting faults and giving instruction for right living. Its purpose is that everyone who serves God may be fully qualified and equipped for every kind of good work' (2 Timothy 3:16–17).

The aims of this book

In this book I have three aims.

First, I want to introduce the habit of reading the Bible regularly and making its message our own. Its message is too important, too life-changing, to be left to chance. Each Bible passage selected is accompanied by comments designed to help the reader think about and act upon the biblical passage. In this way we can deepen our relationship with God and develop a Christian view on life and its challenges.

Secondly, the careful selection of passages from different parts of the Bible is intended to help the reader get a sense of how the different parts 'fit together'. Most people find the Bible's size daunting. 'I don't know where to begin,' they may say. Or, 'If I try to read it I get stuck in all those peculiar bits about sacrifices or wars or genealogies.' Or, 'I can't see what the Old Testament has to do with faith in Jesus.'

This book guides you through different sections of the Bible, helping you to travel on a journey of faith with the Israelites of the Old

Testament and with the followers of Jesus in the New Testament. It will explain how the story unfolds from the earliest times, and how God unfolded his purpose to his people.

Thirdly, the passages for reading are chosen so that in the course of the book the reader looks at many of the main themes of Christian belief and the main aspects of Christian discipleship. In this way the book will help you to be confident about what you believe and will offer guidance for Christian living.

I hope the book will be helpful in these three ways to people who have recently begun the journey of faith and are eager to discover more of what that journey is about. I also hope that it will prove a useful 'refresher course' for people who want to have another look at the foundations on which their lives are built.

What the book is, and what it is not

To choose 130 passages from such a big and richly varied book as the Bible is an almost impossible task. Other people would have made different choices. Everyone will take issue with some of my choices. The passages which I have chosen are included to try to meet the aims explained above.

This book is not, therefore, a collection of favourite passages, or famous passages. I have not chosen passages because they were easy or difficult to understand. I have chosen them to give readers a sense of the developing story of the Bible, and of the different kinds of material which can be found within it. So if your favourite Bible story is excluded, please forgive me! It can safely be left for another time.

There are several books of the Bible from which no passages have been chosen. This is not because they are less important but simply because I had to be selective. Rather than choose, say, two passages from each biblical book it seemed much more helpful for us to take examples from different parts of the Bible and read enough of them to get the feel of what they are saying.

The most obvious example of this is the Gospels. There are no readings from Matthew or Mark, and only one from John. But there are twenty passages from Luke—enough to give us a sense of what a Gospel is about and what the story of Jesus can mean for us. If we learn what to look for in Luke, we can go back to the other Gospels another time and get excited by learning from them also.

The book is not a discussion of who wrote the books of the Bible or when they were written or whether every detail can be accepted as 'true' or 'historical'. Those are important questions but they are not questions for now. I want people to appreciate what the Bible actually says and feel its impact on their lives before I want them to ask those other kinds of questions. However, where I think it directly helps our understanding of a passage I do comment on the date or the author or other issues of that kind.

I have not always organized the readings in the order in which they appear in our printed Bibles. It helps to get the sense better and to follow the story if we read the passages in chronological order. By that I mean not the order in which the biblical books were written (often we can only guess at that), but the order of the events which they report or the times to which they relate. How this works out will be obvious enough as you read, so I need say no more about it now. If you aren't sure about where to find a book in the Old Testament, the contents page at the beginning of your Bible will help you.

Why read the Old Testament?

I was leading a study group for some Christians who were keen to learn about the Bible. Looking around the room at the Bibles they had brought with them, I noticed that some of them had those big Bibles with floppy leather covers and tinted edges to the pages. It was immediately obvious from the tinted edges that the New Testament part of their Bibles was well used. The Old Testament part looked as though it had hardly been opened. Why?

People have many reasons for neglecting the Old Testament. 'It is long and forbidding.' 'It has been replaced by the New Testament, so we don't need it.' 'It tells of a God of judgment, very different from the New Testament's God.' 'It is full of rules about animal sacrifice, what you can and can't eat, and all kinds of other things that have no bearing on today's world.'

More than half of this book is taken up with readings from the Old Testament. Yes, many of the more difficult parts are excluded, because they are not the place to begin. But someone who claims to be interested in Jesus can hardly ignore the Bible which Jesus used, which guided his life and which is so often quoted in the New Testament.

The Old Testament includes ideas about God, about society and politics, about suffering and prayer and other aspects of life which the New Testament hardly touches on. The New Testament is silent on these matters not because they no longer matter but because they are taken as given by the early Christians. The Old Testament was their Scriptures and there was no need to repeat what they already had.

Of course the coming of Jesus changes our perspective on the Old Testament. The New Testament makes clear, for example, that the

Jewish food laws are not binding on Gentile Christians. But to regard the Old Testament as an ancient text which has little to say to Christians is to shut ourselves in to a narrow view of life. We are for ever in debt to the Jewish people to whom the living God revealed himself and from whose rich tradition came the saviour of the world.

I hope that the passages chosen from the Old Testament will persuade you that there are rich resources in it for developing Christian life and thought. You will find here the struggles, the questions, the hope and despair, the praises and prayers of a believing community. Don't be too eager to read them in a 'Christian' way. Try to understand them as they came first to their Hebrew readers long ago and feel yourself part of that believing community. The notes will then help you to relate them to life today.

Let me add one other note on Old Testament passages. Some of the ones selected are quite long. That is because they are stories, and stories aren't always short. It's a pity to break them up just for the sake of creating bite-sized chunks. We wouldn't read two pages of a novel and then put it down until tomorrow! I hope you will find that these passages are long enough to get into the story, but not *too* long as not to be manageable. If you find their length a problem, you can always spread them over two days.

Down to business

This book is designed for daily use. But there are no dates and no deadlines, so there is no need to feel guilty if you miss a day, or if you devise a different pattern of reading which suits you better! Here, then, are some practical suggestions about how to get the most out of it.

First, find a time and a place which suit you for regular reading. It may be in the morning when you get up, or late at night, or during a quiet period in the daytime. Choose a Bible which you feel comfortable using. Any version can be used with this book. I have in fact based it on the New International Version (referred to in the notes as NIV), but I have also kept an eye on the Revised English Bible (REB).

When we read the Bible, we need to have an attitude of *listening to God.* We expect to be taught, fed and guided by him as we read and think about what we have read. So *pray for God's guidance* as you read. Briefly ask him to show you through the reading something about himself, something about his love for you and about what he requires of you today.

Then *turn to the passage for the day.* Usually the Bible passage to be read is stated in the heading for that day's reading. If so, read the

10

Bible passage and see whether you feel that God is saying anything particular to you through it. Then read my comments, which aim to help with any difficulties in the passage and to suggest ways in which the passage may speak to our situation today. If God has spoken to you through the Bible passage before you read the comments, that's fine. My comments are there not to replace what the Bible says but to point you back to it, to help you grasp its significance for you. If you want to disagree with my comments, that's fine also!

Some days you will find that the Bible passage is not stated in the heading. In that case, read my opening comments which are designed to lead you into the Bible passage—sometimes, for instance, to give you some historical information which will help you understand it better. The instruction to read the Bible passage then comes after my opening comments, and is followed by further comments on the reading itself.

Where place names and dates are mentioned—particularly in the Old Testament—keep an eye on the maps and timecharts on pages 274–279. These will help you to get a sense that you are reading about real events involving real people. They will help you see how different biblical events relate to each other. Even to know that Moses came 250 years before David will turn out to be a useful piece of information!

When you have read and thought about the Bible reading and the comments, think how you can move from the reading into *prayer and action*. For some days' readings, the comments end with a specific prayer which you can use or a suggestion about what kind of action the reading might point to. On other days it is important to give yourself time to follow up the reading in whatever way you think is appropriate.

Some people find it helps to have a notebook in which they write down what they want to pray for, or what action they think God is pointing them to. The act of writing helps them not to leave their reading at the level of vague thoughts, but to translate it into specific prayer and action.

In prayer, you may want to thank God for showing you in the passage something about himself. You may need to come to him in confession for wrongdoing or wrong attitudes which the passage has exposed in you. (Reading the Bible can sometimes be painful, but the pain is always a way to to new beginning, a new discovery of God's grace.) You may want to pray for people who have come to mind because of what you have read. You may want to ask God to guide you about particular actions you should take because of what you have read.

The Bible is never meant simply to be read. Reading is of little value unless it leads to action. So try to find in each day's reading something which you can put into practice. It will not always be a particular thing you can do today which you did not do yesterday. Sometimes the reading will suggest general attitudes which God wants to become part of our make-up. It will take time for those attitudes to become 'second nature' to us. But gradually, by the help of God's Spirit within us, he will transform us so that we respond to issues and situations in a truly Christ-like way.

What then?

If you work through this book daily it will take you between four and five months. What happens after that? I hope very much that by then you will have come to appreciate the value of regular reading of the Bible in this way. It will be natural then to explore other parts of it which are not covered here.

Several publishers issue, at regular intervals, Bible reading notes which follow a similar pattern to the one used here—though usually guiding you through a whole biblical book stage by stage, rather than adopting the more selective approach of this book. In your church there is probably someone who acts as an agent for these Bible reading notes, and can supply them regularly to you if you ask.

You can find out about notes supplied by the Bible Reading Fellowship on page 280.

1

BEGINNINGS

Jesus, the centre of God's purpose

John 1:1–18

Imagine a world without words. For a moment it might seem attractive—no more arguments in the family, no more being shouted at by unfeeling bosses, no more empty promises of politicians. But it would quickly become a nightmare, because words express our deepest thoughts and feelings. If we can hear no one say to us, 'I love you,' our lives have little meaning. If those who love us cannot explain themselves to us, we can never really know them.

People have felt the same about God. Unless the creator of the world can somehow speak to us, we are in the dark. We cannot know him, we cannot see the point of life, we are like a raft drifting aimlessly on an endless ocean.

But in fact God has spoken. John knows how people of all times and places long for a sure word from their creator. So he begins his Gospel by showing how Jesus, whose story he is about to tell, is the climax of God's communication with the world.

He has spoken through *the created world* (verses 3–4). In the world we see reflected God's power, his greatness, his love of colour and variety, his infinite care for detail. Yet the world remains an ambiguous signpost to God. For in it we see also suffering and pain. It makes us not only adore God but also ask questions about him.

But he has spoken also through *the experience of the Jewish people*, represented here by Moses (verse 17) and by John the Baptist (verses 6–8, 15). This John (not the author of the Gospel) was the last of the line of Hebrew prophets whose role was to point forward to God's fuller revealing of himself in the future.

And now, finally and decisively, God has spoken through *his Son, Jesus* (verses 9–14, 18). He has taken upon himself our flesh and blood; he has exposed himself to our temptations. For in the end what we need is not just words or actions, but a person who will express to us the heart of God. All that we need to know of God and his plan for our lives we can see in Jesus, because he is 'the human face of God' (John Robinson).

Why has God gone to such lengths? To bring life in place of death, light in place of darkness (verses 4–5, 9). To bring people into a new kind of relationship with God. To enable us to become children who find our life and security not in a human decision but in the Father whose care and commitment to us is total and untiring (verses 12–13).

To say that 'the Word became flesh' is to say something very important about Jesus. Right through this astonishing passage John is suggesting that the man Jesus is closely connected with the way in which God has been acting and speaking since the world began (verses 1–3, 14). By affirming that the Word of the eternal God became the flesh of the man Jesus of Nazareth, John is setting Jesus in the context of God's eternal purpose.

John's message also says something very important about the world. If 'the Word became flesh', God has linked himself inseparably with the world. We cannot choose God and dismiss the world as of no importance. We cannot try to improve the world and dismiss God as irrelevant. God accepts no division between the 'spiritual' and the 'material'. God is not more concerned with the religious activity of his people than he is with science and politics, the world of work and the cry of a hungry child for bread.

To think about

Words from a Christmas sermon by Mark Frank (seventeenth century):

> The infinite greatness of this day becomes so little,
> eternity a child,
> the rays of glory wrapped in rags,
> heaven crowded into the corner of a stable,
> and he that is everywhere wants a room.

2
The world and its creator

Genesis 1:1—2:3

As soon as we begin to read the first chapter of the Bible we see where some of the language of John 1:1–18 comes from. We see that John

14

was deliberately echoing the first words, 'in the beginning ...'. We see God creating through his word—'and God said ...'—and we see the contrast between light and darkness (verses 1–5).

But so familiar is the fact that the Bible begins with the story of the world's creation that we rarely ask why this is so, or think how odd it is. Winston Churchill did not begin his *History of the English-speaking Peoples* with an account of the creation of the world. Yet the story of God's dealings with Israel begins in this striking way. Why? Because the fact that God made the world is his reason for being committed to its salvation. What he has begun, he will see through to the end.

People often argue about how the Genesis story is to be squared with modern science and the theory of evolution. But Genesis 1 is not about *how* the world was made, but about *God's intention* in making the world. It is not in competition with science. Science has its own contribution to make to our understanding of the origins of the world. The Bible has something to say about the beginnings of the world which science cannot say.

People may look at the world in many different ways. Some, for example, think that everything can in principle be explained in terms of scientific cause and effect: there is no room for a creator, and no meaning in existence apart from meaning we may make for ourselves. Others see the world as being of the same 'stuff' as God: divinity is attributed to nature itself and there is no God over and above nature. The Bible asserts that the world is distinct from God, and that it has value and meaning because it is made by God. The whole passage is full of implications of this great truth.

The passage tells the story of creation in seven days. Because it is not about how the world was made, we need not wonder about questions such as whether the days are meant 'literally', or why light appears on day one whereas the sun does not appear until the fourth day. Instead we can concentrate on what the chapter says about God's purpose in creation.

There is a regular pattern to the activities of each day. Each stage of creation has its origin in God's command—'And God said, "Let there be ..."'—and its conclusion in God's delight—'God saw that it was good'. (There seems to be no particular reason for omission of this last phrase on day two.)

Human beings tend to be most interested in their own place in God's creation. But most of the story is given over to the rest of the created order. Humanity is the climax of God's creative plan, but not the be-all and end-all. Only in verse 26 does the human race arrive on the scene.

What is meant by 'Let us make man in our own image, in our likeness'? Genesis 1:26–28 suggests three things. First, it means that God intends humanity to 'rule over' the rest of creation. He entrusts the world to our care and invites us to use its resources creatively. This does not mean we may exploit the world, turn forests into desert, make animal species extinct and pollute the atmosphere with the consequences of human extravagance. 'Ruling' is the role of a king, and in the Bible a king is expected to exercise power as God exercises power—with care for those committed to his charge.

Secondly, this 'ruling' is committed to humanity as a whole. It gives no authority to one particular group (rich nations, for example) to exploit the world's resources at the expense of other groups. Humans in community, not human individuals, reflect the image of God.

Thirdly, humans as male and female express God's image. In this way Genesis affirms that our sexuality is a part of God's good creation.

The passage ends with the creator's rest from his work. The people of Israel observed the sabbath as a day of rest because they believed in a God who is confident enough in his creative work to take a rest. They were declaring that life does not depend on our feverish activity to make ourselves secure by amassing possessions. There can be a pause in which life is given to us simply as a gift.

3

Humanity goes wrong   *Genesis 3*

In Genesis 2 the creation story is developed, with much more attention to God's purpose for the human race. There we read that God has called people to live in his world on his terms. Adam—his name simply means 'humankind'—has a *responsibility* to care for the garden (2:15). He has *permission* to enjoy its fruits (2:16). He is given *boundaries* beyond which he may not go: he may not eat from the tree of the knowledge of good and evil (2:17).

The story does not explain what the tree 'means'. It is a story, and must be allowed to convey its own power. We can no more explain it than we can explain a great painting by analysing the chemicals of which it is made, or Handel's *Messiah* by describing the wave-forms of the notes.

Chapter 3 tells of Adam and Eve's reaction to God's terms for human existence. It does not explain how evil came into human experience. It observes how evil is experienced. It does not say why the serpent takes the role of tempter (though the New Testament sees it as an agent of Satan, the devil—Revelation 12:9; 20:2). As a story, it asks simply to be listened to.

Verses 1–7 describe the temptation of Eve. If we ask why it is the woman who falls to temptation, we must remember that in the ancient world stories were told from the man's point of view. And he is looking for someone to blame (see verse 12)!

Notice how the tempting proceeds. First, the serpent invites Eve to question God's word: 'Did God really say…?' (verse 1). At the same time he distorts God's word, for God never had said, 'You must not eat from any tree in the garden' (see 2:16–17). And in the process God becomes an object of discussion instead of a provider and protector to be lovingly obeyed. In her reply Eve exaggerates the boundary which God has set by adding the idea that the tree may not be touched (3:3). Then the serpent invites a straight denial of what God has said: 'You will not surely die.' And he promises great gain from disobedience: 'Your eyes will be opened, and you will be like God…' (verse 5).

Step by step, the God who made humankind, who provided for them, gave them freedom to explore the world and gave boundaries for their security, has been turned into a killjoy. The responsibility and permission described in 2:15–16 have been set aside, and the secure boundary of 2:17 is now presented as an oppressive restriction. Freedom to express myself, freedom to assert my independence— these have become the goals of humanity. The writer of Genesis did not know that people around AD2000 would have magazines with titles like *Me* and *Self.* But he would not be surprised to be told.

In a sense, of course, the tempter was right. Adam and Eve do not die. Their eyes are opened (verse 7). Stepping over God's boundaries does offer something attractive, and that is why it is so tempting. Rarely do people pursue evil simply because they know it is evil. They pursue it because they see something which will be 'good' for them— freedom, power, wealth. What they lose in the process does not always appear immediately.

But they do lose. Verses 8–13 present the cross-examination by God. Notice how often in their replies the couple say 'I'. Having abandoned trust in God they are turned in on themselves. But now they must bear responsibility for the choices they have made.

The sentence is set out in verses 14–24. Life outside the garden (verses 20–24) suggests human existence without the caring presence of God. Verses 14–19 illustrate what this may involve. For example, there is pain and effort in work (verses 17–19). And in relations between men and women the equality and mutual support of chapters 1 and 2 is replaced by the tendency towards male domination (verse 16).

But even in this tragedy, the gentleness of God is present. He himself provides clothes for them (verse 21). And in the mysterious words of verse 15 the early Church found a promise of the coming of Christ, who would crush the power of the serpent and open afresh the way into God's presence (see Romans 16:20).

To think about

Sin is our refusal to be what we were created to be—sons of God, images of God. Ultimately sin, while seeming to be an assertion of freedom, is a flight from the freedom and the responsibility of divine sonship.

Thomas Merton

4

The flood: God's judgment on human evil
Genesis 6:5—7:24

Everyone knows the story of Noah and the flood. We all have pictures in our minds of the building of the ark, the animals going in two by two under Noah's fatherly direction, the rain falling and the floods rising. Yet a few moments' thought raises uncomfortable questions. Children ask, 'Didn't the cats chase the mice in the ark? What happened to the bodies of all the people who drowned? How could the sea go so high up the mountains?' Adults wonder, 'Can I believe in a God who devastates the world like that? Did anything like this ever happen? Or is it just a primitive fairy story?'

The story may reflect genuine distant memory of catastrophic flooding, perhaps at the end of the last great Ice Age around 10,000BC. But we need a new way of looking at it which breaks through the traditional assumptions. The story which everyone thinks is about God's power to destroy is also about God's anguish at human wrongdoing and about the possibilities of a new humanity. Let us notice four phases of the story.

First, God saw how great man's wickedness had become (6:5).

18

God had great hopes for his creation, as we saw in Genesis 1. But the world has refused to live as his creation. And so God makes the terrifying decision, 'I will wipe mankind, whom I have created, from the face of the earth...' (6:7). This expresses one of the constant themes of the Bible—that human wrongdoing leads to God's judgment. God cannot be indifferent to evil.

But how does he react to it? Vividly describing God in terms of human emotions, the writer shows how God feels about the corruption and violence which he sees. He is not like an angry tyrant but like a troubled parent, disappointed when a child ruins his life. The evil in human hearts troubles the heart of God (6:6). When the Bible speaks of God's judgment on men and women, it is speaking also about the pain God feels at our distortion of his purpose for his world.

The second phase begins when Noah appears on the scene (6:8). For judgment is not God's final word. Here is a man who embodies a new possibility for the world. His special role is described from both the divine and the human perspective. From God's viewpoint, Noah was special because God showed favour to him—he set his love upon him and chose him for a special task (6:8). From the human angle he was special because he was righteous (6:9). He stood out as different. He refused to go with the crowd. Like a chorus through the story, the writer underlines Noah's obedience to God (6:22; 7:5, 9).

Noah was the first of many individuals who, apparently single-handed, have been used by God to carry out his purpose and to make a crucial difference in the world. In these pages we shall read about Abraham, Moses, Elijah, Jeremiah, Mary the mother of Jesus and others who said 'Yes' to God's call. And the list goes on. Even today people famous and unknown are making a difference in the world simply by trying to obey God rather than taking the easy option. They have refused to be bullied into believing that what they do makes no difference.

So God's plan is revealed to Noah. He is to build an ark. The word does not normally mean a boat at all. It is a chest, a box for keeping things safe. The very choice of word underlines the purpose of the enterprise. Noah and his family, and representatives of the animal kingdom, are to be kept safe for the future. Another word—the first occurrence of the word 'covenant' in the Bible (6:18)—adds to this sense of promise for the future. Noah enters the ark not merely as a survivor but as the bearer of God's promise for a new beginning. The content of the covenant will be revealed in chapter 9. Meanwhile, when all were safely on board, 'the Lord closed the door on him' (7:16)—another vivid touch to highlight God's care for Noah's safety.

In the story humans and animals are saved together. The creation story reminded us that we are creatures alongside the animals and have responsibility for them. Now the flood story suggests that we are charged with ensuring the survival of animal species. Our future on the earth is bound up with theirs.

The third phase is the flood itself, bringing judgment on human evil and preparing the way for a fresh start.

To think about

In the New Testament Noah is remembered as a man of faith (Hebrews 11:7) and a preacher of righteousness in an ungodly world (2 Peter 2:5). His being saved 'through water' is seen as a symbol of Christian baptism (1 Peter 3:20–21).

5

Hope beyond disaster

Genesis 8:1—9:17

The fourth part of the flood story begins with the announcement that 'God remembered Noah' (8:1). This speaks of God's constant love, his timely intervention. All of us know times when we feel forgotten by others, and by God. We wonder whether our circumstances will ever change. The good news in this story is that God does not forget. He waits for the right time to act in a new, creative way. At this point the mood changes. All the energy of God is committed to making a fresh start with his creation.

We see Noah testing out when it will be possible to leave the ark. When the dove returns with an olive leaf (8:11) he knows that fresh vegetation is emerging from the earth to feed the animals. They can begin again to breed and spread across the earth (8:17).

Noah's reaction is to offer animals and birds in sacrifice (8:20). In the ancient world to kill an animal and burn it on an altar was a normal way to express thanks for deliverance from danger. It is just as well Noah had taken the precaution of bringing seven pairs of 'clean' animals (the species of animals used for sacrifice, 7:2). Otherwise his task of ensuring the survival of the different species would have been doomed from this point on!

So the story moves to its final phase. The God whose heart was filled with pain (6:6) now 'speaks in his heart' (8:21) and promises a new future. Humanity is still hopelessly inclined to evil (8:21), but there is hope in God's commitment to his world (8:21–22). The promise of regular seasons and harvests (8:22) does not abolish natural disasters. But it does limit them, so that the human family may overcome them by planning and cooperation (as in the story of Joseph, Genesis 41) and by generous compassion (as in the collection which Paul made for famine-stricken Christians in Judea, 2 Corinthians 8–9).

Now that God has resolved to stay with his world and not to give up on it, he develops both his instructions and his promise. His instructions reaffirm the command of Genesis 1 that humanity should preside over creation (9:1–7). But now people are permitted to use animals for food. And yet the command not to eat meat with the blood still in it is a way of saying that the animals still belong to God, who gave them life (9:3–4). There is no permission for the outrageous exploitation of animals and the hunting to the point of extinction practised today both by ruthless poachers in safari parks and by high-tech fishing fleets.

Though humanity continues to trouble God's heart (8:21), they are nevertheless made in his image (9:6). So the violence and murder which has brought about the flood is forbidden as an offence against God himself. The massacres which take place in wars, the cynical killing of political prisoners, the mindless violence against innocent bystanders in our own cities—all these are the acts of people who have forgotten that every human person bears the stamp of the creator and is uniquely precious to him.

After the instructions, the promise. God makes a 'covenant', a solemn commitment, to preserve life on the earth (9:8–11). Usually in the Bible a covenant is an agreement involving commitment from both sides—God's promise to bless his people and their promise to respond in obedience. Here the focus is all on God's promise.

And God provides a sign of the covenant he is making, a sign of his commitment to his world for all time (9:12–17). The interesting thing is that the rainbow is not said to be a reminder to *us* of what God has promised, but a reminder to *God himself* (9:15–16). It is like a memo on his desk, an alarm clock set to go off regularly, to remind him of what he has promised to do.

The flood story which began with God's decision to destroy the human race ends with God's decision never again to destroy the human race. It thus holds together the themes of judgment and mercy which lie at the heart of the biblical understanding of God. But its final word is a word of hope beyond judgment.

The seas have lifted up, O Lord,
the seas have lifted up their voice;
the seas have lifted up their pounding waves.
Mightier than the thunder of the great waters,
mightier than the breakers of the sea—
the Lord on high is mighty.

Psalm 93:3–4

6

The call of Abraham *Genesis 11:27—12:9*

From Genesis 3 to Genesis 11 the story is one of continual gloom. Even Noah and his family turned out to be a problem rather than a solution (9:18–29). How are God's hopes for his world ever going to be realized?

Nothing has prepared us for the shock of the new departure which the story now takes. God makes a fresh beginning by choosing a man to be the father of a race through whom he is going to renew the world.

This new story begins in Mesopotamia (Iraq), probably around 1900BC. A man called Terah moved from Ur near the mouth of the Euphrates to Haran further north. There was no word of God to guide him, no promise to keep him going. It was simply, perhaps, part of the migration of ancient peoples. Contrast that with the emphatic word to his son Abram, later to be called Abraham (12:1–3). To a single individual, God speaks a costly command and a promise loaded with hope. To respond to the command would be madness, if it were not for the promise.

The promise involves *a land* (12:1). Land means home, space, security, prosperity. Only, perhaps, when we see refugees of war on our TV screens do we begin to realize what it means for us to live securely in a land.

The promise involves *descendants* (12:2). Immediately we are struck by the contradiction with the painful statement of 11:30. How can Abraham be the father of a great nation when he isn't the father of anyone? His family has reached a dead end.

22

The promise involves *blessing for all nations* (12:3). God does not choose Abraham for his own sake, but as a way of bringing blessing to the world. All who seek blessing from Abraham's God will find it. All who refuse it will lose it.

Abraham heard the promise and obeyed the command. And so he became not only the father of the Jewish people but also the first of all those who risk everything in obedience to the call of God. He discovered beforehand the truth of Jesus' words, 'Whoever wants to save his life will lose it, but whoever loses his life for me and for the gospel will save it' (Mark 8:35).

Why should anyone take such a risk? There is no reason to do so, except for the character of the God whom Abraham discovers. The story invites us to reflect on God and his call to us.

God is a God who speaks. When the Bible reports God's speaking it does not normally explain how such messages are communicated. It may not mean that God spoke in the past through any different method from the way he speaks to people now. If modern Christians say, 'I felt the Lord was speaking to me that day,' there may be many different ways in which they have sensed God challenging and guiding them. But whatever the method used by God to convey his message, the Bible's vivid statement that 'God said . . .' affirms his intention to communicate with humankind.

God makes new beginnings out of old situations. In our scientific age we have learnt to think that the world is predictable. We easily feel as though we are locked into a treadmill world, like the hamster going round and round in its cage. The story of Abraham invites us to believe that God has the power and the will to change our situations, to create something new out of nothing.

The life of faith is a journey, an adventure. If we believe in this kind of God, then it is all right to set out on an unknown journey because he can be trusted to see us through. It is all right abandoning security and familiar territory because he has new things for us to discover which can only be discovered by taking the risk of faith. As Christians, we are called to 'follow Jesus'. And you cannot follow anyone by standing still.

So Abraham and Sarah journey into what was later called Palestine. From the north they travel through Shechem, Bethel and Ai—already ancient settlements before their time—and onward to the Negev, the dry area south-west of the Dead Sea (12:4–9).

They are in the land but do not yet possess it, for the Canaanites are there (12:6). How is this land, already occupied by a race with no understanding of Abraham's God, to become the home of his descendants? He doesn't know. His calling is simply to live among them and to worship the God who has called him. He is to express God's presence and let the promised blessing be there for any who are open to discover it.

7
God's covenant with Abraham

Chapters 12–14 show Abraham and Sarah living their faith in the real world. To save his own life Abraham deceives the Egyptian Pharaoh, telling him that Sarah is his sister. He is involved in arguments about land with his nephew Lot. He wins a pitched battle against local kings to rescue Lot and his family who have been taken hostage. He is certainly no pious saint, but a man like us who has to work out his faith among the strains and confusions of life.

But now we see him confronting again his basic dilemma.

Read Genesis 15

Despite God's promise and Abraham's faith, Sarah's barrenness remains. How do you trust God when the evidence is against you? How long can can you wait for an answer before you give up, concluding that you misunderstood the promise? In verses 1–6 Abraham wrestles with this problem in response to a vision from God.

God speaks to Abraham: 'Don't be afraid, I am your shield. Your reward will be very great' (verse 1; this translation is preferable to the NIV). To one who has just been in a battle, the picture of God as a protecting shield is reassuring. But the mention of reward, which must refer to the promise of land and descendants, only sharpens the problem.

So Abraham protests (verse 2–3). 'What kind of reassurance is that, when I have no heir and the only person who can inherit my property is an adopted slave-boy?'

The voice of God is heard again (verse 4). 'Believe me, your heir will be a son of your own flesh.' And God 'took him outside' and showed him the stars in the night sky. 'Your descendants will be as numerous as that.'

'And Abraham put his faith in the Lord, who reckoned it to him as righteousness' (verse 6). Abraham who in verse 2 could only protest at God's promise is now full of faith. What has made the difference? God hasn't produced any more arguments to persuade him. It is not reason, but revelation, which has changed Abraham's attitude.

And so it is sometimes in our experience. We move from doubt to faith not because we have been convinced by arguments but because God has touched our lives and awakened trust within us. This does not mean that reason and argument are unimportant. But the deepest things in life are not decided by rational argument. I am persuaded that someone loves me not by a list of arguments but by my experience of her love.

Abraham has given up depending on what he can see and control for himself and has put his future in God's hand. Through his faith he is declared to be pleasing to God ('credited with righteousness', verse 6). But Abraham's faith was not a human achievement which he arrived at on his own. It was a response to God's grace, his generous revealing of himself and his love. That is why, for Paul, Abraham's experience is the great foreshadowing of Christian response to the grace of God (Romans 4:1–8).

God's renewal of his promise to Abraham is underlined by the making of a covenant (verse 18). The strange ritual described in verses 9–11, 17 was an ancient way of binding two people or groups together in solemn commitment to each other. Though to us it may seem entirely mysterious, we perhaps need reminding that the activity of God is mysterious, and we can never control it or fully understand it.

The covenant (verses 18–21) expresses God's faithful commitment to provide a land for his people. The Israelites never did settle in all the territory described here. But under Kings David and Solomon, nearly a thousand years after Abraham, they did control it all by conquest.

But the dream of verses 12–16 warns Abraham that he will not himself live to see the promise of a land come true. Israel's journey will be sidetracked into Egypt before the nation comes to settle in the Promised Land. The biblical account does not hide the fact that faith involves waiting, often for a long time. This is a message not easily received in our culture, where the credit card slogan, 'Take the waiting out of wanting,' sums up a whole attitude to life.

Faith is not a tap for turning on instant miracles. It is trust in a faithful God, who knows what he is doing when he asks us to wait.

8
The ultimate test

There are still more twists and turns to Abraham's story. Unable to wait any longer, he and Sarah agree that he should have a child by her servant Hagar. That would be better than no child at all! So Ishmael, to whom the Arabs trace their ancestry, is born (Genesis 16). God repeats his promise of a child to Abraham and Sarah, and circumcision is introduced as the sign of God's special relationship with Abraham and his descendants. It is at this point in the story (Genesis 17) that the original names Abram and Sarai are changed to Abraham (which means 'father of many') and Sarah ('princess').

At last 'the Lord did for Sarah what he had promised. Sarah became pregnant and bore a son to Abraham in his old age' (Genesis 21:1–2). We can imagine the devotion lavished upon this miracle child by adoring parents. And then the horror of God's intolerable demand . . .

Read Genesis 22:1–19

The story is both beautiful and savage, poignant and perplexing. The problem is not only that Abraham is being asked to kill his precious son—which would contradict all human sensitivity as well as the ruling of Genesis 9:5–6. But Isaac is the child of promise, without whom God's plan of making a great nation will come to nothing. In Genesis 12 Abraham said goodbye to his past. Is he now with a blow of his knife to say goodbye to his future also? Have all his struggles been for nothing? It doesn't make sense. God seems to be contradicting himself.

It is a mistake to try to explain the story so that we can somehow feel comfortable with it. Our own experiences of the contradictions of faith can help us enter into Abraham's dilemma.

God's purpose is to *test* Abraham's faith—not to catch him out but to strengthen him for the continuing journey of faith. He wants to know whether Abraham's devotion is to God's promises and God's gifts or to God himself. That is a question which comes sooner or later to all who claim to believe in God: once I have received something for which I longed and prayed, do I become content with the gift rather than devoted to the God who gave it? But Abraham doesn't know that God is testing him. To him there is only puzzlement at what God seems to be saying to him and anguish at the danger to his son.

At least, that is what we presume. But the narrative itself does not tell us what went on inside Abraham. It tells us only that he obeyed. For that is what the narrator wants us to think about. As in Genesis 12 (contrast the stories in between!) the old man's response is wholehearted and immediate. The character of his faith is brought out in what follows.

Abraham was willing to give up what was most dear to him, because nothing is as dear as God himself.

He obeyed even when he could not see how God's plan would work out. He did not ask to see the end from the beginning. He trusted God to provide even when he did not know how this could happen (verse 8). From the other side of this experience—but only from the other side—he could see that God's intention was to bless him and enrich his faith. And he could give the place a name which would for ever declare that 'the Lord will provide' (verse 14).

If we only had this story about Abraham, we might say that his faith was an unquestioning faith. And we might conclude that unquestioning faith is a dangerous thing when it attributes to God outrageous demands and obeys them whatever the cost. But we have seen that Abraham's trust in God was not always unquestioning or heroic. And so in this episode, for all its difficulties, we can see an example of someone who grows through his struggles and risks everything for the sake of obedience to God.

In this way Abraham foreshadowed Jesus, who risked everything in obedience to God. Paul has the story of Abraham and Isaac in mind when he writes, 'He who did not spare his own Son, but gave him up for us all . . .' (Romans 8:32). Abraham in the end did not have to go through with the sacrifice of his son. For Jesus there was no last-minute reprieve. But still, like Abraham, he trusted that somehow God would fulfil his promise. The pattern of testing and providing in Genesis 22 becomes the pattern of crucifixion and resurrection in the Christian gospel.

To think about

How does the writer to the Hebrews describe the faith of Abraham (Hebrews 11:8–19)?

9
Joseph the dreamer

When Sarah died Abraham bought a field with a cave near Hebron in which to bury her (Genesis 23). This, the first piece of property in

Canaan actually owned by Abraham, was a sign of the 'possession of the land' which was God's goal for his family. The promise of descendants was fulfilled in Abraham's son Isaac and in his son Jacob. Now Jacob had twelve sons, and the eleventh of those was Joseph, whose story fills the last part of the book of Genesis.

It is a dramatic and deeply satisfying story. A spoilt, conceited boy escapes death at the hands of his jealous brothers, makes good in a foreign land and is finally reconciled to his family. Behind it all is the hidden hand of God, moving forward his purpose for his people.

Read Genesis 37

We are plunged straight into family conflict. The scene is repeated often enough in human experience. The elderly Jacob dotes on his young son and spoils him (verse 3). Joseph feels resentful that his elder brothers have established their position in life and tells tales about them (verse 2). The brothers begrudge Jacob's favouritism towards Joseph and are full of hate for their younger brother (verse 4). How can God's hopes for his people survive such destructive conflict?

The dreams only make matters worse (verses 5–11). Not surprisingly, the implication that Joseph will reign over the brothers meets with their seething hostility. He is trying by an underhand way to threaten their position in the family 'pecking order'! Jacob, too, is alarmed (verse 10). But he is not ready to squash the dream. He will wait and see (verse 11).

There is no mention of God in this narrative. But as the story unfolds, the dreams will turn out to be his way of being involved in it. Joseph may be spoilt and arrogant, but that will not stop God using him. God's plan is hidden in those dreams.

Dreams can express the hopes of the powerless. They provide a vision of a way of living which lies beyond present possibilities. We often recall Martin Luther King's words, 'I have a dream that my four little children will one day live in a nation where they will not be judged according to the colour of their skin but by the content of their character.... I have a dream today.' That Christian vision of a nation living as God meant it to live opened the possibility for a different future. It kept him going when things got tough and dangerous.

But where there is no such 'dream', nothing happens. People remain locked in the past, closed to new possibilities. The dreams of the young for a different kind of world, or a different kind of church, may sound unrealistic or threatening to their more world-weary elders. But such dreams need to be heard and cherished. They may express God's hopes for the future.

Finding grazing land for flocks often demanded travel over large distances, as it still does for the Bedouin. Joseph's journey north along the hilly ridge of central Canaan to find his brothers could have taken three or four days (verses 12–17).

In the next section (verses 18–31) the brothers' jealousy turns into drastic action. Reuben, the eldest, knows the seriousness of murder and feels responsible, but cannot stop their evil intent. Judah persuades them that they can avoid the taint of murder and make a profit in the process. So a group of travelling merchants becomes the means of Joseph's life being saved. (In verse 28, 'Ishmaelites' is a general term for the Israelites' nomadic cousins; 'Midianites' were a specific group among them.)

The final scene shows the grief of Jacob (verses 32–35). Nothing— not even the mock-grief of his sons—can comfort him. How else can a parent feel about the loss of a dear son at the age of seventeen? So much hope, so much promise brought to nothing.

Verse 36 closes the episode, and at the same time gives us a clue that there is more to come.

10

The integrity of Joseph— and of God

Genesis 39

We now meet Joseph in the home of one of Pharaoh's officials. For the first time his dependence on God, and God's care of him, is stated (verse 2). And God's blessing reaches not just to Joseph himself, but to Potiphar's whole household and all his enterprises. Potiphar knows he can be trusted and gives him a position of responsibility (verses 3–6).

It is an encouraging picture of how a person of godly integrity can influence his surroundings and hold the respect even of those who do not share his faith or his values. Sometimes we are tempted to think that all we can manage is to preserve our faith in a hostile world. Joseph's story challenges us to make a positive contribution at work and in society, bringing a Christian perspective to everything in which we are involved.

But Joseph's integrity is to be tested in a quite different way (verses 7–20). Notice how the woman—whose name we are never told—turns up the temperature as the story develops. Infatuated with him, she tries the enticing invitation (verse 7). Not put off by his refusal, she attempts to wear down his defences, constantly reopening the question which he has closed (verse 10). Then comes the opportunity to trap him, but he springs the trap (verses 11–12). Finally admitting the failure of her scheming, she accuses him of her own crime (verses 13–20).

We need not presume that Joseph is unmoved by the woman's attention. But he resists the temptation to surrender to her wiles. But think of his dilemma. Loyalty both to his master and to his God require that he resists her. But if he refuses to do what she wants, she has the power to get him into deep trouble. And so she does.

The reasons which Joseph gives for refusing her (verses 8–9) are the same reasons that another man might give for yielding to her. Another might say, 'The boss has left me to do as I please within the house. So what's the harm in saying yes to her, just this once?' But Joseph calls adultery by its proper name: 'How could I do such a wicked thing and sin against God?'

In a society bombarded with sexual imagery and obsessed with sexual self-expression, the pressures are all around us. 'Why need you be different from all the other teenagers?' 'If you don't come away with me for the weekend there will be no promotion for you.' 'What can be wrong about making each other happy?' And the old-fashioned values of faithfulness, trust and loyalty—without which family and society disintegrate—are traded in for the short-term gains of self-expression and self-fulfilment.

Joseph's example of moral integrity can guide us not only in sexual matters. The pressure to compromise comes to us in many guises. A businessman was offered a deal which would have brought his company much-needed income at a difficult time. But the legality of it was questionable. He refused, strengthened by the fact that he had been looking at this passage in a Bible study group the previous evening.

For all his integrity, Joseph lands up in prison. Death would have been a normal penalty for the crime of which he was accused. Perhaps Potiphar had a sneaking suspicion that his wife was not telling the whole truth.

But God has not forgotten him. Notice how verses 20–23 mirror verses 1–6. 'The Lord was with Joseph' (verses 2, 21, 23). And 'he showed him kindness' (verse 21). This word 'kindness' or 'faithfulness' or 'steadfast love' is one of the great words of the Old Testament, denoting God's unswerving commitment to the care of his people. So just as Potiphar had trusted Joseph to control his household, the prison governor put him in charge of the other prisoners.

This chapter, then, places Joseph's experience of life in the world (verses 7–20) in the context of his experience of God (verses 1–6, 21–23). We are tempted to keep these things apart. There are Christians who live 'in the Spirit' and do not engage with the tough issues of human experience in society. There are Christians who live 'in the world' and are inclined to think of prayer and worship as not being 'where the action is'. Neither attitude is a true reflection of the God who is Lord of all life. Joseph's story invites us really to rely on God and really to engage with the world.

11

Pharaoh's dreams and Joseph's promotion

In prison, Joseph has been dealing in dreams once again, interpreting accurately the dreams of fellow-prisoners. In accordance with their dreams, the chief cupbearer has been restored to Pharaoh's favour, whilst the chief baker has been hanged (Genesis 40). The stage is set for Joseph's reappearance.

Read Genesis 41

Verses 1–8 portray Pharaoh's problem. He has been dreaming too, and all his advisers have failed to deliver an interpretation. Even a great empire is limited in its power to understand and control its problems. And since Pharaoh derives his power from his ability to harness the Nile's water to bring life and fertility to the country, any dream which calls in question the land's fertility is deeply disturbing.

In verses 9–36 Joseph interprets the dream and proposes a solution. Notice the confidence of Joseph's response to Pharaoh's dilemma. But it is a confidence in God, who is giving a glimpse of the future so that precautions can be taken (verse 16). So confident is he that he doesn't wait to hear Pharaoh's reaction to his interpretation of the dream but rushes straight on to how the crisis should be dealt with (verses 33–36).

There is no hint that Joseph sees himself as the one to be chosen as Minister of Agriculture and Food Distribution, but God knows. Pharaoh, faced with a problem he can't handle, gladly puts Joseph in charge of the whole operation and even admits the power of Joseph's God (verses 37–40).

So the boy who only just escaped death at the hands of his brothers and only just escaped from an Egyptian prison is now the second most important person in the world. His dream of ruling (Genesis 37:7, 9) has come true.

Verses 46–57 round off this narrative and prepare for what follows. Notice the emphasis in verses 46–49 on the total success of his policy. The names of his children (verses 50–52) allude to the two sides of his experience. He can now forget the painful past, and look forward to a fruitful future.

Since Egypt was was irrigated by the Nile whilst neighbouring areas such as Palestine were watered by rainfall, it was rare for harvests to fail in both places at the same time. But that is what now happens (verses 54–57). Universal disaster is avoided by the efforts, under God, of one man.

We see in this chapter how God can create new possibilities for the future when human leaders are confused and powerless to bring about change. Throughout the Bible he shows himself to be a God of new beginnings, who meets a dead end with the power of resurrection. That is why, when the politicians seem helpless in the face of national and international crises, the solution lies not simply in finding different politicians. We are called to pray, and to go on praying, that God will give wisdom to our leaders and that he will himself bring change.

But God normally acts with human cooperation, not without it. So Joseph is an example of someone who makes himself available for the fulfilling of God's plans in a nation's life. He acts with wisdom, integrity and compassion for the people, and he doesn't hide the fact that his guidance and his motivation comes from God.

Most of us are relieved that we don't have Joseph's influence or responsibility. But we also often feel that our actions are pointless because we cannot see how our efforts can change the world. Compared with people in his position, what we can achieve seems so trivial, like trying to empty Loch Ness with a teaspoon. But it is never trivial to live in integrity and obedience before God. One word of encouragement to a young person, one letter to a Member of Parliament, one act of support to a single parent, can make a difference. Our calling is to live as God's representatives in society, whether our sphere of influence is great or small.

For prayer

Pray for political leaders, that they may serve the people with God-given wisdom.

12

Joseph's brothers go to Egypt

The story now marches towards its conclusion. It can be read and enjoyed with little comment from me. I will simply link together the sections which have been selected, and draw attention to the key points.

Read Genesis 42

The scene changes to Jacob and his family in Palestine. Once again the promise which God had made to Abraham is under threat. If the famine kills Jacob's family (verse 2), the promise is finished. So the journey to reconciliation with Joseph is set in motion.

Observe how the main characters in the story are portrayed.

Joseph is something of a puzzle. His words and actions may seem to us small-minded and vengeful. Why does he call his brothers spies (verse 9), put them in prison (verse 17), and take Simeon as a hostage (verse 24)? Why does he play tricks with them by putting back in their bags the silver they had brought to pay for the grain (verse 25)? Is he being spiteful, or playing games for the fun of it? Or does he perhaps understand his brothers better than we do, and know what is necessary if there is to be genuine reconciliation?

Certainly we should notice that, although Joseph seems to be 'getting his own back' on his brothers by tantalizing them, there is a genuine affection for them (verse 24). And his first thought of keeping all but one in custody is replaced by his keeping only Simeon (verses 16–19). Sending back the silver was an enigmatic act rather than a vengeful one. If vengeance had been his real motive he might have filled their bags with sand rather than with grain! Actually, he is working on a plan to bring the whole family together, but he cannot reveal it yet.

The brothers unknowingly begin to fulfil Joseph's dream of the corn-sheaves and the heavenly bodies (Genesis 37:7, 9): they bow down to Joseph (verse 6).

Inwardly they are anxious and guilty, trapped by their own past. At last their wrongdoing is catching up with them, and they know it (verse 21). As often happens, their guilt turns into accusation of each other (verse 22). But they are beginning to see where they stand before God (verse 28). At last they understand that evil has its pay-off. No one gets away with it in the end.

Perhaps Joseph knows this too, and knows that if there is to be genuine restoring of family relationships there must first be genuine repentance for the wrong that has been done. His policy may be unusual, but its effectiveness is seen in the way his brothers are beginning to change.

Jacob is the other main character. (His alternative name Israel—see verse 5—was given to him in Genesis 32:28 and 35:10. It thus became the name of the nation which traced its ancestry to him.) Despite his age, he is the one with a clear vision of what needs to be done (verses 1–2). Though nothing has been said, he lives with the suspicion that the disappearance of Joseph was no mere accident and refuses to entrust Benjamin to the care of his other sons (verse 4).

When the brothers come back from Egypt with their story and without Simeon, he is overcome with anxiety. His sons have deprived him of Joseph. Now Simeon is gone too. One more tragic loss, and he will die of grief (verses 36–38).

_13_
Benjamin is brought to Joseph

Genesis 43

Continuing famine requires desperate measures. Judah prevails upon his father Jacob to allow Benjamin to go to Egypt under his care (verses 1–10). For Jacob knows that, according to the terms reported by his sons, the ruler of Egypt will not release food until he has seen the youngest brother. And without food Benjamin and the whole family will perish. Jacob must risk losing Benjamin in order to save him.

Jacob hovers between resignation to disaster and faith in God's protection. 'If I am bereaved, I am bereaved,' sounds as though he has surrendered to fate. Yet he takes comfort in an old name for God: 'May El Shaddai (God Almighty) grant you mercy before the man' (verse 14). With this name God had reassured Abraham of his faithfulness towards this family (Genesis 17:1–2). So Jacob dares to trust that God's faithfulness will find a way through the present crisis.

On arrival at Joseph's home the brothers fear the worst. Being nomadic herdsmen, they are a bit out of their depth when confronted by the power and wealth of Egypt. They are even frightened that Pharaoh's right-hand-man, like some small-time tribesman, might have designs on their donkeys (verse 18).

The heart of this chapter is the bringing together of Joseph and Benjamin (verses 16, 29–30). Jacob's prayer that God Almighty would have mercy (verse 14) is answered by Joseph's prayer for Benjamin: 'God be gracious to you, my son' (verse 29). Joseph is deeply moved by the sight of his younger brother (verse 30). But it is not time yet to reveal his identity.

When food is served Joseph eats separately from his brothers (verse 32). This is probably not for social reasons but because the Egyptians' believed that foreigners would (in a religious sense) defile the food. It is similar to the later Jewish refusal to eat with Gentiles.

The meal (verse 32–34) only increases the suspense for the brothers. How does this stranger know precisely the order of their ages (verse 33)? And why does he show such favour to Benjamin (verse 34)? Yet the secret remains undiscovered.

In chapter 44 (which we are omitting here), Joseph's identity remains hidden. He continues to play games with his brothers. This time he orders his steward to hide his silver cup in Benjamin's sack, allows the brothers to set off on their homeward journey, and then tells the steward to give chase, to find the cup and accuse them of stealing (Genesis 44:1–13). When they are all brought back to Joseph he declares that because of the 'crime' Benjamin must become his slave (verses 14–17). At this Judah pleads that Benjamin be spared, lest their father's grief should reach breaking point, and asks that he himself, rather than Benjamin, should submit to slavery (Genesis 44:18–34).

Now Joseph can bear the suspense no longer. The brothers who had sold him for twenty pieces of silver have resisted the temptation to preserve their own freedom by abandoning Benjamin. They have learnt their lesson. The stage is set for the climax of the drama.

The great reunion

The story has told of Joseph's daring dream, the brothers' betrayal, the fall and rise of Joseph in Egypt, the relief of famine, the awkward encounters between Joseph and his brothers. And now comes the grand reunion.

The moment of disclosure is too intimate, too emotional for Egyptian eyes and ears. Joseph wants to share it with his brothers alone (verses 1–2).

It is hardly surprising that the brothers are frightened as well as shocked (verse 3). After all, how do they know what Joseph is going to do next? Maybe he is going to exact a terrible revenge for what they did to him so long ago? Certainly his trickery since they came to Egypt has not encouraged them to have confidence in him. But Joseph's speech (verses 4–13) contains the seeds of a new future. Here are the key features of what he says.

First, he sees God acting through what has happened (verses 5, 7–9). Perhaps Joseph himself has not been conscious of this until this moment of reunion. But now he can look back on experiences which were frightening, negative and meaningless, and see that God has used them for good. His removal to Egypt had resulted in deliverance from famine for Egyptians and Hebrews alike. For us, this is not a reason to pretend that tragic events are not tragic. But it is an invitation to see that ultimately God is not defeated by human failure and destructiveness. He has a way of picking up the threads and weaving them into his tapestry.

Secondly, it is because God is at work that a new beginning is possible.

The dream that Joseph would rule over his family has come true. But it doesn't matter any more, because God has brought the family together and their relationships are transformed. The past is left behind as a new future is opened up. The new situation means the end of the brothers' guilt (verse 5), the father's grief (verses 9–11), Joseph's urge to dominate—for God has given him the power to rule for a more creative purpose (verses 5–11). Providing has become more important than dominating (verse 11). Reconciliation is complete (verses 14–15). In our experience also, it is when we are enabled to see that a different kind of future is possible that we are given the power to let go of past grudges and hatreds. But we do not create the new situation. We receive it from God, who has been working in us and around us to make it possible.

Thirdly, Joseph enables the whole family to come together, as he urges his brothers to bring Jacob to live in Egypt so that they may all be saved through the famine. This secures the survival of the family and of God's promise to Abraham.

In verses 16–20 Joseph's plan for his family receives Pharaoh's enthusiastic backing—a measure of Egypt's gratitude for Joseph's contribution to the nation. And so (verses 21–28) the brothers go back, laden with gifts, to fetch Jacob. His first reaction on hearing the news is shock. For over twenty years he has believed his favourite son was dead. It is too good to be true. But the impossible has happened. 'My son Joseph is still alive' (verse 28). Grief turns to joy. A father has all he could wish for.

Genesis 46–50 tell of Jacob's journey to Egypt with all his dependents, his tearful reunion with Joseph, the family's settling in the region of Goshen, Jacob's final blessing of his sons, his death and his burial in the family tomb near Hebron, and finally the death of Joseph.

The musical *Joseph and the Amazing Technicolor Dreamcoat* is an exciting re-telling of Joseph's adventures. Its one flaw is that it manages to tell the whole story without a mention of God. It tells a biblical story and totally misses the biblical perspective. For the whole point of this narrative has been that Joseph is not left alone, his experiences do not happen by chance. They involve the actions of an unseen but caring God who is patiently working out his plan for Joseph, his family and ultimately through them for the whole world. Take away that perspective, and you take away the only sure ground of hope, the only key to the meaning of life.

To think about

The New Testament's comment on this providential care of God through the difficult and puzzling experiences of life is Paul's words to the Christians at Rome: 'We know that in all things God works for the good of those who love him, who have been called according to his purpose' (Romans 8:28). As you look back on your own experience, can you see this principle at work?

The call of Moses

The book of Exodus picks up the story some four hundred years after Joseph's family settled in Egypt. Times have changed. 'A new pharaoh, who did not know about Joseph, came to power in Egypt' (Exodus 1:8). And the Israelites' life in Egypt, which had begun as deliverance from famine, became the oppression of slave-labour on Pharaoh's building and agricultural programmes (Exodus 1:11–14).

To limit their population growth Pharaoh ordered Hebrew male babies to be drowned (Exodus 1:22). But one baby was hidden by his mother in a basket among the reeds growing at the edge of the Nile. He was found by Pharaoh's daughter, who felt sorry for him and brought him up. She named him Moses (Exodus 2:1–10). Like Joseph's narrow escape from death at his brothers' hands, this turn of events is loaded with hope for Israel's future.

When he had grown up Moses killed an Egyptian whom he saw beating a Hebrew, fled the country eastwards and settled in the desolate land of Midian where he became a shepherd (2:11–22). But God had other plans for him.

Read Exodus 2:23—3:22

In response to the cries of the Israelites (2:23), God 'heard their groaning', 'remembered his covenant', 'looked on the Israelites' and 'was concerned about them' (2:24–25). He knows what his people are going through. So what will he do about it?

Enter Moses. He has brought his sheep to Mount Horeb (3:1; Horeb is traditionally identified with Mount Sinai). In the midst of his ordinary tasks, he is confronted by a vision of God.

'The angel of the Lord' (3:3) is a being not clearly distinguished from God himself. It is an Old Testament way of referring to God's acting and revealing himself in the world. Notice how the 'angel' of verse 3 becomes simply 'God' in verse 4. So here we have a description, vivid yet mysterious, of God's making himself known to Moses. At first Moses is simply curious: this is hardly what he expected when he set out with his sheep to find pasture! But curiosity leads to call. He hears his name (verse 4).

The account of Moses' call is moved forward by three short statements from his lips. In verse 4 he says, '*Here I am.*' He is ready to listen. What he hears overwhelms him as he becomes aware that this really is the living God, who has guided the destiny of his ancestors (verses 5–6). He hears also promise: God is going to rescue his people from their sufferings and bring them into the land of the Canaanites (verses 7–8). But Moses hears also a command: 'Go. I am sending you' (verses 9–10). God will not act on his own, but through a human agent. He accepts the risk and the complications of working *with* humans, because only in this way can he bring people into genuine liberty and maturity.

The command provokes another word from Moses: '*Who am I?*' (verse 11). Deliverance for the Israelites sounded a good idea. But now that the job description has been outlined he is understandably reluctant. After all, where is the wisdom in telling a man who fled from one Pharaoh (2:15) to go back and confront another? He is full of self-doubt. His earlier sense of awe before this mysterious God now gives way to questioning.

God's response is simple and decisive: 'I will be with you' (verse 12). God takes Moses' worries seriously. Moses' questioning leads him to a greater awareness of God and his resources. Unthinking or unquestioning acceptance of what we are told is not necessarily the way to maturity or to effectiveness in the service of God. Through our doubting, arguing and asking questions, God can lead us into further insight.

The promise of God's presence is not accompanied by a sign which will prove its genuineness immediately (verse 12). If the truth of everything were proved in advance, what would be the place of faith? But by the time Moses stands again on Mount Sinai (see Exodus 19–20), he will know that God really has sent him. So it is often in our experience. The path which seems very uncertain when we set out is seen, when we look back later, really to be the way of God for us.

But Moses has another question: '*Who are you?*' (verse 13). Having been away so long, he is not known to most of the Israelites. To establish his credentials with them he must be able to name the God for whom he speaks. God's reply is mysterious and difficult to translate (verse 14). Most likely it means, 'I will be who I am,' or, 'I am who I will be.' The very name of the God of Israel means that he will be for ever what he now is: he is committed to his people for ever.

There is an important point here. This word translated 'I am who I will be' underlies the Hebrew name of Israel's God, 'Yahweh'. Most English Bibles translate this name as 'The LORD' (as in verse 15, using capital letters to indicate that it represents the Hebrew 'Yahweh'). The English 'Lord' suggests to some readers the privilege of class ('House of Lords'), or powerful domination, or even masculine oppression. But 'Yahweh' is a personal name. There is a huge difference between a title and a name. To the thirteen-year-old pupil, the school's headmaster may be a figure to be respected, feared and avoided. But if that pupil is also his daughter who knows his name is John, the relationship is very different.

Israel's God is not an abstract principle behind the universe, nor a distant ruler interfering occasionally in human affairs. He is a person who makes himself known, makes himself vulnerable and commits himself faithfully to those who trust him.

16
Escape from Egypt

All Moses' attempts to get the Israelites out of Egypt by negotiation with Pharaoh fell on deaf ears (chapter 5). Even a devastating series of plagues failed to soften Pharaoh's heart (chapters 7–11). But God did not run out of ideas.

Exodus 12 reports the first Passover, when the Israelites were protected from the final plague on the Egyptians—the death of their first-born sons—by daubing the blood of lambs on the door-posts of their homes. To this day Jews observe Passover to celebrate their liberation from Egypt and God's continual care for them as a people.

At last Pharaoh had had enough of the troubles brought on him because of the Israelites, and he told them to go (12:31). The great escape, or 'exodus', was under way.

Read Exodus 13:17—14:31

God is the chief actor in this narrative. He plans a route for the journey back to Canaan (13:17–18). He leads and guides the people (13:18, 21). He intensifies the hardening of Pharaoh's heart so that his plans to prevent the Israelites' escape issue in self-destruction (14:4). He opens the way miraculously for Moses and the people to flee to safety. Yet, as we have seen before, he does not act on his own but *interacts* with human and natural agents.

Exodus 13:17–18 shows him working within the confines of the military and political situation. Though we might expect God to take the most efficient route to achieve his purposes, he is shown here as limiting his power to take account of what is realistic in the human context. He uses his power in cooperation with human possibilities.

But what is the route implied here? There is a problem with locating the water crossed by the Israelites. The Hebrew phrase translated 'Red Sea' (13:18) means 'Sea of Reeds'. But there are no reeds in the salt-water of the Red Sea. Many scholars have therefore suggested that the crucial event took place not at the Red Sea (somewhere in the Gulf of Suez), but at one of the freshwater lakes which lie between the Gulf of Suez and the Nile Delta, on the present route of the Suez Canal. If the Israelites later thought of the event as taking place at the Red Sea itself, that need not concern us unduly. It is perhaps a sign of the *importance* which they attached to this mighty act of God in their history.

The pillar of cloud and the pillar of fire (13:21) also raise questions for modern readers. It has sometimes been suggested that it was a burning brazier held aloft at the front of the Israelites as a symbol of God's presence. But such a brazier would hardly be big enough to do what the pillar of cloud does in 14:19–20. Yet the meaning of this language is not in doubt: it is saying that God is with his people to lead and to protect them.

When the narrator speaks of God hardening Pharaoh's heart (14:4) he does not mean that God manipulates Pharaoh like a puppet. He has already said that Pharaoh hardened his own heart (8:15; 9:34). God's way with those who persistently resist him is to give rein to their evil ways so that ultimately they reap the harvest of their own wrong choice. He allows a dictator, a Hitler, to overreach himself until his empire comes crashing in on itself. No oppressor freely lets go of the colonies or the slaves who serve his whims and create his wealth. So Pharaoh, not surprisingly, changes his mind about letting the Israelites go. And that is his undoing.

To the terrified Israelites the slavery of Egypt suddenly looks quite attractive once more (verses 10–12). When the enemy is as close as that, God seems far away. But Moses has a different perspective. His words to the people offer instructions based on confidence in the character and power of God (verses 13–14).

'Do not be afraid', 'stand firm', 'be still'. Such instructions would seem pointless to a badly armed bunch of escaped prisoners in face of advancing chariots. Pointless, apart from the promise of what God is about to do: 'You will see the deliverance the Lord will bring you today.' 'The Lord will fight for you.'

God works the miracle of the exodus through a human leader who is in tune with his plan, through a natural phenomenon (verse 21), and through the walk of faith across the temporarily dry land.

The scene has more dramatic images than any film director would dare hope for. But behind the images there is a fundamental conviction which lies at the root of Jewish and Christian faith: God has acted in history to accomplish his purpose for the world.

1 7
The covenant at Sinai

Exodus 19:1–8

After a journey of three months the Israelites reached the foot of Mount Sinai, in the south of the Sinai peninsula. Here, near where Moses had met with God at the burning bush (Exodus 3), the relationship between God and Israel entered a new phase.

The passage speaks of the *covenant*, or 'special relationship', between Yahweh and his people. This is not some new arrangement now devised by God or by Moses. It is the covenant which God had already established with Abraham (Genesis 15), now given fuller content. It does not establish the Israelites as God's people: they already are his people (see Exodus 3:7, 10). So what does the passage say about this covenant, and how might that apply to those who call themselves God's people today?

The covenant stems from God's action in history. God himself has taken the initiative in acting for the good of his people (verse 4). It is a common idea among Christians that, according to the Old Testament, salvation is achieved through human effort, whereas in the New Testament it is a result of God's grace. Nothing could be further from the truth. Human experience of God and his blessings has always depended on God's grace, God's initiative in reaching out to us.

This passage puts it beautifully. God acted like a mother eagle, caring for Israel and protecting them when they were especially vulnerable. He was like the mother bird teaching the fledglings to fly, pushing them out of the nest but always swooping to catch them on her own strong wings if they should falter.

But what God did for Israel involved also his action towards the Egyptians. His action in history is not a private affair between himself and those who claim him as their Lord. He is at work in the affairs of nations, weaving his plan for the world. History is not 'a tale told by an idiot, full of sound and fury, signifying nothing' (Shakespeare, *Macbeth*). History is 'his story'.

The covenant involves the obedience of the people. Grace came first: God did for the Israelites what they could not do for themselves. But his gift of love calls for a response of loving obedience (verse 5). At this stage no content is given to this obedience, no list of rules to follow.

That is because our relationship with God is first and foremost a *personal* commitment. We open ourselves as persons to God who is personal. We trust him even when we do not know what specific instructions he may be going to give us. Because of what he has already done in bringing us into relationship with himself, we say 'yes' to his laws even before we know in detail what they are. He is the only one to whom we can safely write a blank cheque.

Admittedly, the demands of God will soon be fleshed out in the Ten Commandments and other laws which follow, just as in the New Testament there is plenty of specific guidance about behaviour. But whenever such laws or teaching become treated as rules for their own sake, the personal nature of the relationship with God is obscured.

The covenant involves a particular kind of relationship between God and his people. When the text says, 'If you obey... you will be ...' (verse 5), it does not mean that Israel must obey God in order to *attain* to this special relationship. That would contradict what has gone before. It means that they are to obey in order to *express* what is involved in being God's people. Their special character is shown in three phrases.

They are God's *treasured possession*. Chosen out of all the nations, they have a special place in God's heart (verse 5). They are a *kingdom of priests*: the whole nation (not just a special group of priests) is to serve as bridge-builders between God and the people of the world (verse 6). They are a *holy nation* (verse 6). 'Holy' means basically 'set apart'. Israel is set apart from other nations, specially dedicated to God. But their goal is not simply to be separate, but by being distinctive to serve God's purpose for the world.

The covenant is between God and the people as a whole. The text assumes a covenant with the community rather than between God and individuals. Christians may assume too easily that an individual

43

relationship with God is superior to what early Israel experienced. But we are the poorer when we underplay the fact that belonging to God's people is a fundamentally communal relationship.

To think about

The apostle Peter applies these same three pictures to Christian believers (1 Peter 2:9). What do you think these pictures imply for the life and activity of a Christian church today?

18

The Ten Commandments

Exodus 20:1–17

Jesus said that the whole law is summed up in love of God and love of one's neighbour (Matthew 22:34–40). So it is helpful to see the Ten Commandments, and the more detailed instructions which follow, as expressing what it means to love God and my neighbour in various specific situations. The meaning of these Commandments is easily distorted if we do not remember certain things about them.

First, they are set in the context of God's activity towards Israel. They are part of his gift to them: having delivered them from Egypt he is not going to leave them without guidance for their lives under his care. The fact that the law springs from God's saving activity is underlined in verse 2.

Secondly, it is a mistake to think of the Ten Commandments as a list of negative 'Thou shalt nots'. Although eight of the ten begin with 'You shall not . . .', their intention is entirely positive. God is providing boundaries within which the people are to live. Within those boundaries there is freedom, not imprisonment, because these laws protect society from behaviour which would destroy it. Where there is no general acceptance of such laws, humanity is constantly threatened by violence, mistrust and exploitation.

Thirdly, the commandments are addressed to individuals in the community. The old words, '*Thou* shalt not . . .', make this clear. Even though God's covenant is with the people as a whole, each member is responsible for keeping the commandments so that the health of the community is maintained. No one can hide behind the excuse, 'It doesn't make any difference what *I* do'. One small hole in a boat is enough to sink it.

Fourthly, these commandments are not a complete guide to human behaviour. But they provide a framework for how life is meant to be lived. The first four describe our duty towards God, and the other six are about our relationships with others. Let us look briefly at their significance to Israel at Sinai, and to us.

Only one God. Yahweh has proved himself to be the living God who acts on behalf of his people, so he alone has the right to their love and loyalty.

No idols. The living God is not to be compared with, or represented by, a lifeless image.

Misuse of God's name. Any action which devalues God's reputation is a denial of the power and love which he has shown towards his people. This command applies not only to the abuse of God's name in swear-words. It is also a warning against claiming God's blessing for some questionable cause, for example when people fighting a war of aggression claim that God is on their side.

The sabbath. Delivered from slavery, Israel must protect a day of rest. The Bible has much to say about protecting the rights of workers.

Honouring parents. The family structure (though this may take different forms in different circumstances) is basic to the health of society. 'Honour' includes the care of adults for elderly parents, as well as the obedience of young children.

No killing. Life was cheap in Egypt. Israel must value human life as God values it. 'Kill' in the Old Testament is a wider term than 'murder' in English. For example, it includes what we would call manslaughter. But it is never used of killing in war.

Marriage. Adultery is a crime against another person and distorts God's good gift of sexuality. It is not a casual matter, affecting only one or two individuals. It destroys trust, cheapens loyalty and undermines the stability of society as a whole.

No stealing. The Hebrews thought of theft as violation not merely of property but of persons. Anyone whose home has been burgled knows how it affects their inner selves. Respect for what belongs to others is necessary for an open, harmonious society. But 'theft' has

45

many forms in modern society. An employer who pays unreasonably low wages, for example, is depriving workers of what they have a right to expect for their labour.

Truth and integrity. Freed from the injustice of Egypt, Israel must protect truth, especially in legal cases. Without honesty and integrity, the fabric of society collapses. When someone spreads rumours about a workmate, or a politician abuses the reputation of an opponent, mistrust and division are sure to follow.

Contentment. The final commandment moves from outward actions to the inner motives of the heart. Out of greed or envy or the lust for power spring so many of the evils described in the other commandments. In an affluent society, few things are more urgent than that people should discover the joy of contentment with a more limited number of possessions.

19

When the going gets tough

The later chapters of Exodus and the whole of Leviticus set out further regulations for Israelite society and for their worship of God.

The next book, Numbers, gets its name from the census returns in chapters 1–4 and 26. But its original Hebrew name, 'In the wilderness', is a more sensible description of its contents. It portrays the forty-year wandering of the Israelites in the wilderness of Sinai before their entry into the Promised Land.

Within months of receiving the Ten Commandments, they reached the borders of Canaan. Under God's direction, Moses sent twelve spies to check out the nature of the land and the strength of its inhabitants (Numbers 13:1–25). They reported back that the land flowed with milk and honey, but that the people living there were powerful and their cities heavily fortified. They spread fear among the Israelites, announcing that even the land itself ate people up, and that they themselves felt like grasshoppers in comparison to the huge men of Canaan (Numbers 13:26–33).

Read Numbers 14:1–25

Verses 1–4. Having come all the way from Egypt to the borders of the Promised Land, the Israelites are overcome with panic. And they do what every church, every football team is prone to do when things go badly: blame the manager (verse 2). They are so desperate about their prospects of survival against the tribes living in Canaan that they propose offering themselves as slaves again to the Egyptians. They are so disillusioned with Moses that they suggest appointing another leader (verses 3–4).

But such proposals involve rejecting God's promise, his whole rescue plan for the world. For it is by getting his people into the Promised Land that he is to carry forward his promises to Abraham. So the issue facing the Israelites is not simply, 'What strategy does military intelligence suggest?' It is, 'Will God's people trust his word, even when the circumstances seem to cast doubt upon it?'

In a sense, the whole Old Testament story, and the history of the Christian church too, is the story of people wanting to cling to the securities of the past, looking back through rose-tinted spectacles to past acts of God. And the message which God is constantly trying to bring home to his people is that he is not to be found in the past any more. He is always out in front of us, asking us to take risks of faith, calling us forward towards some new act of his astonishing grace.

Verses 5–10. Two of the spies, Joshua and Caleb, tell a different story from the other ten. They see the same obstacles as the others, but they see also that God has promised victory over them. They have faith which rises above merely human perspectives. But the Israelites are unimpressed: they think Joshua and Caleb are bearing false witness and propose killing them with stones, the penalty for such a crime.

Verses 10–25. The Lord comes to the rescue, just in time. The people sense his presence around the Tent of Meeting—a portable worship centre carried by the Israelites through the wilderness. There follows a conversation between God and Moses which, like some stories in Genesis which we have already read, has a very 'human' feel to it, with arguments passing to and fro.

God's first thought is to destroy the Israelites because of their refusal to trust him despite all he has done for them, and to make a fresh start with a small nucleus of people around Moses (verses 11–12).

Moses' counter-argument is that if Yahweh acts in this way he will reduce the reputation he has built up among the Egyptians and other nations by defending Israel against their oppressors (verse 13–16).

And in prayer he appeals on behalf of the unfaithful Israelites to God's love and forgiveness (verses 13–19). Christians today can find a model here of the prayer which pleads for God's mercy on a nation which is in trouble because it has abandoned biblical faith and biblical values.

Verses 20–25. God answers Moses' prayer by declaring forgiveness for the people. They will not be destroyed. Yet they are not ready to enter Canaan. They must approach the Promised Land by a devious route—which will take them another forty years. As often in the life of a nation, prayer and repentance do not lead to an immediate change of circumstance. The consequences of previous wrong choices must be worked through before better times can come.

This episode marks a watershed in the story of Israel. The generation which came out of Egypt will not live to see the the Promised Land. That role must be left for a new generation, made strong in faith through their wilderness experience.

20
Love the Lord your God

Deuteronomy ('Second Law') is presented in the form of speeches by Moses just before the people enter the Promised Land. He reminds them of God's covenant with them, his constant love for them, and their responsibility to remain in obedience to him. Chapter 5 repeats the Ten Commandments of Exodus 20.

Read Deuteronomy 6:4–25

Known as the *Shema* (the Hebrew word for 'hear'), verses 4 and 5 are at the heart of Old Testament faith. To this day Jews recite them morning and evening. This is not a pious ritual but a declaration that the whole of life is to be lived consciously under the care and direction of God.

The *Shema* begins not with a demand but with a claim, 'The Lord our God, the Lord is one.' This identifies the God who lays claim on Israel's loyalty. He is the Lord ('Yahweh') who has revealed himself to Abraham and to Moses, rescued the Israelites from Egypt and bound himself in covenant to them. Whereas other nations believed in gods who competed with each other for power over the world, Israel's God was the single creator and ruler of the world.

When the Israelites declare, 'The Lord is one,' they are offering him their undivided loyalty. They are accepting their responsibility as the people chosen by this God to carry out his purpose for the world.

After the claim comes the demand (verse 5). Deuteronomy is particularly fond of the word 'love' as a description of humanity's response to God. It does not mean an emotional feeling so much as a total giving of oneself to another. To love God with all one's heart, soul and strength is to be committed to him with every fibre of one's being. Jewish interpreters have suggested the following explanation:

- ◆ heart—to love God with undivided loyalty

- ◆ soul—to be committed to God even to the point of death or martyrdom

- ◆ strength—to recognize that one's wealth and possessions truly belong to God and are to be used in his service.

The message of the *Shema* is that there can be only one ruler in our life. Though we have responsibilities to our family, our job, our country, and to other things, none of these can have *ultimate* importance for us. They take their place as an *expression* of our love for God. If there is conflict between, say, our obedience to God and the requirements of our country, then loyalty to God comes first.

The importance of remembering this demand is underlined in verses 6–9. They are to be passed on carefully to children and discussed among adults (verse 7; on children see also verses 20–25). Still today many Jews carry out literally the instruction of verse 8 by wearing at the synagogue small leather boxes (*tefillin*) containing the words of Deuteronomy 6:4–9 and other short passages from Exodus and Deuteronomy. And they place similar Scriptures in little boxes nailed to their doorposts (verse 9).

Why is such remembering so important? Because God knows how easily we forget! When things go well for us and life feels more comfortable, God may seem a little less necessary to our daily lives. We attribute the good times to our own hard work. Then more than ever we need to remember that we are dependent on God's goodness to us. He has given us more than we deserved (verses 10–12).

In particular, we remember that our experience of God's blessing depends on what he has done in history. For the Israelites this meant referring back constantly to the deliverance from Egypt (verses 12, 20–23). For Christians it also means recalling that the death and resurrection of Jesus is the basis of our experience.

To think about

'Remember' or 'do not forget' is a frequent theme in Deuteronomy. It is an important perspective for Christian living. As we call to mind what God has done for us we open ourselves to his influence upon us. The following examples from Deuteronomy and elsewhere can be used for personal reflection.

'Remember that you were slaves in Egypt and that the Lord your God brought you out . . .' (Deuteronomy 5:15).

'Remember how the Lord your God led you' (Deuteronomy 8:2).

'Remember Jesus Christ, risen from the dead' (2 Timothy 2:8).

'Remember what you have received and heard' (Revelation 3:3).

21
Entering the Promised Land

When we begin a new phase of life or take on a new task, questions flood into our minds. Am I taking on more than I can manage? How will I cope? The Israelites now face one of these critical moments. A new generation stands on the borders of Canaan. The qualities of their new leader, Joshua, and the readiness of the people to follow him, are about to be put to the test.

Read Joshua 1

This passage may be read on two levels. First, it expresses God's promise to Joshua that he will give the land of Canaan to the Israelites. After being landless for so long, they will at last receive the promise made to Abraham.

For those of us who live secure in our own countries it is hard to imagine what it feels like to be a people without a land. But we can glimpse something of the insecurity of Kurds or Armenians today. We can wonder at the deep fears which have driven Serbs and Croats and Bosnians to fight a bitter struggle for land. We can understand the longing of Jewish people under Nazi oppression for a land of their own. We can sympathize with Palestinians who feel their own land is being taken away.

The God of the Bible is committed to giving a land to his people. He knows that human beings need not only a spiritual freedom but also a measure of earthly security. But the size of the land was rarely as great as the area described in verse 4. Only during the reigns of David and Solomon (about 1000–930BC) was this whole area under Israelite control.

The books of Joshua, Judges, 1 and 2 Samuel and 1 and 2 Kings tell the story of how the Israelites gained the land, lost parts of it, regained them and finally lost the land to foreign powers. The common theme of these books is that their hold on the land depended on their obedience to God's law. Obedience ensured God's protection. Disobedience left them exposed to foreign aggression. This call for obedience is stressed here at the beginning of the campaign (verses 7–9, 13, 16–18).

Entering the land, of course, involved fighting. This presents problems for us. Would God really tell one group of people, the Israelites, to gain security in the land by throwing out another group of people, the Canaanites? Is such killing any different from the actions of Serbs or Muslims in former Yugoslavia, or of those in Northern Ireland who claim the blessing of religion on their aggression? There is no tidy answer to such questions, but three comments may help.

First, the Old Testament insists that the Israelites are the objects of God's special care and protection. This is not for their own sakes but so that 'all peoples on earth will be blessed' through them (Genesis 12:3). But if they are ultimately to convey this blessing, they must be preserved as a people.

Secondly, Old Testament writers say that the reason for Israel's sometimes ruthless treatment of the Canaanites was because the corruption of their religion and society might otherwise lead the Israelites astray (see Deuteronomy 7:1–6; 20:16–18). Where Canaanites were responsive towards the Israelites, they were welcomed into the Israelite community (Rahab in Joshua 2; 6:22–25).

Thirdly, the studies of archaeologists suggest that when Joshua came into the land its towns were governed by Canaanite kings who oppressed the peasant population. Civil unrest was on the increase. So when Joshua arrived he came not as the ruthless destroyer of a whole Canaanite nation but as liberator of the oppressed from their oppressors. This helps to explain how Joshua's army was successful so quickly. It also provides an example of a theme which runs through the Bible: God is on the side of the oppressed. As in the case of Pharaoh, Hitler and the Soviet system, God works through the tyrants' hardness of heart until their whole system collapses and the oppressed go free.

But this whole chapter can be read on a second level, as a word from God to anyone setting out on a new and challenging venture and needing God's reassurance. In such circumstances, God urges us to be true to our calling and not to turn aside when the going gets difficult (verses 6–9). And he promises his constant presence to guide, to protect and to strengthen us (verses 5, 9).

When the risen Jesus commissioned his followers to make disciples throughout the world he promised, 'Surely I am with you always, to the very end of the age' (Matthew 28:20). Missionary pioneer David Livingstone called this the promise of 'a perfect gentleman, who never breaks his word'. And in that confidence he set out declaring, 'I will go anywhere, provided it be forward.'

22
Gideon versus Midian

The rest of the book of Joshua tells the story of Joshua's conquest of Canaan (chapters 2–12) and his arrangements for Israelite society now that they have a settled homeland (chapters 13–24).

The conquest seems to be a swift and unqualified success—until we read the book of Judges. Here we discover that people hostile to the Israelites still threaten their safety. The basic victory won by Joshua was described in broad brushstrokes in Joshua 2–12. The book of Judges tells of the Israelites' constant struggle to keep control of the land.

During this period they were an alliance of twelve tribes bound together by their shared descent from Abraham and their shared commitment to Yahweh. When their security was threatened they banded together under a leader chosen from one of the tribes. These leaders were called 'judges', a word which conveys the idea of 'ruler' or 'deliverer'.

Gideon was one such leader who led Israelite forces against attacks by the nomadic Midianites. His is one of those biblical stories illustrating the truth that 'God chooses the foolish things of the world to shame the wise' (1 Corinthians 1:27).

Read Judges 7

Gideon's army is encamped below Mount Gilboa. The Midianites are five miles to the north, on the other side of the broad valley of Jezreel which stretches from the foot of Mount Carmel to the Jordan valley (verse 1).

So that there will be no doubt that victory in battle is due to God's action rather than to Gideon's skill, his army of thirty-two thousand has to be drastically reduced. One way to do that is to dismiss any who are filled with fear. There is sense in this, since fear is contagious and very damaging to an army's morale. Even so, Gideon must have wondered what kind of an army he had when he discovered that more than two-thirds of them had no stomach for a fight (verse 3)!

But still ten thousand is too many for God's purpose. God's next instructions for reducing the numbers are hard to understand (verse 4–5). What exactly does it mean to 'lap like a dog', and why is that more acceptable than kneeling down to drink? If lapping like a dog means getting your head right down to the water's level, might not the soldiers who do this be caught off guard by the enemy? Or is that precisely the point of God choosing these three hundred rather than the others? Perhaps, in line with his plan in verse 2, he wants to use 'the foolish' rather than those who know all the correct military survival techniques?

So Gideon gets his three hundred men. What a contrast with the forces of Midian, extravagantly described in verse 12! But God is at work on Israel's behalf. He even suggests to Gideon that a visit during the night to the Midianite camp will give him confidence of victory. Though his heart may have missed a beat or two on the way, Gideon arrives at the camp just in time to hear a soldier interpreting another's dream (verses 9–14). The time for action has arrived.

What follows seems more like an elaborate prank than the precisely calculated tactic of crack troops. But the effect is devastating. Surprised by the din in the darkness, the Midianites are convinced that the noise and the torches are those of a great army. Movement in the camp makes them think that the Israelites have already penetrated their defences, and in the confusion they begin to lash out with their swords at anyone who looms up in the shadows (verses 21–22). The rout of the Midianites is soon complete (verses 23–25).

To see the importance of what God tries to teach through this incident we only have to look to the next chapter. In Judges 8:22 the people say to Gideon, 'Rule over us—you, your son and your grandson—because you have saved us out of the hand of Midian.' Despite the manner of the victory, they attribute it to Gideon himself rather than to God. And so they urge him to become their king and to establish a permanent dynasty. Such a plan may seem to offer greater national security. But from the perspective of the writer of Judges, and of Gideon, it is an abandonment of faith in God as the one who rules over and protects Israel: 'I will not rule over you, nor will my son rule over you. The Lord will rule over you' (Judges 8:23).

The lesson of Psalm 115:1 needs to be constantly learnt and relearnt: 'Not to us, O Lord, not to us but to your name be the glory, because of your love and faithfulness.'

2

PROPHETS AND KINGS

23
Israel asks for a king

The two books of Samuel describe how Israel changed from being a loose association of tribes into being a monarchy with a centralized government. The books take their name from one of the three key personalities whose stories are told here, the others being the kings Saul and David. Samuel was the last of the 'judges' of Israel, who also functioned as a prophet.

During the period of the judges the Israelites became increasingly harassed by the Philistines. These people inhabited the coastal plain to the west of the hill country which the Israelites had occupied. They possessed the skill of iron-working, which made their armaments superior to those of the Israelites, who still made weapons of bronze (see 1 Samuel 13:19).

Against this background, the clamour for a king kept coming back.

Read 1 Samuel 8

Two reasons for wanting a king are mentioned by the representatives of Israel (verse 5). First, they know that Samuel's days are numbered and that his quality of leadership is not sustained by his sons. Godly wisdom is a fine quality in parents, but even that cannot guarantee the good character of their children.

Secondly, they want to be 'like all the other nations' (verses 5, 20).

They see the strength of surrounding nations where kings exercise control from a central power base, and pass on that power to their sons. They want someone to give strong leadership, someone to fight their battles for them.

Samuel is reassured by God that their call for a king represents a crisis of confidence in God himself (verses 6–9). He tells the people what will happen if they have a king (verses 10–18).

They only need to look more closely at other nations to see what monarchy actually does to a people. It is characteristic of monarchy to 'take', he says. Notice how often this word appears in verses 11–17. A centralized government will mean conscription into the army, the forcing of young men and women into the royal service, the confiscation of land for royal use, the imposition of taxes in the form of a levy on crops grown and animals reared.

In effect, all this will mean that the people will become the king's slaves (verse 17). How ironic that this nation,who two hundred years earlier escaped from being slaves of Egypt's tyrannical monarch, should now want to entrust themselves to such a system of government! How sad that this nation which was meant to be different from other nations should now want to be like them!

Samuel's speech does not consider whether it is possible for monarchs to rule to the real benefit of their people, without exploiting them. It simply draws attention to how monarchy actually worked in nations around Israel at that time. It is an eloquent warning about the abuse of political power.

It can encourage us to reflect on government as we experience it. What happens when too much power is 'given away' by ordinary people to a government seated hundreds of miles away? Does it mean that we cease to take responsibility for our own and our neighbours' lives, and our experience of society becomes more impersonal? Is is always true that 'power corrupts, and absolute power corrupts absolutely'? What are the genuine advantages of a centralized government? How can these best be enjoyed, and the corresponding disadvantages kept to a minimum? What are the particular temptations of people in power, and how should we therefore pray for them?

Similar questions can be asked about power and leadership in the church. Do churches too readily try to build their power 'like the nations'? Do we look for systems and programmes and powerful leaders who will make us feel safe and successful? Does our longing for such things undermine our sense of responsibility for our own lives before God? Are we looking for a predictability about life which stops us being open to the God of surprises, who holds our future in his hands?

When the people remain unmoved by Samuel's argument, he turns once again to God. And God's answer is surprising. 'A king', he seems to say, 'is a bad idea. But let them have one anyway' (verse 22).

God has a habit of not being defeated by human sinfulness or stupidity. When we take a wrong turning in life, we are not condemned to a life-time of 'second best'. He finds a way of working out his purpose for us by an alternative route. He knows that there are some advantages in kingship, and he can use them for his own purposes. Perhaps he already has his eye on David, the king from whose family the Messiah will one day be born.

24
Saul is made king
1 Samuel 9–10

These two chapters tell the story of how Saul became the first king of Israel. There are two stages in the process. First, Samuel seeks him out and tells him that he is to be leader of God's people (9:1–10:16). He symbolizes this appointment by pouring olive oil over Saul's head (10:1). Secondly, Saul is acclaimed as king by the people (10:17–25).

The first part of the story is not entirely what we would expect in an account of a king's appointment. Saul looks like a king. He is handsome and stands head and shoulders above his contemporaries. But we first meet him looking for lost donkeys! This reminds us how even wealthy people at that time lived close to the land. Animals rather than consumer goods represented prosperity.

Saul and his servant wander around the hill country of central Palestine, but fail to find the donkeys. Saul is on the point of giving up when his servant reminds him that they are close to the home of Samuel, who has God-given powers of insight (9:5–6). So the search for donkeys brings Saul into contact with Samuel, who turns out to have more to tell him than he bargained for!

God, who has decided that Saul is to be king, has already let Samuel in on the secret (9:15–17). When Saul and Samuel meet the prophet reassures Saul that the animals have been found and hints that bigger issues are now at stake (9:19–20). Saul utters the classic reply of Moses and all reluctant servants of God down the ages: 'But I'm of no significance. Why should God pick on me when he wants to do something important?' (9:21).

Some people are naturally ambitious. They want to get to the top, to make an impact, to have influence in the world. That is not wrong in itself. When harnessed with a spirit of service, ambition can produce people who achieve much good in the world. But maybe God has a special place in his heart for reluctant leaders who do not seek responsibility but have it thrust upon them. Leaders who didn't want the job but whose gifts are detected by others may offer a style of leadership which is effective because it gives room for others to contribute rather than dominating them.

Saul's appointment is confirmed for him by a series of signs. He will be reassured that his donkeys are safe (10:2). He will be offered bread (10:3–4). He will become a changed man by receiving the gift of prophecy (10:5–6). Such signs will confirm that God is with him (10:7). God does not always give signs in this way, but sometimes in his love he meets our human uncertainty with the traces of his presence.

Once the people have seen that Saul is a changed man it is time for the public proclamation of his kingship. Samuel calls the people to assemble at Mizpah (10:17). He reminds them again that their desire for a king is in some sense a questioning of God's kingship (10:18–19), but proceeds with the ceremony because God has now chosen Saul to deliver and protect his people (9:16; 10:1). By the drawing of lots God's choice of Saul is confirmed once more (10:20–21). But Saul still can't see himself as king and is hiding among the baggage (10:22)!

He is dragged out and declared king, with the enthusiastic approval of the people (10:24). What follows is very interesting. Israel is not after all to have a king 'like all the other nations'. For there are 'regulations of the kingship' written down and deposited in a place of worship (10:25). In other words, the king does not have absolute power. There are limits to his authority, and he is responsible to God for his use of power.

The story of Saul's appointment as king shows God allowing his own plans to be influenced by the weaknesses of his people. When his love meets with resistance he does not abandon his people in anger or depair, but finds a way of working with their weaknesses to carry forward his plans in a different way.

Yet despite divine appointment and public approval Saul does not have everyone on his side. There are cynics who doubt his ability to rescue Israel from the Philistines (10:27). His troubles are beginning already.

25

David spares Saul's life

Saul demonstrated his kingship by winning battles against the Philistines and other enemies of Israel. But he began to defy the regulations which Samuel had laid down for him, until the time came when Samuel solemnly declared to him: 'Because you have rejected the word of the Lord, he has rejected you as king' (1 Samuel 15:23).

God 'was grieved that he had made Saul king over Israel' (15:35), and through Samuel chose the young David to succeed him (1 Samuel 16:1–13). After being rejected by God Saul became increasingly subject to periods of depression which sometimes verged on madness. Ironically, David the musician was appointed to provide comfort for Saul's melancholy, and so their lives became intertwined (16:17–23).

After David became a national hero by killing the Philistine Goliath (1 Samuel 17) Saul became jealous of him and tried to kill him (1 Samuel 18–19). David had no choice but to become an outlaw, supported by a band of fugitives who lived on the margins of Israelite society.

So David knows that Saul is an irrational ruler whose days are numbered. He knows that he himself is to become king. He is living as an outlaw in the desert, constantly pursued by Saul's men. And now the opportunity to resolve the situation presents itself.

Read 1 Samuel 24

By an amusing coincidence Saul goes to relieve himself in a cave near the Dead Sea where David and his men are hiding. The commander of three thousand soldiers is vulnerable to a bunch of outlaws on the run. The pressure on David from his men and from his own survival instincts must have been enormous. But instead of killing Saul there and then he stealthily cuts off a corner of his robe (verse 4).

Immediately he is conscience-stricken (verse 5). Even though Saul is his enemy, he is still to be respected as the king whom God appointed. To cut his robe is to make him look ridiculous and so to undermine his royal status.

Then David calls out to Saul (verses 8–15). By showing that he could have killed Saul but did not, he declares his innocence. He is not a rebel intent on destroying Saul's rule. Why does it take three thousand men to pursue someone who is no more of a threat to Saul than a dead dog or a flea (verse 14)?

David's speech shows generosity towards his enemy. Under pressure to to take revenge and to make his own future more secure, he opts for mercy. He is content to leave justice in God's hands (verse 15).

But his speech is also shrewd. He knows that Saul will sooner or later destroy himself. He can wait for God's timing. Meanwhile his own innocence is dramatically demonstrated.

Saul's reply expresses his sad realization of how the tide has turned against him (verses 16–21). A life of great potential has turned empty. Even he now knows that nothing can stop David becoming king. He extracts a promise from David: 'Swear to me that you will not cut off my family and my future in the way you cut off my robe.'

In this part of the story there is no constant reference to God's activity. Yet the purpose of God is working itself out slowly as the events unfold. David will not try to speed up the process. He will not kill Saul or challenge him to abdicate. He will receive the crown only as a gift, when God's moment comes.

People who are confident of God's involvement in events do not need to fret or manipulate circumstances. They can be at peace, knowing that God's will is being worked out. That is different from simply resigning oneself to whatever happens. It is different from saying, 'Whatever will be, will be.' It is a positive embracing of God's purpose. It is a willingness to cooperate with God whilst allowing him to take the lead. It is the attitude of Jesus who said, 'My food is to do the will of him who sent me' (John 4:34).

To think about

Am I involved in a situation or a relationship where it is 'natural' to take revenge, to 'get my own back' on someone else? Does this story of David suggest a different way forward?

26
God's promise to David

Saul's reign ended when the Philistines defeated his army on Mount Gilboa. Critically wounded in the battle, he committed suicide

(1 Samuel 31). David was then declared king over his own tribe, Judah, and then over all Israel (2 Samuel 2, 5).

He captured Jerusalem, which until then had always remained in the hands of a non-Israelite people, the Jebusites (2 Samuel 5). This move was both militarily spectacular and politically shrewd. For it enabled him to unite the twelve tribes of Israel and lessen rivalry between them by ruling from a city which did not belong to any of them.

Read 2 Samuel 7

This chapter records one of the most important developments in the story of Israel—God's promise that he would establish the rule of David's descendants 'for ever'. It begins with David reflecting on his new situation with Nathan, prophet and adviser to the king (verses 1–3).

Until then the central shrine of Israel had been a moveable tent (or 'tabernacle') in which was kept a box containing the Ten Commandments ('the ark of the covenant'). It symbolized the presence of God guiding his people. But now David wonders if it is right for him to live in a palace while God lacks a solid and permanent shrine.

Nathan is not inclined to contradict the king's idea. But he remains open to God and receives from him a different message (verses 5–16). It begins by asserting the danger of building a temple. Throughout their history the Israelites have experienced God 'on the move', leading them forward on their journey of faith. The moveable tent symbolized this. But a temple will fix God in one place. It will make rulers think they can tame and control him. It will narrow people's vision of what the Lord of all the earth can do (verses 5–7).

But God has better news for David. Having looked after David from the moment he chose him as Israel's future king, God will give the nation security and prosperity under David (verses 8–11). And instead of David building a house for God to dwell in (a temple) God will build a house for David (a dynasty) so that his descendants will rule permanently (verses 11–16).

God's commitment to David and his descendants is expressed most vividly in verse 14: 'I will be his father, and he will be my son'. It is a promise without strings attached, a gift of God's generosity. Individual kings may go wrong and suffer for it (verse 14). But God will preserve the dynasty as a whole because it is important to him (verses 15–16). Even though his servants are unfaithful, he remains faithful to his purpose of love.

Despite the earlier warnings about the risks of having a permanent temple, God permits David's son to build a temple in Jerusalem (verse 13). Just as he permitted the monarchy to be established though it was less than ideal, he permits the temple and will use it as the focus of his presence among his people.

'Your throne shall be established for ever' (verse 16). In the Bible 'for ever' can mean 'for a long time', and that promise was fulfilled by David's family ruling in Jerusalem for four hundred years. Even after their rule was brought to an end by the Babylonian conquest (586BC), the hope remained that a future 'son of David' would bring a new era of peace and liberation. The New Testament from the start (Matthew 1) stresses that Jesus is 'the son of David' and declares that his reign will literally be for ever.

It is a great moment for David and for Israel. The Philistines have been driven off, the economy is beginning to prosper, Israel is united in accepting David's rule. God has given his approval for the building of a temple and asserted his faithfulness to David's descendants. His prayer reflects his confidence in God (verses 18–29).

He responds to God with humility (verse 18). His rise from his simple origins was due less to his own abilities than to God's goodness. He expresses thanks and wonder at God's generosity (verse 19–21). He praises God as the only one worthy of worship (verse 22). He remembers how God has acted to deliver Israel (verses 23–24). Finally David boldly urges God to keep the promises he has made (verse 25–29).

This mixture of submissive dependence and insistent demand is a characteristic of Old Testament prayer, which we meet often in the Psalms. Having expressed wonder at the scale and extravagance of God's promises, David almost impudently demands that God should deliver what he has promised. He has learnt that God invites that kind of relationship.

2 7
David and Bathsheba

After God's promise to David comes David's unfaithfulness to God. The Bible does not gloss over the failures of its heroes.

Whilst others fight his battles, David remains in his hill-top palace in Jerusalem, master of all he surveys. And that includes the woman whom he sees bathing on the flat roof of her house lower down the slope. His desire for her provokes instant action. 'He sent messengers to get her. She came to him, and he slept with her' (verse 4). The words, 'She had purified herself . . .' indicate that she was not pregnant by her husband Uriah.

Notice how after verse 3 she is not named but is simply 'the woman'. That is all she is to David. There is no hint of care and affection. He does not call her by name or even speak to her. But then the moment of lust brings its consequences. David was not the last person to have his world shattered by those words, 'I am pregnant'. But he does not think of the anguish this has caused Bathsheba, but only of the implications for himself.

He summons Uriah back from the battlefield and tries to get him to sleep with Bathsheba so that the baby will be assumed to be his (verses 6–13). But Uriah is a man of principle—unlike David who is prepared to sleep with the wife of a man risking his life in David's war. He is not on leave and he will not relax with his wife while his comrades are fighting a war. Even when David tries to weaken his defences by getting him drunk, again Uriah remains firm.

David will now stop at nothing. Uriah goes back to the battle carrying his own death warrant (verses 14–15). Joab is the kind of hatchet man that rulers need to do their dirty work, and he duly carries out David's instruction and reports it back to the king (verses 16–24).

The job has been done. David is relieved. His need to kill Uriah has made reckless tractics necessary, and other wives have lost their husbands as a result. But no matter. Better that a whole regiment be lost than that David's sin be found out. His message back to Joab is cynical and heartless (verse 25). 'People die all the time in war. It's just one of those things. Don't let it upset you.'

In truth Uriah's death was not an accident of war but a sinister requirement of royal power. When the king wants something he gets it, overriding the rights of others. When his action needs covering up to protect his authority, he can do it whatever the cost to others. Sexual temptation and the ruthless desire to get our own way lurks not far below the surface in many of us. But people in positions of influence face particular dangers here, just because they have more power to satisfy their desires.

The story shows how, once the path of wrongdoing is taken, one thing leads to another. Lust leads to adultery. Adultery leads to deception. Deception will resort even to murder in trying to cover up its tracks. But David has reckoned without God's verdict on the matter (verse 27).

Read 2 Samuel 12:1–14

Nathan has a tough assignment. If he speaks God's truth to him, will David act as ruthlessly towards him as he did to Uriah? Or will he respect him as a man of God and be changed by his painful message? Nathan's method of delivering the message is a brilliant use of parable, as searching and devastating as those of Jesus.

There is no hint to David that it is a parable. It sounds to him like one of those awkward cases from the local courts on which, as the country's chief judge, he is expected to give his verdict from time to time. Hearing the story he cannot fail to take sides. The rich man is ruthless and deserves to die, he declares.

Then comes the thunderbolt. 'You are the man!' (verse 7). The game is up. David, like most men and women, has a keen sense of justice when it comes to pronouncing on the weaknesses of others. Now it is time for him to stop making allowances for his own crimes and to recognize the horror of it. Despite all God's goodness to him he has broken God's law. The sword which has been his instrument of murder will bring conflict in his family (verses 7–12).

David finally acknowledges that he must bow to a greater King. Though the consequences of his actions must still be faced, genuine repentance meets with real forgiveness. God has not given up on David (verses 13–14).

28
Solomon's temple

By one of God's ironies, it was from the marriage of David and Bathsheba that Solomon was born to continue the dynasty and build the promised temple. On David's death Solomon became king, and in the fourth year of his reign the building of the temple began. The details of the work, which took seven years, are described in 1 Kings 6–7. Chapter 8 tells the story of its completion and dedication.

Once the building was completed, Solomon organized the opening ceremonies at a time of festival when large numbers of Israelites were gathered in Jerusalem (verses 1–2). Priests carried the ark of the covenant to the temple which stood on a new site to the north of the city. In this way the old symbol of God's presence and container of his law became part of the new structure. The new period of stability and prosperity had made possible the building of an imposing temple as the official centre of Israelite religion. But the people were not to forget that the God whom they worshipped had brought them out of Egypt and led them through the wilderness to the land of promise (verses 3–9).

In verses 10–13 the cloud represents the presence of God, 'taking up residence' in the temple. Just as God's presence with his people during the Exodus period had been conveyed to them by a cloud, so now the temple became the place where he dwells.

Solomon reminded the people how the newly built temple brought into being what God had promised to David (verses 15–21). It was an occasion for celebration, and a proud day for Solomon himself. It is worth reflecting on the gains and losses of this new development in Israel's religious practice.

On the credit side, the temple gave a new and impressive focus to Israel's faith. It conveyed something of the greatness of God in the same way as a medieval cathedral does. And it assured the people that God was always in their midst. That was its function, to guarantee God's presence at the centre of the nation's life.

But there is a debit side as well. The temple was built with forced labour (1 Kings 5:13). In that sense it was an expression of the tyrannical side of monarchy of which Samuel had warned. Like many a great building, it had something to do with the glory of Solomon as well as the glory of God. It was not simply a natural development from the moveable tent of the earlier period. It was also an expression of religion serving the interests of the state, a building to match Solomon's new royal palace. There are times when a state looks to its religious institutions to provide support for its political acts, such as the fighting of a war. When state and church are as close as this, the church is able to be heard by the state. But it may be harder for the church to be critical of the state.

And like all religious buildings and rituals, the temple raises questions about *the presence of God*. Can God's presence be guaranteed by a building? There were certainly people in Jerusalem later who thought that God's presence in the temple guaranteed their safety from enemy attack, and the prophet Jeremiah tried to warn them of this dangerous delusion (Jeremiah 7:1–11).

Solomon knows that God is not so predictable as this. He cannot be boxed in to suit our requirements. He knows that God 'dwells in a dark cloud' (verse 13). He remains mysterious, beyond our reach. He can surprise us by coming to us in new ways. He certainly cannot be controlled by religious rituals, or by 'saying the right words' or 'singing the right songs'.

Because a church is a place where people come to God in faith, and where baptisms and weddings and funerals and other significant events take place, an expectancy can develop that God's presence may be known there in a special way. But the New Testament suggests that this is not so much because of the special nature of the building as because the people themselves, gathered together before God, are 'God's temple' the place where God's Spirit dwells (1 Corinthians 3:16).

And here in 1 Kings 8 it is clear that to know the presence of God involves not merely attending the temple ceremonies, but living in obedience to God's will. For at the heart of the temple is the ark containing the Ten Commandments (verse 9).

29
Solomon's prayer
1 Kings 8:22–66

Solomon's prayer of dedication gives further insight into what the temple meant to the Israelites. But it goes beyond that and suggests how our relationship with God may be expressed.

Solomon begins by affirming Israel's central conviction, that Yahweh is the only God. He has bound Israel to him in a covenant and keeps his promises to them. His habit of fulfilling promises gives the king confidence to claim his promises for the future (verses 23–26). To appeal to promises which God has made in the Bible is a good way of praying. All our praying expresses trust in the promise, 'Come near to God and he will come near to you' (James 4:8).

Verses 27–30 reveals a big view of God. Just when we suspected that the temple was being built to contain and control God, we find Solomon declaring that God is so great that the whole universe cannot contain him. God is not restricted to religious places, he is free from the control of religious professionals. And it is *this God* who is able to help us in our need.

This understanding of God is not negative towards the temple. Verse 29 pictures the temple like a kind of relay station: people pray towards the temple and God, whose eyes and ears are fixed on the temple at all times, picks up their messages. He responds to their needs and forgives their wrongdoing.

Verses 31–45 surveys a whole series of troubles which may be taken to God in prayer. These include personal disputes (verses 31–32), wars (verses 33–34, 44–45), drought, disease, and famine (verses 35–40). Underlying this passage is the assumption that troubles frequently arise through unfaithfulness to God's will. So again the focus on forgiveness is important. There is no area of life about which it is irrelevant to ask, 'What does it mean in this situation to obey God?' There is no area of life which is beyond his power to forgive and transform.

In verses 41–43 there is a remarkable affirmation of the place of foreigners within the Israelite community. If people come from afar to worship Israel's God, they will find him as generous towards them as to any Israelite.

Verses 44–53 look forward to the possibility of exile from Palestine, pleading that God will forgive the sins which bring on this disaster. Because he knows that God is not *confined* to the temple, Solomon can have confidence that prayer from a distant place is heard by God. We are never so far from God that he cannot reach us in our deepest need.

Confidence that prayer will be answered is based on Israel's special calling (verses 51–53). God, who has rescued them from Egypt and made them his own, will not let them down. Because we can 'praise him for all that is past' we can 'trust him for all that's to come' (Joseph Hart).

Solomon's final words (verses 56–61) are a fine summary of themes which have been prominent in this chapter—the goodness and the promises of God, the longing for God's protective presence, the importance of obedience to God's demands, the need for God's grace to enable us to please him.

The whole ceremony ends with extravagant celebration (verses 62–66). The altar cannot cope with the number of animals for sacrifice and feasting (verse 64)! Joyful thanksgiving to God is the keynote (verse 66). Thanksgiving is the beginning and end of prayer.

A prayer of thanksgiving

Thanks be to thee, my Lord Jesus Christ,
for all the benefits thou hast won for me,
for all the pains and insults thou hast borne for me.
O most merciful Redeemer, Friend and Brother,
may I know thee more clearly,
love thee more dearly,
and follow thee more nearly,
day by day. Amen.

St Richard of Chichester, 1197–1253

30
The kingdom is split in two

After the glory comes the fall. Solomon was famous for his wisdom, his buildings, his military achievements. But his alliances with other nations brought to Israel worship of foreign gods. His personal lifestyle was as extravagant as that of any modern dictator. Forced labour was the price which the nation paid for Solomon's grandiose achievements. Samuel's warning about the cost of having a king (passage 23) came true with a vengeance. The harvest of oppression was about to be reaped.

Read 1 Kings 11:41—12:33

When Solomon died the question bubbled to the surface: Will his son Rehoboam continue the oppression, or will he learn a different way to rule? When representatives of the Israelite tribes met at ancient Shechem to affirm his kingship, the question was put bluntly to him by Jeroboam (12:4).

For Rehoboam there was a choice. Whatever the influence of family and upbringing on a child's behaviour, the son does not *have* to follow in his father's footsteps. He consulted two sets of advisors. The older officials knew, like Jeroboam, that there is another way of exercising power (12:7). True leadership involves service, not domination. It wins people's loyalty, even their affection.

Rehoboam's contemporaries, intoxicated by their new-found

influence, urged even greater oppression (12:10–11). They won the day, and the fortunes of the nation were changed for ever. The statement in verse 15 that 'this turn of events was from the Lord' does not mean that God approved the attitude of Rehoboam, but that he used the events to bring on Solomon's family the judgment of which he had warned (1 Kings 11:9–13).

Verses 16–24 describe the split between the ten tribes of northern Israel and the tribes of Judah and Benjamin around Jerusalem, who remained under Rehoboam's rule. The slogan of verse 16 expresses northern hostility to domination by David's dynasty in the south. Rehoboam's attempt to squash the rebellion came to nothing (verses 18–24). Aiming at total control, he lost most of his subjects.

From that time there were two kingdoms—Israel in the north and Judah in the south. The remaining chapters of the Books of Kings tell the story of these two kingdoms. The conflict between them which began with Jeroboam's rebellion rumbled on until there was little left to fight about.

The writer explains how Rehoboam's aggression was curbed by the warning of a prophet (verses 22–24). Even tyrants are ultimately subject to God's control. They cannot do what they like for ever. However unlikely the prospect may seem, the oppressed will find their freedom—as recently in eastern Europe and South Africa.

But Jeroboam too gets only limited approval from the writer of 1 Kings. As the bringer of liberation for the northern tribes he was truly the agent of God who hears the cry of the oppressed. But the consequences of his revolt were spiritually disastrous.

Having cut links with Jerusalem, he knew there was a problem. If people from the north went to Jerusalem to offer sacrifice at the temple their affections would revert to Jerusalem and to Rehoboam. They would surrender their independence for the sake of access to that special place of God's presence (verses 25–27).

Jeroboam's solution was to set up alternative shrines at Dan on the northern edge of Israel and at Bethel near its southern border with Judah. In each place he set up a golden calf (verses 28–30). Probably these calves were not meant to represent God, but to be a kind of throne on which the invisible God was believed to stand. Canaanite gods were often represented as standing on calves or bulls as symbols of their strength.

But the attempt to provide an alternative focus of worship opened the door to the introduction of pagan rituals. Jeroboam softened the distinctiveness of Israel's faith: 'The Lord our God, the Lord is one.' He built other shrines on 'high places'—hilltop sites where there had been Canaanite places of worship—and broke the traditional rule that priests must come only from the tribe of Levi. He introduced a new festival to divert his people's thoughts away from the great festivals in Jerusalem (verses 31–33).

The verdict of the story-teller is that Jeroboam compromised Israel's true faith for the sake of political expediency. Like many political leaders down the centuries he tried to harness the power of religion to bolster his own régime. As we shall see, his policy sowed trouble for the whole nation.

To think about

Compare Rehoboam's attitude with the comment of Jesus: 'The kings of the Gentiles lord it over them; and those who exercise authority over them call themselves Benefactors. But you are not to be like that. Instead, the greatest among you should be like the youngest, and the one who rules like the one who serves' (Luke 22:25–26). In any group or organization with which you are involved, what would it mean to take Jesus' words seriously?

31
Elijah, God's man in a hostile world

Jeroboam was followed by a number of rather undistiguished rulers of Israel. Then in the ninth century BC two kings, Omri and his son Ahab, brought political stability and strength to the nation. They were shrewd soldiers and statesmen, but their alliances with foreign nations deepened the crisis of Israel's faith. Ahab married Jezebel, daughter of the king of Tyre and Sidon. A crusading advocate of Canaanite religion, she brought with her 450 prophets of Baal and 400 prophets of his partner Asherah, and tried to suppress the prophets of Yahweh.

Baal and Asherah were nature gods. They were believed to guarantee the fertility of the soil, and so held the key to the continuation of life itself. It is not too difficult to imagine the attraction of these gods to many of the Israelites. Yahweh had rescued them from Egypt and secured their place in the Promised Land. But was he any good at making the crops grow? Wouldn't it be better to hedge their bets and worship the Canaanite gods who had apparently made a success of fertility long before the Israelites arrived? It was not easy to trust Yahweh for everything, to believe that the Lord of history was also the Lord of the harvest.

When such crises come, God usually has someone whom he has quietly prepared to stand up for him in the world. His man this time was Elijah, a leader in the tradition of Moses and Samuel, a prophet who acted as God's mouthpiece in a special way. The writer of 1 Kings gives a lot of space to the conflict between Elijah and king Ahab because he sees that the survival of Israel as God's covenant people depended on their refusal to dilute their faith for the sake of political 'progress'.

Elijah confronted Ahab with the message that God was sending a severe drought on the land, and then ran for cover while the dust settled (1 Kings 17:1–6).

Read 1 Kings 18:1–15

When Elijah at last gets word that the drought will end it is not because Ahab or Israel has repented, but simply because God in his grace has decided to reveal himself afresh to his people (verse 1). The prophet sets off for Samaria, Ahab's capital city, to break the news to him.

The scene shifts to Ahab's palace. The king is planning with his chief administrator. But what is he planning? The mighty king, whose role is to form the nation's policy and to deal with the great affairs of state, is going out to look for grass! But notice why he needs it: to feed his horses and mules (verse 5). These animals are the engines of his military power. Ahab is behaving like a modern dictator who squanders his Gross National Product on supplying his arsenal rather than on improving the life of his subjects.

There follows the meeting between Elijah and Obadiah (verses 7–15). Here are two men dedicated to wholehearted service of God. Elijah is a prophet. His life is in danger because of his faithfulness to God's call and his bold challenge to the king. Obadiah is a statesman, living with integrity in the midst of a government hostile to Israel's traditional beliefs and values. He too has risked his life by hiding prophets from Jezebel's search parties and supplying them with food and water (verse 4).

Together they provide a picture of the kinds of service which God requires. One is called to a 'religious' ministry of speaking God's word. The other is called to 'secular' service in the life of the nation. Just as much as Elijah, he is standing for truth, justice and compassion in a hostile world. He is the buttress preventing the wall of Ahab's

71

régime collapsing into a tyranny which totally defies the will of God. Neither kind of servant is more important to God, more dedicated than the other. Both are needed if God's purpose is to be worked out.

'Go and tell Ahab that I've come out of hiding,' says Elijah (verse 8).

'But if I do, God is just as likely to whisk you off somewhere else,' worries Obadiah. 'Then when he doesn't find you he'll kill me for not arresting you here and now' (verses 9–14).

'There's no danger of that. I have business to do with the king' (verse 15).

And so the scene is set for one of the most dramatic incidents in the Old Testament.

To think about

Are you, or someone you know, in a situation similar to Obadiah, trying to live with Christian integrity in hostile surroundings? What are your spiritual resources for this ministry? How should we pray for our fellow-Christians in these circumstances?

3 2
The contest on Mount Carmel   1 Kings 18:16–46

This is one of those moments when a nation senses that it has a stark choice to make which will profoundly affect its future. It begins with the encounter between the prophet and the king (verses 16–19). Ahab's charge is a serious one: by bringing drought to the land Elijah is destabilizing the whole nation and is guilty of treason. Elijah's reply raises the stakes even higher: the king himself is the source of Israel's trouble. He and this people must find out once and for all who is the real God, and decide whether they are to follow him wholeheartedly.

A crowd representing the whole nation gathers near the top of Mount Carmel, together with the prophets of Baal. We can imagine them sitting and standing in a kind of natural amphitheatre on the mountain slopes as the contest takes place before them. But first comes the challenge of Elijah (verse 21). The word translated 'waver' or 'sit on the fence' is the same as the word for 'dance' in verse 26. Elijah charges the people with hopping from one foot to the other, never making up their mind which God they are committed to.

The rules for the contest are set out (verses 22–24). Elijah and the prophets of Baal are each to prepare an altar for the sacrifice of a bull. The real God will reveal his identity by sending fire to kindle the altar. The Canaanites believed Baal was responsible for thunder, lightning and rain, whilst in Israelite faith Yahweh was the source of weather as of everything else in creation (see Psalm 104:3–4).

The prophets of Baal take their turn first (verses 25–29). 'No firelighters, no cheating', says Elijah. 'Just pray to Baal and see what happens.'

So the prayer and ritual dance begins. Like a joker in the crowd at a football match, Elijah taunts the opposition. Actually, in doing so he shows knowledge of the myths about Baal. The suggestion that he is asleep, for example, alludes to the Canaanite belief that Baal slept through the winter and was roused when crops were sown in the spring. But the satire is more savage than that. 'Perhaps he is busy, or on a journey' is probably a polite way of suggesting that Baal has gone to the toilet. A rather crude joke to make about a god, perhaps. But it underlines the fact that, far from being a great god, Baal cannot rise above the ordinary functions of a human being.

A whole day of frenzied appeal to the god. No reply. Then it is Elijah's turn (verses 30–39). Symbolically he places on the altar twelve stones, for what is happening today concerns the whole of Israel and Judah, not just the ten tribes of the north. To prove there is no cheating, he pours water on and around the altar. The water is probably from a well on the mountain which even today does not run dry during times of drought. And he prays that the Lord will act decisively, to turn people's hearts back to himself. Three times his prayer speaks of 'the Lord'—Yahweh, the God of the Exodus, the God to whom the Israelites owe everything, if only they would recognize it.

Imagine how Elijah feels as he begins his prayer! If God does not respond, he is a dead man. Sometimes prayer has to stake everything on the faithfulness of God to respond, refusing to contemplate the alternative.

The effect is immediate. The fire falls, the wood on the altar is kindled, and the people shout their enthusiasm for Yahweh. There is no point speculating how the miracle happened. We are simply confronted by the story and invited to respond. We see the contrast between the people's speechlessness at the beginning and their acclamation at the end (verses 21, 39), between the god who gave no response and the God who answers by fire (verses 26, 38). We see the fugitive Elijah carry the day, while Ahab and Jezebel's prophets are humiliated.

We shudder at the slaughter of the prophets of Baal (verse 40).

Elijah is in fact carrying out the sentence set by the law for prophets of pagan gods (Deuteronomy 13:12–18). Perhaps the danger was seen as so great that they had to be stamped out to save the rest of the nation.

To think about

'No-one can serve two masters. Either he will hate the one and love the other, or he will be devoted to the one and despise the other. You cannot serve God and Money' (Matthew 6:24). These words of Jesus express the same theme as Elijah's 'How long will you waver between two opinions?' Why do you think we are so inclined to try and have it both ways?

33
An enemy general is healed

A decade later another king ruled Israel, and Elijah's prophetic mantle had been passed on to Elisha. If the drama of Elijah on Mount Carmel gives the impression that Israelites are meant to hate and fear foreigners, the following story casts a different light.

Read 2 Kings 5

Naaman is a successful general in the army of Aram (Syria). But he is afflicted by a chronic skin disease (not necessarily what is called leprosy today). As an Aramean he is an enemy of Israel—though the present episode must have occurred during a comparative lull in hostilities. In his own house is a slave girl from Israel captured in a border raid. And this unnamed teenager becomes the key to his healing (verses 1–3). She doesn't appear again in the story. But she represents those countless people of God who never become famous but are doing God's will, saying a word for him when it matters.

Imagine the story now from Naaman's viewpoint. You get the king of Aram's permission to go to Israel (verses 4–6). He sends you off with a note to the king of Israel, asking him to arrange the cure. You also take with you a gift of about 350 kilos of silver, 70 kilos of gold and ten changes of clothing. You are determined to make a good impression! Or you are desperate to get healed and will pay any price. But Joram, king of Israel, sees all this as an elaborate ploy to pick a quarrel (verse 7).

While you are wondering what to do next a message comes from Elisha (verse 8). When you arrive at his house with all your horses and chariots he doesn't even come out to say hello. He just sends instructions to wash in the Jordan. You are outraged. Surely a man of God would come out and perform some impressive ritual to make the healing happen? And why should a great man like you get wet in a muddy little river like the Jordan (verses 11–12)?

At this point some other unnamed people play their part in the sequence: your servants persuade you to swallow your pride. You go to the Jordan in obedience to the prophet and your skin is wonderfully restored (verses 13–14).

In a short time you have moved from desperation to hope, to anger and pride, to submission and now to gratitude and recognition of the power of Israel's God (verse 15). Elisha refuses your gift. He wants you to know that God's healing and all his gifts are free. They are to be bought neither with money nor with impressive acts. They are given on God's terms to people who will receive them as he directs. And they are for all the world—even for those whom the 'insiders' fear as their enemies.

This theme of God's purpose for the whole world is one which keeps surfacing in the Old Testament. It was there in the promise to Abraham that 'all peoples on earth will be blessed through you' (Genesis 12:3). It will reappear in other writings to which we shall come later. It will reach new heights in the experience of the early Christian church, recorded in the New Testament. For religious groups, whether Jewish or Christian, there is always a temptation to make God 'one of us' and to resent the intrusion of 'outsiders'. Naaman's vivid expression of faith (verse 15) is a challenge to that mentality. God himself refuses to be boxed in by our boundaries.

Naaman's request in verse 17 is often thought to express the ancient view that a god could be worshipped only on the soil of the country to which he 'belonged'. But perhaps he simply wants a visible reminder of his visit, as pilgrims today often bring back a bottle of water from the Jordan or soil from the Holy Land. Either way, it signals Naaman's determination to worship the God whom he has now discovered.

Unfortunately the story doesn't end there. Gehazi is the type of religious professional for whom the activity of God is no longer a source of wonder but an opportunity to make money (verses 19–27). While his master is introducing people to the magnificent grace of

75

God, he is round the corner selling postcards of the place. Worse than that, he resorts to deception in order to get what he wants and to cover up his unprincipled behaviour. With poetic justice, he becomes a leper.

But we need not dwell too long on this part of the story. Earlier, the message has been about a God whose concern for people knows no boundaries, a God who gives himself to the humble. And it has been about the vital part which 'unimportant people' play in bringing his plans to their goal.

34
Uncomfortable prophet

As we have seen, prophets such as Nathan, Elijah and Elisha played a significant role in Israel's life. But a few such men were regarded as so important that their words were gathered together into special collections. The earliest of these so-called 'writing prophets' were Amos and Hosea, who prophesied to the Northern Kingdom about a hundred years after Elisha.

Prophets had an intense awareness of what God wanted to say to people. Through their own closeness to God, or through dreams and visions, they picked up his message and declared it with a confident 'This is what the Lord says...' They spoke in poetry, often with great vividness and power. Their purpose was to show how the nation had turned away from their covenant with God and to warn them of the consequences. It was to exhort them to change their ways and rediscover what it meant to be God's privileged and obedient people. Their forecasts of the future were not the fatalistic predictions of a fortune-teller, but promises and warnings of the consequences of obedience and disobedience to God's will.

Amos was a truly disturbing character. Under king Jeroboam II, the Israelites were enjoying peace and prosperity, thanks to the decline of power in surrounding nations. Their control of key trade routes brought new wealth, and a property boom ensued. A farmer from Tekoa near Jerusalem, Amos crossed the border from Judah to Israel uninvited and unannounced. His blistering messages came like a blast from a blow-torch to the complacent people of Israel. We read the following passage first because it includes reference to his call to be a prophet.

Read Amos 7

Amos receives three visions (verses 1–9). The first two depict the terrible devastation which God's judgment on Israel will bring. God's witholding of the judgment in response to Amos' plea shows that God's activity in the world is not 'programmed' according to an unalterable plan. Precisely because he longs to bring blessing rather than destruction he responds to the prayers of his people. This is an encouragement to Christians to keep praying for justice and compassion in the life of their nation.

But the third vision brings home the sober truth: a constantly rebellious nation cannot avoid God's judgment for ever. God has measured Israel against his standard of righteousness. And, like a tottering wall, Israel is fit only to be knocked down. Corrupt worship-centres and the royal household itself will feel the weight of God's anger.

Not surprisingly, the religious establishment is alarmed at Amos' message and his insolence at bringing it. It is as if an Irish sheep-farmer were to confront the Dean in Westminster Abbey with the news that the Abbey was to be destroyed and the whole royal family and Her Majesty's government were to meet a violent death. The traitor must be deported before his subversive message poisons the people any further. Amaziah, the high priest at Bethel, tells him to get back to Judah and earn his living as a prophet there (verses 10–13).

But Amos stands his ground (verses 14–15). 'I'm no professional prophet,' he retorts, 'earning my bread by issuing prophecies at the temple or the court of Judah. Sheep and cattle are my business. But the Lord took hold of me and commanded me to prophesy to Israel.'

Notice the contrast: Amaziah says, 'Go, prophesy in Judah'. God says, 'Go, prophesy to my people Israel.' That, for Amos, is the difference between a divine call and a human arrangement. Amaziah doesn't mind Amos prophesying, as long as it is in a safe place where it won't disturb him. Amos is overwhelmed by the sense that, despite his lack of training, he has been chosen by God as the bearer of a devastating message. He takes no pleasure in it but, like Martin Luther in his stand against the corrupt practices of the medieval Roman Catholic Church, he 'can do no other'. That deep sense of call sustains us when we serve God in difficult places.

How do we know that a man with such a message is a man of God and not a crank? There is no easy answer. Amos was in due course shown to be right because his warnings of destruction came true—and so were written down for the benefit of later generations. But we are wise not to dismiss too quickly the warnings of those who shake us to the foundations by challenging the values by which we live. By undermining our cherished hopes they may be messengers of true and lasting hope.

By refusing to listen, Amaziah seals his own fate (verses 16–17). The exile to another land, to which he alluded in verse 11, will indeed be his own fate and the fate of Israel itself.

3 5
'Let justice flow like a river' *Amos 5*

We see here in more detail what Amos's disturbing message was. In verses 1–17 he laments Israel's condition and calls for repentance.

First, Amos *laments* Israel's fall from grace (verse 1–3). Like a mourner at a funeral, he grieves over the death of a great nation. He shares God's sorrow over Israel's refusal of healing. 'Virgin' (verse 2) underlines the sadness of Israel's premature death. She should have had a whole life of love and fruitfulness before her. The cause of Israel's death will be invasion, destroying all but a fraction of her army.

Secondly, he *exhorts* Israel to turn back to God (verses 4–6). They think that going to the worship centres at Bethel and Gilgal, or making a pilgrimage to Beersheba in the south, will boost their standing with God and secure the nation's safety against attack. Far from it, says Amos, these shrines have distorted true worship. Instead of providing a way to God they have become a substitute for God. 'Seek the Lord himself, and you may yet survive the judgment that is coming.'

Thirdly, he *accuses* Israel by putting his finger on what is wrong (verse 7). Because God acts in justice and righteousness the people of his covenant are meant to do the same. But in their legal decisions and their dealings with each other they show how they despise God's will.

Fourthly, he *celebrates* God's rule over the world (verses 8–9). The God who sustains the world is the Lord who guides Israel's history. If he chooses, he can do against Israel what he has previously done for Israel. There is no hiding from his justice.

The following verses have the pattern of verses 1–7 in reverse order.

Amos *accuses* Israel of wrongdoing (verses 10–13). We see now how justice is being perverted. People are putting pressure on those responsible to maintain truth and justice in the law courts. And, as is always the case when prosperity comes, it does not come to all. The rich are trampling on the poor by extorting unreasonable rents from tenant-farmers. They are building expensive houses and lush vineyards. They are using their wealth and influence to ensure that the complaints of the poor against them don't get a proper hearing in court.

Amos *exhorts* Israel once again (verses 14–15). To declare in worship, 'The Lord is with us', is empty syllables if the worshippers are not seeking and loving good. The only test of true devotion to God is obedience to the will of God.

Finally, he *laments* Israel's expected fate (verse 16–17). So great will be the calamity that farm-workers will be drafted in as extra mourners. The vineyards in which the wealthy prided themselves will echo with cries of grief. For God himself will come in judgment.

In verses 18–27 Israel's comfortable assumptions are overturned. They 'long for the day of the Lord' when God will bring permanent victory over their enemies. But they are in for a surprise. Because they have scorned the demands of their covenant with God his victory will be against them, not for them. Amos's devastating images need no explanation (verses 18–20).

In their worship the people think they are celebrating and looking forward to this great day of victory. But this worship means nothing to God because it is a smokescreen for their heartless indifference to their fellow-Israelites. 'They are *your* feasts, *your* assemblies, *your* sacrifices, *your* songs,' says God. 'They have nothing to do with me' (verses 21–23). Worship without obedience worked out in daily living is an insult to God. To despise a fellow human being is to despise the God who made her.

What matters above all else is that Israel should practise justice and righteousness (verse 24). 'Justice' means righting wrongs and punishing wrongdoers. 'Righteousness' involves ensuring right relationships in society. And that includes protecting the poor against the power of the rich, and making sure the vulnerable are cared for. Here is a vision of society which contrasts sharply with the individualism of Western societies today. The person who says, 'I never do anyone any harm', and thinks that is an adequate guide for living, is a million miles away from the prophet's understanding of God's purpose for human society.

In verses 25–27 Amos points out that from the beginning Israel's relationship with God was based on obedience rather than merely on worship rituals. Now their disobedience has led them to idolatry. The judgment of exile to foreign lands is surely on its way.

To think about

'Concern for the rights and welfare of all [God's] people flows, like a mighty river, from his own heart. Whoever would truly serve him must go with that flow' (D.A. Hubbard on verse 24). What aspects of our own society might Amos denounce as unrighteous?

36
A marriage made in heaven

Unlike Amos his contemporary, Hosea was a native of the Northern Kingdom. In a daring and deadly serious piece of drama, God told him to marry 'an adulterous woman' (Hosea 1:2). It is not quite clear what this means. Was she a prostitute? Or a 'cult prostitute', employed at a Canaanite shrine to perform sexual intercourse in a cultic act designed to persuade Baal to bring fertility to the crops? Or was she a woman who simply found it impossible to remain faithful in marriage?

Whichever of these she was, God instructed Hosea to marry her. He was not playing games, but was using Hosea's experience to dramatize his own anguish at Israel's unfaithfulness to him. If the people would not listen to prophetic words, would they perhaps respond when they saw God's grief and God's love acted out before them?

The following passage uses Hosea's experience of marriage and unfaithfulness and persistent love as a picture of God's relationship with Israel. Hosea's vivid poetry defies logical analysis, but the power of the message is unmistakable.

Read Hosea 2:2–23

Divorce proceedings (verses 2–5). God is speaking, as though he were a husband making accusations in a divorce court. Like Gomer, Israel has proved unfaithful. The reality has gone out of her relationship with God. Her defence is the familiar plea of the unfaithful partner, that her other lovers can satisfy her in a way that her husband cannot (verse 5). She believes that Baal, not Yahweh, will make the earth fruitful and supply her needs in life. Lured by the powerful symbolism of an earthy religion which makes no moral demands, she cannot believe that Israel's God is the supplier of all her needs.

Divine restraint (verse 6–13). There are times when God allows us to reap the consequences of our own wrong choices. For him to do other than that would be to make a mockery of our freedom. And yet somehow there are times when in love he restrains us. He limits our freedom to go wrong. He protects us until we learn from our past mistakes.

That is what God is suggesting here. Israel's search for security and satisfaction from Baal will come to nothing. She will return to Yahweh because 'then I was better off than now' (verse 7). This is not a very lofty motive for returning to God. But it offers hope of a fresh beginning.

Yet it will be a painful process. Verses 11 and 12 hint at the destruction which exile will bring. Religious festivals celebrated at Israelite shrines will become a thing of the past. The land will be devastated—perhaps by drought, perhaps by invading armies.

The door of hope (verses 14–23). The mood changes. The language of love returns. Israel's exile may be a 'wilderness experience', but there they will recapture the excitement of the young love which they felt when they first came out of Egypt. God will once again win the heart of his beloved. The place of trouble (Achor was a place of disobedience at the original entry into the Promised Land, Joshua 7:26) will become the door of hope (verses 14–15).

In verses 16–17 Hosea plays on the fact that '*baal*' or 'master' was used in Hebrew to mean 'husband' as well as the god Baal. No longer, he says, will God's 'wife' Israel confuse him with Baal. She will love him with undivided devotion.

The day will come when the harmony between humanity and nature will be restored, and peace will reign (verse 18). God will commit himself afresh to Israel, with an engagement present which overflows with generosity (verses 19–20). Israel will now receive from God—their true source—all the blessings which nature provides (verses 21–22).

The passage ends by reversing the significance of the names of Hosea's children (verses 22–23). Hosea 1:3–9 described how the

81

three children born to Gomer were given names symbolic of Israel's spiritual condition. His son was called Jezreel (meaning 'God scatters')—an allusion to God's judgment on the royal household. Now that name is reinterpreted as 'God sows'—a promise of Israelites newly 'planted' in the land after exile.

Hosea's daughter was called Lo-Ruhamah ('Not loved') and his second son Lo-Ammi ('Not my people'). Now the threats implied in those names are turned into blessings. And—like a bride at a wedding service—Israel will respond to God's promise of commitment to her: 'You are mine' (verse 23). God's love at last is met by wholehearted response.

The good news in Hosea is that nothing can squash God's ability to restore us to himself. Upbringing, failures, wrongdoing, broken relationships, despair, the habits of a lifetime—beyond all these there is a door of hope where God says, 'I love you. You are my people.'

37

'How can I give you up?'   Hosea 11:1–11

Verses 1–4. God and Israel are now portrayed not as husband and wife but as parent and child. God adopted Israel as a helpless baby in Egypt, taught him to walk, cared for him with enduring love. At the end of verse 4 the image changes to that of a farmer tending his animals. Some translations, however, translate, 'I lifted them like a little child to my cheek', and thus continue the parent-child picture.

But Israel has become like an adolescent anxious to distance himself from his parents. He doesn't want to acknowledge what he owes to them. He has embraced Baal instead of the God who rescued him from Egypt (verse 3).

Verses 5–7. Judgment therefore is certain. Verse 5 probably alludes to diplomatic moves which Israel was involved in in an attempt to prevent invasion. Ironically, their turning away from Yahweh who rescued them from Egypt may result in their return as refugees to this place of slavery.

Verses 8–9. After the expected word of judgment comes the shock of God's inner conflict. Defiance of God brings its inevitable consequence. Yet God cannot let it happen! He cannot find it in him to let Israel (also called Ephraim) suffer the fate of Admah and Zeboiim (destroyed with Sodom and Gomorrah, Deuteronomy 29:23). Notice the repeated 'not' in verse 9. God recoils from dismissing his rebellious child from his presence.

Verses 10–11. These verses, however, presuppose that Israel has gone into exile. Like a mighty lion, God now leads them home once more. So verses 8–9 cannot mean that God simply cancels the expected sentence for Israel's sins. It means that Israel experiences the judgment of exile, but is not utterly destroyed. God will make a fresh start with them.

Why does he not allow them to be destroyed once and for all? 'For I am God, and not man.' By human logic death means the end. But by divine logic the creator can bring about resurrection. Rebellious though they are, he will not let go of those to whom he is committed. He will make a new beginning with them. The agony which we glimpse here in the inner conversation of God was to reach its fullest expression at the crucifixion of Jesus. There God in Christ took on himself all the pain of human wrongdoing so that we may be brought into a new relationship with him.

Whereas Amos had much to say about the *moral* failures of Israel, Hosea's prophecy concentrates more on the *spiritual* crisis which underlies them. Israel has walked out on her husband, and has found other lovers in Baal and the gods of Canaan. What might his attack on Israel's compromise with Canaanite religion suggest to us?

First, Canaanite religion was for them what technology and the management of the economy have become in our society—essential for prosperity and the increase of the Gross National Product. In seeking the success which these things offer we, like they, lose our focus on the living God. Our lives are shaped by what we worship. And if worship involves giving attention to the object of worship, the gods of our society have names like Economy, Success, Self-expression, Sex.

Second, if we stay with the prominence of sexual imagery and sexual activity in Canaanite religion, we are not far from the obsession of our times. At least the Canaanites seriously believed that such expressions of sexuality were necessary to ensure that the gods kept making their crops grow. In our day the infatuation with sexual self-expression, the prominence of pornography and the calculated use of sex to sell things are signs of a society which has lost its way.

Thirdly, in having one god for rain, one for corn, and so on, the Canaanites had a fragmented view of the world. The Israelites muddled this even further by trying to add this collection of gods to their belief in Yahweh. All this time, says Hosea, they are refusing to recognize that Yahweh is responsible for all things. He is the creator and sustainer of the world as well as the Lord of Israel's history.

What is important here is that the Hebrew belief in one God provides a coherent view of the world. It is not ruled by a collection of competing powers (gods), each to be wooed by human persuasion. Nor is it simply a closed system running like clockwork on its own predetermined path. The world is a single, harmonious system, of which everything—including the fertility of the soil, the possibilities of technology, the 'laws of nature'—owe their origin to a single creator.

To think about

What, in your view, are the 'gods' which people worship today? What do you think is their proper place in God's world?

38
Isaiah of Jerusalem

There were prophets in Judah too. Isaiah lived in Jerusalem and prophesied over many years, advising, encouraging and accusing the king and the nation. By looking at the account of his call we may use his experience to reflect on our own calling as servants of God.

Read Isaiah 6

The context (verse 1). 'In the year that king Uzziah died . . .'. It was about 740BC and the fifty-year reign of Uzziah (called Azariah in 2 Kings) was over. It was a year of destiny in which prosperity gave way to uncertainty. For it was the time when Assyria was beginning to bring its menacing power to bear on Israel and Judah.

If we sense a shaking of the foundations—in the world or in personal experience—such as confronted Isaiah in his time, it is a time when God can break through. As we sense the urgency of the need around us and the weakness within us, we can be open to a fresh vision of God.

The vision (verses 1–4). Isaiah is at worship in the temple. Suddenly his senses are led beyond the grandeur of the building and the worship to a glimpse of God himself. The choir singing in the temple becomes the heavenly choir, the smoke of incense becomes the smoke which signifies God's presence. It is as though a screen which normally hides God from earthly view is drawn back to reveal the Lord in all his glory.

The seraphs are winged attendants of God, two of whose wings serve to protect their faces from the brightness of God's glory. Their song (verse 3) impresses two great themes on the prophet. First, God's *holiness* means his complete 'otherness' or distinctiveness from his creation. The repetition of 'holy' stresses that he is utterly distinct from us. This fact brings both awe and hope. Awe, because we are overwhelmed by our own smallness and sinfulness in comparison with him. Hope, because we need someone different from ourselves to deliver us from our plight.

Secondly the seraphs sing, 'The whole earth is full of his glory.' This must have come as a surprise to Isaiah, disturbed as he was by the thought that the earth was full of sin and despair. But a vision of God brings a new vision of the world. A glimpse of God's majesty in worship enables us to see that he has not abandoned the world to darkness. He is everywhere at work, inviting us to uncover for ourselves and for others his hidden presence.

Repentance and forgiveness (verses 5–7). The vision makes Isaiah deeply aware of his sinfulness. He doesn't say, 'I can't help it, I'm a product of my environment.' He identifies with the failures of his country. The reference to unclean lips perhaps invites us to ponder especially on how much human sinfulness is expressed through words—anger, lying, abuse of others . . .

God's forgiveness is conveyed to him by a strange but vivid ritual. To be forgiven and purified by God is a prelude to our serving him.

Commission (verses 8–10). In his vision Isaiah overhears the conversation between God and his heavenly servants. Unlike Moses (passage 15), he doesn't shrink from the task to be done. He interrupts the divine conversation and offers himself immediately! Being overwhelmed by God's holiness and renewed by his forgiveness leads to obedient and thankful service.

But the task is utterly daunting (verses 9–10). As if despairing of them, God calls the people of Judah 'this people', not 'my people'. He warns the prophet that the people will take little notice of his message. To us it may seem as though God is actually instructing Isaiah to prophesy *so that* the people's hearts will be hardened against him. The ironic language is a way of warning Isaiah that his mission is tough—but he is still to go.

When as Christians we face a difficult task it is important to know that we are called by God to do it. It is also a source of great strength to know that God understands how tough it is. It is a puzzle why people in Europe or the Middle East today do not respond to the Christian message as readily as people in Africa or Korea. But the difficulty of sharing Christ in these places is not a reason for pulling out.

Ray of hope (verses 11–13). Isaiah is told that exile will be the fate of God's rebellious people. Devastation will be almost total. And yet even out of the stump of a single tree new life can begin. Faithful service may see little response, yet God will not give up.

To think about

How is the sequence of context, vision, repentance and forgiveness, and commission reflected in your own experience?

39
The ideal king

Isaiah's hope lay in a future king whose rule would contrast with the often faithless and inadequate kings of Israel and Judah. Christians see Jesus as the fulfilment of this hope, the Messiah descended from David. Jesse (verse 1) was David's father.

Read Isaiah 11:1–9

Because in Christian thought these words are so closely associated with Jesus, we need to make a conscious effort to see that Isaiah's hope is focussed on an earthly ruler. Perhaps we can do this by rewording part of his prophecy in a way which highlights the qualities which he longs for in an ideal ruler.

² The Spirit of the Lord will endow him with all the gifts need for
his office—
wisdom and understanding in political affairs,
skill in diplomacy and strength in negotiation,
discernment and insight.
In his actions he will always take God's purposes into account

³ and will promote an atmosphere of godliness in the land.
In administering justice he will discern people's inner motives
and uncover deception.

⁴ He will pay attention to genuine grievances
and will champion the cause of those who are powerless to
defend themselves.
Like a rod his verdict will strike the ruthless.
He will not shrink from imposing severe penalties when
necessary.

⁵ His constant aim will be to uphold justice and truth.

In the second part of verse 4 I have followed the Revised English Bible,
which takes the whole passage to be about the king's role as the
righteous ruler of Israel, rather than as a military leader against the
nations ('strike the earth' in some other translations).

On one level, then, we have here a description of an ideal king, a
picture of how a ruler ought to behave. It lists the qualities we should
look for and pray for in our rulers, whether in national or local
government. By implication it suggests qualities desirable in a leader
in any context. And it insists that such qualities grow in a person by the
work of God's Spirit.

There is food here for thought and prayer—prayer for myself and
for others.

The prophecy goes on to say that under this king there will be peace
and harmony not only among people but also in the whole natural
world (verses 6–9). It contrasts with our present experience, where
disorder on the human level increases the disorder of nature. Wars
devastate the landscape and foul the atmosphere. Pollutant technology
is dumped on Two-Thirds World countries. Short-term planning by
politicians fearing that tough decisions will lose them their jobs leads to
increasing holes in the ozone layer and continued global warming.

With such a vision of a world renewed and at peace we clearly move beyond the hope for an ideal king on an earthly, political level. As God's prophet Isaiah spoke deeper truth than he realized. This and other passages in his book express Israel's hope of a Messiah who would transform the world and bring people close to God in a new way. It was a hope which kept them going through centuries of oppression. It is this hope which ties the Old and New Testaments together. For the New Testament shows how this age-old longing was fulfilled in Jesus the Messiah and points forward to the future time when God's purpose for the world will finally reach its goal and 'the earth will be filled with the knowledge of the glory of the Lord, as the waters cover the sea'.

We may be tempted to wonder whether such hopes are simply a case of whistling in the dark, believing that better times are coming simply because, without such a prospect, present experience would be depressing and intolerable. We might respond to that question in two ways.

First, Isaiah himself would insist that his confidence for the future was based on what God had already done in the past. Because God led Israel out of Egypt he can be relied on to do similar acts of salvation again (see Isaiah 11:16). Because he is the Lord of history he is the Lord of its end as well as of its beginning. Having declared his purpose for the world he will bring it to completion in his own creative way.

Secondly, to have your eyes focussed on the future is not escapism from the present. Quite the opposite. Martin Luther King's vision of a future free of racial discrimination ('I have a dream...') was what drove him to action and kept him working for that goal when anyone with a less clear vision would have given up. When I focus on the Bible's vision of God's coming kingdom I am inspired to live by the values of that kingdom now. Biblical hope is the mainspring of our service in the world.

40
The fall of Samaria

We now resume the story in 2 Kings. During the period of Hosea and the early years of Isaiah several kings of Israel reigned and died—mostly assassinated by their successors. Meanwhile, north-east of Israel, Assyria was building its military strength and looking for places to extend its control.

Read 2 Kings 17:1–23

In verses 1–6 Israel's fate is told with a sombre economy of words. Already in 743BC the king had been forced to pay an enormous amount of money to the Assyrian emperor in order to keep him at bay (2 Kings 15:19). Then in 727 Shalmaneser became ruler of Assyria. King Hoshea of Israel played the risky game of trying to make alliances with Assyria and Egypt at the same time (verse 4).

Shalmaneser's response was swift. In 722 Samaria was captured and, in accordance with the normal policy of the Assyrians, Israelites were driven in thousands into exile in distant parts of their empire. Later that year Shalmaneser was succeeded by Sargon, who in his official records claimed the capture of Samaria as his own achievement and said he deported 27,290 Israelites.

In verses 7–23 the writer's understanding of God's part in these events comes to the fore. 'All this took place because...' (verse 7). Israel is not just the victim of a power-hungry dictator. Assyria is actually serving God's purpose by bringing the threatened doom on Israel's disobedience. This is where Hoshea went wrong. He thought the Assyrians were the problem and manoeuvred desperately to keep them away. It never occurred to him—or to our modern governments—that there is someone else standing over their history-making, who holds them to account. The real problem is detailed in several ways.

Israel abandoned trust in the God who gave them a history in the first place. They forsook the demands of the covenant which gave them their identity, their reason for living (verse 7). To a modern society which puts its trust in affluence, free trade and the survival of the fittest, this text dares to ask: What about justice and mercy and care for the powerless?

In particular, they broke the most basic obligation of the covenant by worshipping the gods of the very people over whom God had given them victory. They adopted the pagan rituals of the Canaanites and worshipped images of false gods (verses 7–12, 16). They worshipped the stars and used magical methods to seek God's will (verses 16–17). In desperate times they even adopted the Canaanite practice of child sacrifice (verse 17). In our age we have different ways of compromising our loyalty to God. But they are still our ways of denying his unique claim on our lives.

They refused to listen to the warnings which God sent to them through the prophets (verses 13–14). For a nation whose own peculiar calling was to listen ('Hear, O Israel: the Lord our God, the Lord is one...', Deuteronomy 6:4), that refusal to listen heralded disaster. Such warnings seemed irrelevant to Israel's crises. They always do. 'This is a problem for the politicians. The solution is political. The church has no business meddling in politics.'

The whole sorry tale is traced back to its origins in Jeroboam's rebellion against Rehoboam (passage 30). It was he who opened the door for all Israel's religious compromises to come in (verses 21–22).

Verse 15 provides a summary of the writer's criticism of Israel's failings. In imitating other nations they succumbed to the fate of nations. In chasing worthless idols they became worthless themselves. In setting their hearts on things which have no value they denied their own true value as children of God—like a child who trades his precious teddy bear for money, only to discover that the money in his hands is toy money worth nothing.

The Bible often pictures God's judgment in this way. When people persistently resist God and his care for them, he respects their freedom, withdraws his protection and allows them to reap the consequences of their choice.

Israel learnt from bitter experience that there are limits to God's patience. As we saw in Hosea, God is constantly surprising people with the persistence of his love, which goes on pursuing them when they have tried their hardest to run away from it. Yet such persistence can never be presumed upon. The presumption which says, 'God will forgive—it's his job', has failed to realize that there is no true forgiveness without a change of life in the forgiven one.

Yet still God's purpose was not defeated! 'Only the tribe of Judah was left' (verse 18). The Southern Kingdom remained. Though it shared in Israel's disobedience, it still survived as the bearer of God's promise to the world.

41

Josiah, king of Judah

After the Assyrian conquest of Israel, the Southern Kingdom was well governed by Hezekiah, though the Assyrians came within a whisker of capturing Jerusalem during his reign (2 Kings 18–20). His son Manasseh ruled Judah disastrously for fifty-five years, compromising the nation's commitment to Yahweh in a multitude of ways (2 Kings 21). But Manasseh's grandson Josiah brought radical reform.

Read 2 Kings 22:1–13

During repairs to the temple in 622BC the 'Book of the Law' was discovered where it had lain unnoticed and unheeded for a long time (verse 8). To judge by what follows, this book must have been the Book of Deuteronomy, or a major part of it.

Josiah's reaction to hearing the contents of the book was to repent. Heir to the sorry legacy of Manasseh, he had unwittingly ignored the requirements of God's law. Immediately he began to put things right (verses 11–13).

It is an impressive admission of failure and change of direction by a person in power. In our day such actions would be seen as a sign of weakness, an act of political suicide. No one takes responsibility when things go wrong. As a result we become a nation of cynics, so that the development of a moral vision for our society becomes all the harder to achieve.

How Josiah worked out his reform can be seen from the following selection from chapter 23.

Read 2 Kings 23:1–3, 21–30

Together with his people, Josiah recommitted himself to the covenant with God and to the vision of a just society portrayed in Deuteronomy (verse 3).

Such a response to a religious text seems light-years away from what is possible in a complex modern society where people subscribe to a variety of conflicting creeds. Yet there is a searching for moral guidance, a sense that society needs to find a better way of living responsibly within itself and towards the wider world. Those who are committed to biblical teaching about justice, respect for the neighbour and protection of the vulnerable, have a coherent vision to propose as a basis for public policy. And because we believe that this vision comes from the creator of humanity himself, we may have confidence that—whether people acknowledge this creator for themselves or not—his laws will actually work as the foundation of human life in the world.

Verses 4–20 and 24 detail how Josiah purged Judah's religious life of all the pagan practices which had been introduced during the previous fifty years. Anxiety not to offend foreign powers, fascination with occult practices and astrology, child sacrifice and dismal failure to trust in God had all played their part in this spiritual decline.

The effect of this clean-up operation was to put an end to all the semi-pagan altars and alternative worship centres and to centralize the nation's religious life in Jerusalem. Only at the Jerusalem temple were sacrifices to be offered.

Josiah's reintroduction of the Passover festival, which had fallen into disuse, is significant (verses 21–23). Like people in Eastern Europe rediscovering their history in the nineteen-nineties after decades of communist oppression, the people of Judah now rediscovered their history after the ravages of Manasseh's reign. They remembered afresh how God in the past had rescued them from Egypt and honoured him again as the Lord of the present time.

It is important to remember our past, the roots of our liberation. For Christians, the Holy Communion is our Passover. It is the moment when we recall God's saving action in the past in order to be renewed by him in the present and focus our faith for the future.

Verse 25 summarizes the purpose of the whole enterprise. The words of course echo the commandment of Deuteronomy 6:5, to love God with heart and soul and stength. Josiah, like no other king, sought to live under the rule of God.

Yet there is no happy ending to his story (verses 26–30). The narrator is honest enough to report that Josiah's integrity did not guarantee long life and peace. The evil of Manasseh prevails over the obedience of Josiah (verse 26). God thinks the unthinkable and confirms that exile will still come (verse 27). And Josiah himself is killed in a desperate and perhaps misguided attempt to head off the threat of an alliance of Assyria and Egypt (verses 29–30). Power politics wins over religious and moral reform.

So is Josiah's reform a waste of effort? Surely our response must be that it is never a waste to live with integrity and to do what God requires. Even though our influence seems small, it is always our responsibility 'to do what is right and just, to defend the cause of the poor and needy' (Jeremiah's comment on Josiah, Jeremiah 22:15–16).

4 2
The fall of Jerusalem

After Josiah's death is 609BC the story moves quickly towards its tragic climax. Faithless and competent kings followed each other in quick succession. Meanwhile Babylon had replaced Assyria as the superpower. Its ruler Nebuchadnezzar was tightening his grip on the whole Middle East. The following narrative begins in 598BC.

Read 2 Kings 24:8—25:30

Jehoiachin was king for only three months before Nebuchadnezzar captured Jerusalem in 597BC. He replaced Jehoiachin with a puppet ruler, took treasures from the temple and the royal palace and forced Judah's leading citizens into exile (24:8–20).

Ten years later Zedekiah, thinking that Egyptian support could secure Judah's independence from Babylon, rebelled. Nebuchadnezzar threw all his military power against Jerusalem, and in 587 the end came (24:20—25:7). The temple was destroyed after anything of value had been removed, the city walls were knocked down, and all except the poorest people were taken into exile. Some leading citizens were executed to minimize the risk of futher revolt (25:8–21).

Nebuchadnezzar appointed Gedaliah, a Jew who had won his confidence, as governor in Judah. He urged the people remaining there to accept Babylonian rule as God's judgment on the nation and to rebuild their lives through normal peacetime activities. But he was assassinated by Ishmael, who resented Gedaliah's submission to Babylon and perhaps had designs on the throne of Judah himself (25:22–26).

1 Kings began with Solomon and the building of his temple. Now 2 Kings ends with its destruction. The building which symbolized God's presence among his people is no more. As a judgment on his people, God has indeed 'thrust them from his presence' (24:20). God's law cannot be defied for ever.

We may pause now to think about the message which 1–2 Kings has presented. At first we might think of it as a straightforward record of events from Solomon to the exile. But all history is told from a point of view. *A History of the Wild West* written by a Texas oil millionaire would have a different perspective from one written by a Sioux or an Apache.

The writer of 1–2 Kings interprets the history of Israel and Judah from the perspective of their obedience to God's law. Kings are praised or blamed according to whether they took seriously the demands of the law. Some who made their mark on the international scene by being shrewd politicians or able generals (Ahab, for example) get no credit for that if they paid little attention to their obligations under the covenant with Yahweh. It is a question of what is *really* important.

These books have much to say about the temple, because the temple expressed God's presence with his people and the importance of true worship. The most important test of a king is whether he keeps the worship pure. To allow alien gods and forms of worship to be mingled with worship of Yahweh is faithlessness of the highest order.

Yet worship at the temple can never be separated from the worship of daily obedience, as we see from the life of Josiah. Correcting religious abuse was incomplete without also promoting justice and mercy. The concern which we see in him—to turn to God with the whole of heart, soul and strength—exposes every part of life to God's direction and God's grace.

The story shows Israel and Judah impressed by the success of other nations and tempted to believe that their gods can deliver what Yahweh cannot. Against all such limiting of the scope of God's activity, 1–2 Kings insists that the God who has entered into covenant with the Israelites is the Lord of Israel's history, of the nations and of the natural world. Nothing is beyond the scope of his care and power.

Despite their title, these books are not only about kings but about the interplay between kings, prophets and God's Law. Prophets confront kings with the Law's demands. The Law reveals how they should lead their people. But the message is not just for rulers. All of us, like the kings, may be tempted to use power for our own ends. All of us are confronted by the challenge of obedience to God. All of us may be open to the liberating air of God's Spirit, represented by the prophets.

Finally, even this book has a message of hope. Right at the end we are shown king Jehoiachin, now released from house arrest in exile, being generously provided for by the ruler of Babylon. Despite the catastrophe of exile, this descendant of David is safe, keeping alive Israel's hope of a future ideal king. 'Neither the aggressiveness of imperial power nor the evil of God's own people can finally thwart God's good purpose' (Walter Brueggemann).

43

Unpopular prophet

One prophet whose ministry spanned the period from Josiah's reign to the exile was Jeremiah. His book contains not only his messages of judgment and hope during this momentous period but also reflections on his own experience of being a prophet.

Read Jeremiah 7:1–15

We have heard this theme before, in the preaching of Amos and Hosea and in the story of Josiah. But it comes here with a new urgency. Jeremiah stands in the temple court and addresses the crowds who have come to worship—perhaps at a festival time. His charge against them is that their false forms of worship arise from a false understanding of God.

They have a slogan (verse 4). The threefold repetition suggests that it may be a song they sing in the liturgy. Through unthinking repetition, an expression of faith in the significance of the temple has become no more than a lucky charm.

The trouble was that the temple was celebrated as the place of God's presence. They had songs to express this:

The Lord has chosen Zion,
he has desired it for his dwelling:
'This is my resting place for ever and ever;
here I will sit enthroned, for I have desired it . . .'

Psalm 132:13–14

The apparently miraculous deliverance of Jerusalem when the Assyrians were at its very gate in 701BC had bolstered this conviction. How could God ever abandon the place he had chosen as his home? And so a misguided optimism about God's protection of the temple became the tool of of a government oblivious of the nation's peril. False prophets, whose role was to provide religious backing for government policy, encouraged such delusions. ('Deceptive words' in verses 4 and 8 refers to such prophets.) A misplaced faith in the institutions of religion instead of in the living God became the source of Judah's ruin.

There is always pressure to make religion serve the interests of governments. There is always false optimism about the goods that religion can deliver to people who ignore its moral demands. It happens when a prime minister expects an archbishop to celebrate a victory in war without sensitivity to the moral compromises which the war has involved. It happens when parents bring a child for baptism without any intention to follow the Christian way themselves. It

95

happens when religious education in schools is expected to bear the burden of teaching children 'morals' which are widely ignored by their elders.

To all this the message of Jeremiah is stark and simple: there are no guarantees of security without obedience to God (verse 3). There is a great 'if' before God's promises (verses 5–7). Verses 5 and 6 summarize key elements in God's Law, found especially in Deuteronomy. Jeremiah understands the relation between the Law and the nation's well-being in the same way as 1–2 Kings.

The 'if-ness' of God's promises is a constant theme in the Bible. God is full of generosity, constantly seeking to pour his blessings on people. Yet nothing is automatic. He guarantees nothing to people who want his gifts without his rule.

There is a view among some Christians today that the modern state of Israel is a specific fulfilment of Old Testament prophecy and is therefore to be supported by Christians as the will of God. But even an Israel which is the object of prophetic promises is not exempt from the prophetic demand. The God who gives land to his people Israel also hears the cry of the Palestinian. If he says to Israel, 'I will let you live in this place', he also says, '*If* you do not oppress the alien, the fatherless or the widow and do not shed innocent blood' (verses 6–7).

Despite the 'if ... then' of verses 5–7, the final part of Jeremiah's message seems to assume that the time for repentance is past (verses 9–15). The opportunity has been missed and the destruction is just round the corner. Religious rituals provide no hiding place for people who ignore the Ten Commandments—like those who commit adultery and present themselves unrepentant for holy communion (verse 9–11).

Imagine the impact of verses 12–15 on its hearers. Shiloh, a shrine in the Northern Kingdom, had been destroyed. Jerusalem's fate would be no different! God has no favourites. It is never too difficult to observe the downfall of others and to think of reasons for it. This text challenges us to reckon that our own empires—political or personal—are in danger unless the law of God is our guide.

To think about

In what ways are we prone, like the people of Judah, to place a false reliance on what God did in the past or on religious institutions or rituals, rather than looking to where the living God is leading us now?

44

The potter and the clay
Jeremiah 18:1–12

God is always using everyday objects and the experiences of life to show us truths about himself. For Amos a plumb-line became a sign of God's judgment on his people. Hosea's own experience of marriage became for him a picture of God's relationship with Israel. Jeremiah here receives a message from God through a visit to a potter's workshop.

Because God is both creator and saviour it is natural that he should use the created world to develop our spiritual lives. So, for example, a baby's smile of contentment as she lies secure in a parent's arms may bring to the parent a new sense of the goodness of God. A sandcastle washed away by the sea may help us grasp the completeness of God's forgiveness, removing our sins for ever. Barbed wire may prompt us to pray for those imprisoned unjustly. Bread and wine speak to us of Jesus' life poured out for the salvation of the world.

Of course there is a danger in looking for a 'message' in every little object or incident, instead of just enjoying the world and receiving it as his gift. But insights like these from our everyday experience can be God's way of creeping up on us and pointing us beyond the immediate to all the possibilities of God.

A man that looks on glass,
On it may stay his eye;
Or, if he pleaseth, through it pass,
And then the heaven espy.

George Herbert

What, then, does Jeremiah see here? The potter's complete control over the clay underlines for him God's total sovereignty in human affairs (verse 6). As creator of the universe, God has the right to do what he chooses. He is not at the mercy of human stubbornness. Hence it is not unthinkable that God would abandon his own people to the hands of an invading army.

But we are not left with this simple insistence on God's complete mastery over humanity. The passage takes an unexpected turn in verses 7–10, where again we find the 'if . . . then' sequence which we saw in Jeremiah 7. If a warning of disaster leads to repentance God will avert the disaster. If a promise of blessing is met by complacent disobedience the blessing will turn to disaster.

So in verses 11–12 Jeremiah urges repentance—and then expresses despairing confidence that the people will take no notice of his warnings.

The prophet is not interested in a theoretical discussion of how divine sovereignty can be squared with human free will. His concern is intensely practical and pastoral. How can people who have resisted God for so long be persuaded to turn back to him? He knows that people who keep refusing God access to their lives eventually become incapable of changing their ways. Human freedom is real, yet there is an inevitability about continued wrongdoing which is beyond the power of humanity to control.

From a more positive angle, we sense in our own experience both the sovereignty of God and the freedom of our own wills. When we sing, 'Thou art the potter, I am the clay', we are affirming our faith in the sovereign rule of God, who understands our gifts and our weaknesses and knows what is best for our future. Yet at the same time we are *freely* inviting him to shape our lives according to his creative purpose.

This passage, then, makes clear that Old Testament prophecy is not fatalistic. It is not like the predictions of *Old Moore's Almanack*, forecasting that particular events are predestined to occur at particular times. Though God through the prophet declares where his plans are heading, he allows room for human freedom to affect the shape of the future.

One other point should be noted. Verses 7–10 are not only about Judah. In referring to 'a nation or kingdom' they imply God's involvement with *all* nations. All the peoples whom he has set on the earth are responsible for their behaviour and are subject to his control. We shall see this theme becoming prominent elsewhere in Scripture.

To think about

Does any incident in your experience today give insight into your relationship with God?

45

A prophet's agonies

For forty years Jeremiah warned the people of Judah of the coming disaster. All the time he battled with false prophets. For his pains he was misunderstood, abused and imprisoned for undermining the nation's morale. Who in his right mind would be a prophet! The following passage is the last of his six so-called 'confessions' in which the personal cost of his ministry is laid bare.

Read Jeremiah 20:7–18

When we read long sections from prophets such as Amos, Hosea and Jeremiah, we are perhaps tempted to think that they enjoyed being prophets of doom. Did these constant denunciations of others, these lurid threats that 'the End is nigh', feed something in their own egos which made it impossible for them to stop? This passage suggests that nothing could be further from the truth.

Jeremiah's lament follows the pattern of some of the Psalms (known as psalms of lament), in which individuals or the whole worshipping community protest to God about their suffering and ask for his help. Despite his criticism of the people's attitude to the temple, the prophet has learnt from the temple how to pray.

Verses 7–10. Jeremiah refers back to the time when God called him (Jeremiah 1:4–10). 'You twisted my arm,' he complains to God. 'You promised to be with me and to rescue me. But since that day I've known nothing but rejection and persecution' (verse 7). He holds God responsible for his suffering, since it is his preaching of God's word which has brought it all upon him (verse 8).

He cannot win. If he speaks, God seems not to support him. But if he holds back, God's word burns a hole inside him. Agonizing though it is, he must deliver it (verse 9).

All the time there are people reviling him, nicknaming him 'Terror-on-every-side' because of his doom-laden message. So-called friends—perhaps members of his family—betray him (verse 10).

Verses 11–13. After his complaint, Jeremiah expresses trust in God and pleads with him to counfound his persecutors and show him to be in the right. He even breaks out into praise for God's deliverance (verse 13).

This confidence comes as a shock in the middle of such bitter complaints. But it is typical of Israelite prayer to offer praise alongside lament. Such praise, however weakly it comes from the lips of the one who prays, is a cry of faith. In its bold defiance of the darkness, it opens a gap through which the light of God may shine.

Verses 14–18. But Jeremiah does not end there, neatly tying up the ends. There is no resolution to his pains. In these verses he returns to utter despair. Feeling completely alone, he wishes he had never been born.

There are times when people of faith feel like this. It is particularly true of people who are serving God on the frontiers of Christian ministry, working in unconventional ways and feeling unsupported or misunderstood by their fellow-Christians. Faith is still there (verses 11–13), but it is overwhelmed by depression.

Like Jeremiah, such people feel their friends have failed them. They feel the hostility of those who disapprove of their message or their ministry. When their work seems ineffective they begin to question whether they are in the right place or whether they are delivering the right message. They feel let down by God and resent his call and the suffering which has ensued from it. They are overcome with lone-liness and can see no future for their labours.

There are no instant solutions to such nightmares. But three things suggest themselves. Most importantly, this passage gives permission for the expression of such thoughts. To pretend that they are not there is not faith, but dishonesty. When everything seems dark, God invites his people to express to him their anger, frustration and bewilderment. He is big enough to take it.

Secondly, a major part of Jeremiah's problem is that he feels so utterly alone. A group of friends who will speak the truth and be supportive through thick and thin is essential if ministry is to be sustained in tough places.

Thirdly, God's people must recognize that a ministry which addresses society with the disturbing demands of God's word is not just for the occasional eccentric Jeremiah. Christian faith is not a consumer item, to be picked up if it seems helpful for a happy life. It conflicts with many of the values of Western society. Together we are called to live by a different set of values and to bear the misunder-standing and hostility which this may cause.

A prayer

Out of the depths I cry to you, O Lord;
O Lord, hear my voice . . .

Psalm 130:1–2

46

A new covenant

For forty years Jeremiah tried in vain to shatter the false hopes of the people of Judah. Only when false hopes are smashed can true hope begin to grow. But when the fall of Jerusalem happened, the people who had refused to learn by listening began to learn by terrible experience. So Jeremiah's message began to be about building the future.

Read Jeremiah 31:27–34

Verses 27–30. Jeremiah was called not only 'to uproot and tear down, to destroy and overthrow' but also 'to build and to plant' (Jeremiah 1:10). Now at last the first part of his task is complete and he can address the people devastated by the Babylonian conquest with a message of hope.

In verses 29–30 he clears away one major cause of the people's depression. They have taken to using a proverb to express their feeling that they are suffering for their parents' sins. In one sense, of course, that is true. Children do bear the scars of their parents' wrongs. In a nation, one generation cannot escape the consequences of choices made by the previous generation. We all bear the marks of our history. And yet, insists Jeremiah, each of us remains responsible. The good news is that people in exile, who are suffering because of generations of wrongdoing, are not locked into the old ways. They can choose a new direction. If they choose death, that is their responsibility. But they *can* choose life (verse 30).

The other remarkable thing about this passage is that the promise of a new beginning is for Israel as well as Judah (verse 27). God will not only restore Judah to its pre-587 situation. He will roll back all the years of division and unite the twelve tribes in a renewed nation. God will provide a future which is better than anyone's memory of the past! We shall return to this question of the restoration of Israel and Judah (in passage 49).

Verses 31–34. These speak of the new covenant. The phrase occurs only here in the Hebrew Bible, but of course it is this phrase which provides the name of the New Testament or New Covenant. For this reason it is a key passage in providing a link between the two Testaments.

This promise of God responds to an unspoken question which must surely have been in the minds of Jeremiah's contemporaries: if the people of Israel have failed so completely to keep God's Law and have brought disaster on themselves, what assurance can there be that the same fate will not come to them again? The answer lies in the nature of this new covenant. To understand this, it is tempting for Christians to jump straight to the way this phrase is used in the New Testament. But we must look first at its meaning in the context of Jeremiah and the exiles.

It will not be like the earlier covenant made with Moses (verse 32). Despite God's tender love to them the people have repeatedly broken this covenant. Now God himself will act to change things. How will the new be different from the old?

God's law will be in people's minds and hearts (verse 33). Instead of the law being an external teaching written on stone tablets or in books, God will provide an inner motivation for obedience.

The people will be bound to God as his own people (verse 33). The covenant is about relationship before it is about obedience.

There will be full 'knowledge of the Lord' (verse 34). People will be enabled to love and obey him spontaneously. Because such knowledge of God will be open to all, the least and the greatest are on an equal footing. Each has access to God, and none may claim to be a special channel through which others must come to God.

The burden of past sins is removed for ever (verse 34). The word 'for' which begins this sentence is very significant. It implies that this promise is the basis for all that has already been stated in verses 31–34. All the new possibilities are there *because* God has forgiven the past. He has broken the vicious circle of sin and punishment and committed himself in sheer grace to his people.

We should not underestimate the power of such promises to create a new future for exiled Israel. Yet there was no clear and specific fulfilment of them in the Old Testament period. Jesus spoke of the new covenant being established through his death (Mark 14:24). Reflecting on Christian experience, the writer of the Letter to the Hebrews saw Jeremiah's vision wonderfully fulfilled through the work of Christ (Hebrews 8:7–13). It is our privilege to know the benefits which Jeremiah envisaged.

The field at Anathoth

'Actions speak louder than words,' we say. Jeremiah spoke many words, but they mostly fell on deaf ears. Now, as the Babylonian armies closed their grip around Jerusalem, he performed an action loaded with meaning.

Read Jeremiah 32:1–15

It was 588BC. King Zedekiah had imprisoned Jeremiah in the royal guardhouse to prevent his depressing prophecies being heard any more (verses 1–5). From the king's viewpoint Jeremiah's attitude was at worst treason, at best a threat to the people's morale.

The fact that Jeremiah received notice from God about Hanamel's impending arrival before his cousin came to see him shows that God is at work in this event (verses 6–8). When we are seeking guidance from God about a course of action which we are considering, the convergence of circumstances, of 'hunches' received through prayer and of advice from different sources can be important pointers to God's will.

How did Hanamel get into Jerusalem if the city was under siege? Probably this incident took place at a time when the Babylonians briefly lifted the siege in order to deal with an attack from Egypt (see Jeremiah 34:21–22). But why did Hanamel want to sell his field? Had he fallen into debt in the chaotic economic situation caused by the invasion? Had he decided to flee the country? We are not told, because what matters here is the significance of Jeremiah's purchase, not of Hanamel's sale.

As the closest relative, Jeremiah had first claim on the land. Leviticus 25:25–31 lays down the law governing such transactions, whose purpose was to keep land within the family. It was one of the checks in Israelite law designed to prevent property gradually getting into the hands of fewer and fewer people. From early times the Israelites recognized that under a 'free market' system there are all kinds of factors which gradually result in the rich getting richer and the poor getting poorer. God-given laws like this one were designed to limit the extent to which this could happen and thus to give protection to the poor.

All the proper procedures of the sale are detailed—payment in silver, witnesses, the preparation and filing of documents (verses 9–

14). Baruch was Jeremiah's scribe, who wrote down his prophecies. The clay jar would be similar to the jars which kept the Dead Sea Scrolls intact from the time when they were hidden in caves around AD70 until their discovery in 1947.

The point of the whole episode is revealed in verse 15. Jeremiah's purchase is a tangible expression of his prophecies of hope. Quite literally, he has put his money where his mouth is. In the presence of a nation apparently facing extinction he has acted on his confidence in God's promise of restoration. His little piece of land is a sign of the whole land where in God's time normal economic activity will be resumed.

Jeremiah's bold action is a model for people who believe in 'the God of hope' (Romans 15:13). It is our Christian hope that one day 'the kingdom of God' will come in its completeness, when people of all races will live in justice and peace and and love under the rule of God. That hope must control our action now. If God's kingdom will be characterized by peace, we are to take risks in being peace-makers now. If God's kingdom will embrace people of all races, we are to resist all forms of racist and nationalistic prejudice. If love is the supreme characteristic of God's kingdom, we are to build caring relationships wherever we have influence now.

Such actions may seem foolish in a world where power counts for more than love, where fear prevents people from taking the first step to making peace, where the workplace is full of people being 'managed' rather than related to as human beings. So be it. Jeremiah's action seemed foolish in the extreme. But it made real the purpose of God as no mere words could.

Jeremiah 32:16–44 reports a prayer of Jeremiah and God's response. We will not read it all. But notice how the prophet questions the sense of God's instruction to him to buy the field in the face of the Babylonian siege (verse 25). And God puts a question back to him: 'Is anything too hard for me?' (verse 27). Yes, the destruction of Jerusalem is coming, but beyond that there is a new beginning (verses 36–37). Verses 38–41 repeat in different words the promise of the new covenant.

To think about

What action might be appropriate for us if, like Jeremiah, we are to 'put our money where our mouth is'?

Ezekiel's prophecy against Tyre

Ezekiel was a younger contemporary of Jeremiah. While in his twenties he was among the leading citizens of Jerusalem taken away to Babylon with the first group of exiles in 597BC. Not until about 593 did he receive his prophetic call. So all his ministry as a prophet took place in Babylon.

Like Jeremiah, his earlier prophecies were about the justice of Judah's fate at the hands of the Babylonians, whilst he later brought messages of hope for the nation's renewal. Like Jeremiah and some other prophets, he also uttered prophecies of judgment against foreign nations (Ezekiel 25–32). We shall look at an example of these.

Tyre, which remains today a significant city in Lebanon, was one of the great trading states of the ancient world. Tyrian glass and purple dyes were lucrative sources of income. Earlier Tyre had supplied materials for Solomon's building projects.

In chapter 26 Ezekiel declared that once he had finished with Jerusalem Nebuchadnezzar would turn his attention to Tyre. (This is exactly what he did, though it took a thirteen year siege to subdue it!) Chapter 27 is a poetic lament over the fall of Tyre, portraying it as a trading ship which has finally sunk under the weight of its cargo. Ezekiel then spells out reasons for the disaster which is to befall Tyre.

Read Ezekiel 28:1–19

Verses 1–5. Ezekiel attacks the ruler of Tyre not in his own person but as representative of the city's arrogant power. It claims to have become great by its own wisdom and resourcefulness. Like medieval Venice or imperial Britain it has used these gifts to amass wealth. But that is a distortion of wisdom. It bears no comparison with the wisdom of Daniel, a wise ruler of ancient legend (not the biblical prophet Daniel).

Wisdom as claimed in Tyre is very different from the wisdom commended in the book of Proverbs, which associates wisdom with justice and truthfulness. There, wisdom is to be chosen in preference to gold and silver. It cannot be reconciled with pride and arrogance (Proverbs 8:1–21, especially 7–8, 10, 13).

Verses 6–10. Because of their arrogance the Tyrians will experience God's judgment at the hands of 'the most ruthless of nations', Babylon (verse 7).

Verses 11–19. Here the king of Tyre is described in language which in part echoes the story of Adam in Genesis 2–3. Notice, for example, the reference to Eden (verse 13), to the king's being expelled (verse 16), and to the consuming fire (verse 18) which may allude to the flaming sword of Genesis 3:24. It is as though the prophet is saying that Tyre's economic extravagance is one expression of basic human sinfulness.

The key to Tyre's crime is in verse 16: cut-throat competition turning fair trade into economic and political oppression. Their wisdom is corrupt, their trade dishonest (verses 17–18).

It is clear, then, that Ezekiel is not indulging in the politics of envy, denouncing Tyre simply because it has made money successfully. As Margaret Thatcher was fond of saying, there is nothing immoral about making money: the good Samaritan could not have helped the wounded man unless he had money. But the prophecy against Tyre suggests two perspectives on economic growth which are relevant to our times.

First, it explodes the myth that economic growth is to be pursued at all costs. There are questions of morality and of care for the human community which are ultimately more important. It is the arrogance of Western societies to claim the right to an ever-increasing standard of living. It is the arrogance of Western politicians to think that they can deliver it.

Secondly, in denouncing the distortion of wisdom it raises questions about the use of human ingenuity for trivial purposes. The mail order catalogues advertising costly gadgets to perform tasks which people can perfectly well perform without them are a triumph of human invention and free enterprise—and an indictment of the triviality and moral cowardice of our age.

The prophecies against foreign nations by Ezekiel and other prophets are an expression of Israel's faith in one God. If Yahweh is the God of the whole earth, he has something to say about the history and destiny of nations other than Israel. The violation of respect for other human beings is condemned by God whether it is committed by Israel or by others.

If we ask why Babylon, which was itself an arrogant nation, was allowed by God to destroy other nations in this way, we are asking the same question as the prophet Habakkuk. The answer which God gave to him was that in due time Babylon too would pay for its aggression. In the long term, God interacts with the movements of history to see that justice is done.

The valley of dry bones

Jerusalem has fallen. Its people are in exile. They look around at each other and see nothing but despair. 'Our bones are dried up and our hope is gone; we are cut off' (verse 11). Responding to their hopelessness, God gives Ezekiel a vision (verses 1–10).

What he sees in the valley looks like the bones of a defeated army. They lie unburied, long ago picked bare by the vultures and bleached by the sun. To the question of verse 3 the only sensible answer seems to be 'no'. But the prophet waits to hear God's answer. It comes in the form of instructions to prophesy in two directions.

First, Ezekiel addresses the bones (verses 4–8). This 'preaching' to lifeless bones has the effect of arranging them into corpses, but they remain dead. Then he speaks to the 'breath'. This Hebrew word also means 'wind' and 'spirit' (either the human spirit or God's Spirit, as in verse 1). The text plays with these different meanings, as the prophet is told to summon the life-giving breath from the four winds and give life to this company of corpses.

And the miracle happens. God can take doomed skeletons and turn them into a living army. Perhaps the two roles of Ezekiel in his vision—to prophesy to the bones and to the breath—suggest that preaching to the 'dead' and praying to the Spirit are both necessary to the revitalization of God's people.

In the explanation of verses 11–14, the battlefield has mysteriously changed into a cemetery: 'I am going to open up your graves...' But the message is clear. Like the dead restored to life, God's people in exile will be restored to their land and will be invigorated by God's Spirit. They will be in no doubt that they owe their transformation to God himself.

The vision of the valley of dry bones is a forceful symbol of the power of God to renew his people even in the most desperate and depressing circumstances. Our teaching of God's word and openness to his Spirit play their part. But all depends on the energizing work of God himself.

In verses 15–28 an 'acted parable' leads to a fuller description of what the restoration of the exiles will involve. Ezekiel is told to take two sticks, one representing the Southern Kingdom and the other representing the Northern Kingdom. He is to hold them end to end with his fists covering the joint so that 'they become one in your hand' (verses 15–17).

The meaning of this act is that God is going to bring the divided kingdoms together again into one nation (verses 18–22). The promise inevitably raises the question: How could this be? Didn't the northern tribes pass out of existence when the Assyrians drove many of them into remote parts of their empire? Didn't the Assyrians bring in foreigners to take their place, who intermarried with the remaining inhabitants of northern Israel and thus destroyed the purity of the race? Speculation about what happened to 'the ten lost tribes of Israel' has flourished down the centuries among both Jews and Christians.

It is possible to point out that the ten tribes were never entirely lost. Not all were exiled to Assyria, not all necessarily intermarried. And ever since the kingdom was divided into two there had been some members of northern tribes who had thrown in their lot with Judah (2 Chronicles 11:16; 15:9; 30:1–12).

But Ezekiel's vision is on a grander scale than this. He sees Israelites of all the tribes brought back from various places of exile into the Promised Land (verse 21). They will be one kingdom under one king descended from David (verses 22, 24). Their worship will be purified (verse 23). They will live in obedience to God and in permanent covenant with him (verses 24, 26). God will once more place his temple among them to symbolize the central truth of the covenant: 'I will be their God, and they will be my people' (verse 27). Then the nations will know that God is not dead and Israel is still his people (verse 28).

All this is the kind of language in which the prophets expressed their longing for the future rule of God when earthly conditions would be transformed and a descendant of David would be God's agent of justice and peace (see passage 39).

On one level, therefore, it is a promise to the exiles that their national life would be restored in their own land. But it goes far beyond that. From a New Testament perspective, the golden age depicted here dawned in the coming of Jesus the Messiah. It will come to its final fulfilment when all peoples are brought together under his rule.

3

LIFE AND
WORSHIP

50
Celebrating sexuality

After the serious matters of Israel's history up to the time of the exile, we turn now to some Old Testament books which are not closely tied to any particular period of history. They offer insight into different aspects of life.

To many people, the Song of Songs is the most surprising book to find in the Bible. 'If it's fun, stop it', is their idea of what the Bible has to say about sex. For this reason, this book which speaks the language of sexual love has often been interpreted as an allegory, or picture, of God's love for Israel. Between AD800 and 1500, forty-five commentaries on this little book were written, all explaining how it illuminated the relationship between God and his people! No biblical book received so much attention in the Middle Ages.

But all this is surely to misunderstand the book's intention. It is a collection of love poems in which the lovers speak to each other in turn. The fact that their expressions of love are occasionally interrupted by the comments of friends suggests that it may have been intended for use at a wedding feast. It is the Bible's declaration that human sexuality is a wholesome gift of God. It is not to be denied or abused, but enjoyed.

The title 'Song of Songs' simply means 'Greatest of Songs'. King Solomon is presented as the author (1:1), but this is probably a literary convention.

The lovers' appreciation of each other is expressed in vivid imagery. Some of it is very different from that of a modern love-song, and may seem strange to us. It is sensuous and erotic and yet restrained. The selected passage should be enjoyed as a poem rather than merely analysed for its 'message'. But we can then comment briefly on the understanding of love and sexuality which underlies it.

Read Song of Songs 7:1—8:7

The speakers in these two chapters are:

7:1–9	The man
7:9—8:4	The woman
8:5	The friends
8:5–7	The woman

The following underlying assumptions of these poems may be noted.

Such intimate love is a *mutual* attitude and experience. It is not simply one person's infatuation with, or exploitation of, the other. And it is an *exclusive* relationship, different from wider relationships with family and friends (7:10).

There is an appropriate *spontaneity* about loving. It does not force itself on the other. It does not work by fixed timetables. It creeps up on the lovers and surprises them with its intensity (8:4).

As the grave will never give up the dead, real love will *never surrender* the loved one. Nothing can destroy it (8:6).

Nothing can rival its priceless *value* (8:7).

It is worth observing that in the book as a whole, as in our chosen section, more words are attributed to the woman than to the man. Male-dominated though the culture of Israel was, this literature sees the woman as a *partner* alongside the man, not as his plaything or servant.

An intriguing possibility arises from the final phrase of 8:6. The Hebrew may mean 'the flame of Yahweh', implying that the love between the partners is a gift of God. But we do not have to find this meaning in the poem in order to make it more religiously respectable. It is a *poem*, in which the lovers say what they want to say to each other. It is not a theological statement.

For the same reason we need not worry that it does not say everything that other biblical writers thought were important about love and sexuality. There is nothing in the book, for example, which makes explicit whether the couple are married, or about to be married. But this does not mean that it advocates sexual intimacy outside marriage. It is celebrating love between two particular people, not defining the boundaries of love in general.

Elsewhere, Scripture teaches that the right context for sexual intimacy is a lifelong marriage commitment between a man and a woman. It affirms the wholeness of the single person. It warns of the dangerous potential of sex to ruin rather than to enhance human relationships. But *this* book of the Old Testament rejoices in erotic love as one of God's good gifts to humanity.

To think about

'If it's fun, stop it.' How can the church present to young people a more positive message about sex, whilst warning of the dangers of the irresponsible expression of sexuality?

5 1
Everyday wisdom

Three books of the Old Testament—Proverbs, Job and Ecclesiastes—are called 'wisdom literature'. There were in Israel, as in other countries such as Egypt and Babylon, 'wise men' whose role was to collect wise sayings (see Jeremiah 18:18, where they are mentioned alongside priests and prophets). Solomon was famous for having started this tradition within Israel.

We might call the literature they produced 'reflections on the meaning of life'. They speak about life as it is experienced by human beings in general, rather than by the Israelites in their particular covenant relationship with God. But the three different books we shall look at offer three different kinds of reflection.

The Book of Proverbs collects sayings about everyday experiences of life. It makes observations on attitudes and lifestyle, implicitly asking of each example, 'Is this wisdom or folly?' The fact that many sayings begin with the words, 'My son', suggests that they were used in the education of young people—the Israelite equivalent of personal and social education in secondary schools today.

The proverbs which we are going to look at don't really need comment. They make their own impact and it is up to us then to make the connections between the observations they make and our own lives. So here, first, are some suggestions about how to read from the Book of Proverbs.

A collection of sayings on a variety of themes clearly requires a different style of reading from a story in 2 Kings or a long prophecy in Ezekiel. It may be better to read a few proverbs slowly and think about them one by one, or to read a chapter through and then think about two or three of them which have struck a chord with you.

As you read each one, ask yourself questions such as:

◆ Does it make me smile, or nod in agreement, or raise an eyebrow? If it does any of these, why is that so?

◆ Does it strike a chord with any recent experience?

◆ What does it teach about God or about human nature?

◆ What weakness in me does it expose?

◆ What strength in me does it encourage?

◆ Does it suggest to me any course of action?

Make a note of proverbs on similar themes. Over a period of time you could make your own collection of proverbs organized under theme headings. Then you would have a fruitful source of wisdom on many issues affecting everyday life. For example, in the chapter which we are about to read there are proverbs about words, about readiness to accept correction, about the value of a simple lifestyle, about the depressing effects of hardship, and about God.

There are, as it happens, more references to God in our chosen chapter than is normal in Proverbs. Many of the sayings in this book are common sense, or shrewd observation, or humorous comparison. These don't need God brought in to make them worth saying. On the contrary, they challenge us to recognize that there is sometimes less common sense and wise judgment among believers in God than among others! These proverbs keep us earthed in the realities of ordinary life. They are God's antidote to the over-spiritual approach to life which underplays the importance of ordinary, everyday human needs and experiences.

Yet a belief in God lies behind the whole book and provides a context for its comments and exhortations. Its underlying theme is, 'The fear of the Lord is the beginning of knowledge' (Proverbs 1:7). It shows us how to live in the world with our feet on the ground whilst seeing the whole of life as being under the watchful and caring eye of God.

Read Proverbs 25

52
The sufferings of a righteous man

If Proverbs shows us wisdom reflecting on everyday life, the book of Job takes us up to a deeper, more disturbing level. Here wisdom wrestles with the mysteries of life. Why do innocent people suffer? That is a question which touches most families in very personal ways at some time or another.

Starting from an already ancient story about a righteous man (contained in the introduction and conclusion, Job 1–2; 42:7–17), the writer has constructed a magnificent poetic drama where this question of innocent suffering is explored (Job 3:1—42:6).

Chapters 1 and 2 set the scene. The time and place of Job's life are deliberately vague. He could be anyone. He could be the person next door, or the man you sit next to on the train. He is the man who has everything—nice family, good business, the respect of his whole community. And he is a good man, a serious believer in God who puts his faith into practice.

But does he believe in God because God has blessed him with family and wealth, or simply because God is God? That is a question for all of us. Are we religious because we really love God, or only because of what we can get out of religion? Are we scratching God's back because God scratches ours? Is our relationship with God a personal one or merely a commercial one? Alongside the question of innocent suffering, the book of Job looks at this issue of self-centred religion.

So Job is to be put to the test. Will he still love and honour God when the people and things which make life good for him are stripped away and when he himself is subject to hideous personal pain? His children are killed, his animals destroyed. He himself is covered in sores which disfigure his body. Yet he refuses to curse God.

The mechanism whereby this test is brought about—a dialogue between God and 'the Satan' or 'accuser'—may raise difficult questions for us. But since it is part of a traditional story it would be unwise to try to extract too much theological meaning from it. What is important is that it sets in motion the drama in which the question of innocent suffering is explored. We, the readers, know that the test has been arranged in heaven, but Job doesn't. For him there is only the human agony which comes to all when senseless suffering strikes.

Three friends arrive to comfort him. For seven days they sit alongside him and say nothing. That is a true expression of sympathy, more precious than their spoken 'comfort' later. Job now speaks in their presence.

Read Job 3

Job's despair has much in common with Jeremiah's (passage 45). Gone is the patient Job of chapters 1 and 2. He curses the day he was born. He wishes the night of his conception ('birth' in NIV) could be struck for ever from the calendar (verse 6). He appeals to soothsayers who have the power to awaken the forces of chaos to curse the day of his birth (verse 8, where Leviathan is a mythical sea monster representing the chaos which existed before the world came into being). If only he were dead, for death is the only place of deliverance from his torment (verses 11–19).

Life has lost its meaning. Death seems infinitely preferable. God has hedged him into suffering from which there is no escape (verses 20–23). That is the heart of his agony. God has trapped him into a nightmare from which there is no escape. He is the source of Job's problem. Life is sheer torture (verse 24–26).

Notice how often Job asks, 'Why?' (verses 11, 12, 16, 20, 23). This is not a question looking for an answer, but the cry of a man full of anguish.

His outcry is the mixture of eloquent despair, anger and puzzlement which afflicts people in extreme suffering or in the shock of sudden bereavement. It may not be rational, but it is intensely real. It reminds us that the problem of innocent suffering is a personal and pastoral issue before it is an intellectual issue. The pain cannot be 'answered'. It can only be listened to.

To think about

In this and other speeches Job's agony leads him to ask God many questions. For example:

'Why is life given to those in misery, and life to the bitter of soul?' (3:20)
'Why do you hide your face and consider me your enemy?' (13:24)
'If a man dies, will he live again?' (14:14)
'If only I knew where to find him...' (23:3)
'Oh, that I had someone to hear me...' (31:35)

What kinds of response does the New Testament provide to such questions?

53
Job's comforters

The friends who sat in sensitive silence with Job now become professional counsellors and problem-solvers, and not very helpful ones at that. The first to speak is Eliphaz, who has worked out all the answers. In his view, life follows a simple rule: if you are good you are rewarded and if you are bad you are punished. So the conclusion to be drawn in Job's case is obvious. Bildad agrees with him, and pleads with Job to turn back to God. Zophar is the last to speak.

Read Job 11

Zophar is the kind of man who calls a spade a spade. He has no time for complicated discussion or for ideas about God which aren't black and white. He knows what he believes and can't wait any longer to make this clear to Job. Having listened for a while to Job's tortured questioning he accuses him of 'idle talk' which mocks God (verses 2–3). Such lack of sympathy or compassion is not a promising beginning.

Verses 4–6. Job has been contending that he was innocent (which is also God's view of him, according to 1:8 and 2:3). Now Zophar twists this to imply that Job has been claiming to be totally sinless. 'You're quite wrong, Job,' he says. 'God has punished you less than your sin deserves.' A rather surprising suggestion in view of the extremity of what Job has endured!

Verses 7–9. This assertion of the sovereignty and mystery of God is true enough. Job himself has already said the same sort of thing

115

(9:10–12). But for Zophar it implies, 'It's no business of yours to question the deeds of the Almighty. You must submit to the punishment which he has brought on you.'

Verses 10–12. Zophar is back to Job's sin again. 'No sin ever escapes God's notice. So you'd better own up.' The curious proverb of verse 12 probably means, 'Job, you are stupid. There's no more hope of you understanding your own guilt than there is of a wild ass giving birth to a man!'

Verses 13–20. Finally, Zophar urges Job to repent of the sins which have brought calamity on him. Then his fortunes will change and his sufferings will be only a distant dream. Life will be bright and sunny. He will once again be the respected citizen at the centre of his community.

No wonder 'Job's comforters' is a label we give to counsellors whom we would rather do without. Zophar typifies a certain kind of believer whose advice and support is at best a mixed blessing. From noticing his mistakes we may learn some positive lessons.

He lacked sympathy. He had made his mind up what Job's problem was and had no insight into the feelings of the sufferer.

He rejected Job's sincerity. This made it impossible for him to hear Job's protestations of innocence.

He had a cut-and-dried theology which could not make room for the perplexities of Job's experience. Job's suffering had to be made to fit into his package of ideas. To rethink his theology to take account of Job's experience was too risky. So he defended his views at the cost of love and human understanding.

He had a misguided idea of the rewards enjoyed by those who are obedient to God. His promise that 'life will be brighter than noonday' if only Job repents (verse 17) is a caricature of the believer's life. God provides no guarantee that life will be prosperous and trouble-free.

These attitudes are repeated when people say, 'The reason why you haven't been healed is because there is unconfessed sin in you.' 'You're not healed because you haven't got enough faith.' 'If you prayed hard enough you'd get a job.' In some cases, of course, there might be something in these suggestions. But to turn them into dogmas applicable to all situations is to put God in a box of our own making.

There are mysteries in our experience for which there is no tidy solution. And the most pressing of these is the mystery of innocent suffering. A true friend will not try to *explain* the suffering, as Zophar and the others did. She will listen with sympathy, she will take seriously the sufferer's own account of things, she will know that it is more important to be there than to give answers.

5 4
God speaks to Job

In the course of his dialogue with the three friends, Job has demanded that God should answer his complaints (31:35–37). He has protested that God seems like an elusive enemy who refuses to declare his innocence. Now at last the silence of God is broken. If you have time, read the whole of chapters 38–41. But one chapter will give the essence of what God says in response to Job.

Read Job 38

Earlier Job remarked that if God should ever confront him—which he doubted—he would crush him with a storm and give him no chance to catch his breath (9:17–18, NIV). Now to his amazement God speaks to him directly through a storm.

But God doesn't offer a straightforward answer to Job's complaint. He doesn't behave like a judge in a law court pronouncing him innocent or guilty. Job's questioning meets with a torrent of questions in reply.

'Where were you . . .?' (verse 4) sums it all up. Job was not there when the earth was created and chaos was transformed into an ordered world. It is not by his ingenuity that darkness gives way to light every morning and the regularity of nature is maintained. It is not he who controls the weather and keeps the stars on their course. It is not because of his work that lions and ravens find their food. Throughout chapters 38–41 God takes Job on a tour of his creation and, in effect, says to him, 'Look at my world in all its variety and complexity. Does it not reassure you of my wisdom as the Creator? Do you not see how carefully I look after it?'

What does this line of argument mean? Is God pulling rank on Job, simply saying, 'I know best and you'd better stop asking questions'?

What does he mean by not answering Job's pleas directly? Three comments may help us here.

First, the fact that God speaks is in a sense more important than what he says. The Lord of creation has heard the debate of Job and his friends and now enters into it himself. God is there and he is not silent. He shows himself to people in the crises of their lives. By addressing Job as 'a man' (verse 3) he is not belittling him as 'mere man' but honouring him as one invited to discuss the mysteries of the universe.

Secondly, by widening the picture from a focus on Job's own sufferings to the patterns of the whole created world God is inviting Job to see that the world doesn't revolve round him or even around the human race as a whole. Job, as well as his friends, needs a bigger view of God. Sometimes human questions remain unanswered, but we can trust God's competence to run the world according to his wisdom.

Thirdly, then, although Job's questions are not answered on an intellectual level, he is enabled to see them in a new light. More important than any explanation of the reasons for suffering is the experience of God which comes to him through his struggle. When tragedy strikes people seek to find a meaning in it. '*Why* did it happen to her?' 'Why has my world fallen apart? If only I could make *sense* of it.' But in the suffering, beyond the anger and the questions, they may discover God's presence. Like Job, they may be born again from chaos.

To think about

The book of Job does not so much answer a question (Why is there suffering?) as question an answer (that suffering is always God's punishment).

5 5
Happy ending

Job 42

In his final speech we find Job in chastened mood. There are four key statements.

'I know . . .' (verse 2). Job has come to realize that God's power and purpose go beyond anything he had imagined.

'I know that I don't know...' (verse 3). There are some questions which must be left unanswered, some mysteries which must remain mysterious. 'We live by faith, not by sight' (2 Corinthians 5:7).

'I see...' (verse 5). Job's limited knowledge of God has given way to a fresh vision of him. Head-knowledge has given way to personal experience. This 'seeing' is different from the 'sight' in the quotation from 2 Corinthians in the previous paragraph. For it is the 'seeing' of knowing God's presence, not the 'seeing' of knowing all the answers.

'I repent...' (verse 6). When we discover that God is bigger than we thought, we realize that we are smaller than we thought. Job is not at last repenting of all the sins which his three friends suspected him of all along. He is repenting of his complaining attitude, his refusal to let God be God. He had thought that God was his enemy. Now he has found God as his friend.

The story is now brought quickly to its close (verse 7–17). God gives his opinion of the three friends: 'You have not spoken of me what is right, as my servant Job has' (verse 7). He could hardly underline more clearly his approval of honest questioning and of the doubt which searches out truth, and his rejection of straitjacketed theology which knows all the answers and will not be disturbed by contradictory experience. Yet he is generous towards the friends and uses Job's prayer for their benefit (verses 8–9).

Job's prayer, we notice, occurs before the removal of his own sickness. After all he has heard from the lips of his friends, it is a striking example of the attitude urged by Jesus: 'Bless those who curse you, pray for those who ill-treat you' (Luke 6:28).

Finally Job's fortunes are restored. He gets twice as many animals as he owned before. He has more children to replace those he lost, and lives in contentment to a ripe old age (verses 10–17).

A happy ending, yet it may leave us uneasy. Have we returned after all to the world of Eliphaz, Bildad and Zophar, where suffering is always the result of sin and goodness always guarantees prosperity? Perhaps in the context of the story as a whole, the reversal of Job's misfortunes is a way of making clear that the testing announced in chapters 1 and 2 is now at an end. It is not a promise that suffering is always reversed or that obedience to God always in the end brings earthly blessing.

To reinforce this point we should contemplate what would happen if God always did punish evil with suffering and reward obedience with prosperity. Human beings could not then love God for his own sake. We would find ourselves obeying God only because of what we get out of it. We would surrender to the self-centred religion which was highlighted in passage 52.

Someone might say, 'But you are a believer because of what you get out of it—eternal life in God's presence. Surely that is self-centred religion.' But that is a different matter. Eternal life in God's presence is not the *reward* of our relationship with God. It is the relationship itself. The fact that it is God and his presence, rather than material prosperity, which we hope for, can purify us of the 'love' which is only interested in what the lover can give us. We can love God for himself alone.

The book of Job, then, lays down a challenge: could I, like Job, love God if he seemed to take away everything that provides meaning and security for my life—a job, income, family, health?

And it offers a reassurance: when our lives are rocked by tragedy, God is not remote, blaming us for our wrongdoing. He is waiting to be discovered as the friend who stands beside us in our suffering.

56
'Everything is meaningless'

Ecclesiastes suggests a different view of life from the optimistic everyday wisdom of Proverbs. It is the voice of a sceptic who seems to alternate between a conventional faith in God and a wry criticism of the normal assumptions of his fellow-believers. Like many a modern person, he hovers between faith and doubt, between hope and despair, between enjoyment of life and puzzlement abut life's meaning.

Many are surprised to find such an enigmatic book in the Bible. So much of it seems to reach conclusions about life which don't take God into account. But this book of all books is a document for our times, because it allows us to think deeply about whether meaning in life can be found without God.

Read Ecclesiastes 1

The book's title means 'The Preacher' or 'The Teacher' or perhaps 'The Philosopher'. Although probably writing long after the exile, the author attributes his book to Solomon (1:1). He is imagining Solomon as the writer of the thoughts he is going to present, as if to say, 'Even that great man of wisdom and man of the world couldn't find the meaning of life.'

Verse 2 is the text which the Preacher is going to expound. The word 'meaningless' (NIV) or 'futility' (REB) is the Preacher's theme-tune, repeated over thirty times in the book. The word means a vapour, a puff of wind, something without substance. Life is like that, he says. It doesn't add up to anything solid. He pursues his theme relentlessly, developing it in various ways.

Verse 3 asks, 'What is the point of all our effort? We get up, get on the train, go to work, come home on the train, go to bed, all for the sake of earning money so that we can get up, get on the train . . .' The endless routine of life seems so empty sometimes, so lacking in significance.

Verses 4–7 reinforce this depressing thought. We live out our lives, only to be replaced by the next generation. We are soon forgotten. There is nothing left to show for our effort. The world just goes round like an endless treadmill.

Verse 8 sounds very modern. 'The more you have, the more you want.' Nobody knows better than the advertisers and the marketing experts that we have an endless appetite for change, for something new. We try to get off the treadmill by buying new clothes, new CDs, a new car, new furniture. We look for satisfaction in a new holiday destination or a new home. And before long we are back for more because 'the eye never has enough . . .'. We do not know how to be content.

Verses 9–10 bring us back to the treadmill. The Preacher knows as well as we do that *some* new things happen in the world. Someone runs 1500 metres in less than three and a half minutes. The power of the atom is harnessed to create electricity. People write books on computers.

But constantly there is that sense of *déja vu*. A war in one part of the world is ended as conflict flares up somewhere else. An increase in people living rough on the streets takes us back to the time before the welfare state. The young people complain that the church services are boring and the old people are uncomfortable with the electronically amplified songs. 'So what's new?' asks the cynic. 'Nothing ever really changes.'

Verse 11 completes the depressing picture. People live their lives, they pass into history. And there they stay, totally forgotten. A few famous people get studied in school or quoted by writers or give their name to a building or a make of car. But the rest of us?

There is a tombstone in the churchyard at the bottom of my garden. It says:

In affectionate memory of
Sarah,
Beloved wife of Charles Lang,
who departed this life 17th May, 1877,
aged 42 years.

But who remembers her now? No one. She may have mattered to her friends, her husband, her children. But to today's generation her life counts for nothing. She is meaningless, a puff of wind. And in a hundred years or so I shall be the same.

That is how life feels to many people—we see them portrayed in films and novels. But they are not fictitious: they live in our street. We sit next to them on the bus. Like Job's three friends—before they started giving their cut-and-dried answers—we must sit with them and understand their stories before we suggest that there is another story which can give meaning to their lives.

5 7

The search for meaning

Human beings long for a meaning to their lives. We want to feel that we have some significance which goes beyond our roles as taxpayer and shopper, even beyond our roles as friend, husband, wife, parent and child.

Read Ecclesiastes 1:12—2:26

The search for meaning through wisdom (1:12–18). The writer is serious about discovering the purpose of life. Like the French writer Albert Camus, he believes that the most important question facing all people is 'to decide whether life deserves to be lived or not'. But all attempts to answer it seem to be futile, 'a chasing after wind' (verse 14). There is so much in the world over which we have no control (verse 15). So are we not simply victims of our circumstances, victims of our genes? How can we find a meaning beyond them?

The wisdom referred to here includes what we would call education, philosophy and scientific investigation. The Preacher is not decrying these as a bad thing. But he believes they don't provide ultimate answers. They sharpen the questions, but they also make us see how much we don't understand. They cannot in themselves deliver the truths and the values which we need to make life meaningful.

The search for meaning through pleasure (2:1–11). The leisure industry is one of the growth industries of our time, seeking to satisfy endless varieties of the human search for satisfaction through pleasure. If the writer lived today he would be going to a football match, inviting friends out for a meal, 'working out' at the gym, playing in a jazz band, taking the children to the cinema, having a holiday in the Caribbean.

But he has discovered that there are parts of him that these pleasures cannot reach. He knows what it is like to 'have a good time' and then feel empty afterwards. He has reflected how the comedians who make us laugh are often themselves deeply unhappy (verse 2). He has learnt the dangers of alcohol (verse 3).

So how about some larger projects? He has turned to creativity and has developed a haven of peace for himself. His house and gardens will ensure that his reputation lives after him (verses 4–6). He has become a patron of the arts ('men and women singers', verse 8).

He has found pleasure in power over people and over property (verses 7–8). He has sought sexual fulfilment on a grand scale (verse 8, where REB's 'everything that affords delight' probably refers to a harem). We would probably link only the last of these three forms of power with the search for pleasure. But the desire to have power over men and women and property is a deep instinct which drives many people today, and is a symptom of a restless search for satisfaction.

The Preacher insists that in all this he has not lost sight of his goal: 'my wisdom stayed with me' (verse 9). He has left no stone unturned (verse 10). Yet he has found no holy grail, no meaning to hang on to (verse 11).

The search for meaning through wisdom—again! (2:12–16). The Preacher likes gnawing at a bone. He comes back to his exploration of wisdom and adds another aspect of its inadequacy. Even though the wise man is better than the fool, the same fate comes to all. Tradition has it that wisdom is the path to life. But what is life the path to?

Whether you are wise or stupid, death brings an end to everything. Any significance you may have had is lost for ever.

The search for meaning through hard work (2:17–23). Because of death, all the hard work we put into a job, a business or a project counts for nothing. We may lose sleep worrying over how to make a success of it. Then when we are gone those who come after may fritter away all that we have built up, attaching no importance to our work and our values.

A chink of light (verses 24–26). Having shown that the places where he has searched for meaning don't deliver what they promise, the Preacher hints at a new perspective. Food and drink, work and pleasure are gifts of God. Without him, they make no ultimate sense. 'What spoils them is our hunger to get out of them more than they can give' (Derek Kidner). But when God is at the centre, there is a deep satisfaction and a significance to life which not even death can destroy.

This theme becomes gradually more prominent as Ecclesiastes proceeds. The author's strategy is to strip away our false hopes in order to bring us to reality. But not until we come to the New Testament do we find a fuller answer to the problem of death.

58

A hymn of praise

There are times when we feel like shouting with joy or with anger. There are times when our hearts are full of thankfulness. There are other times when we are in the depths of despair. The Psalms are for people like us.

The Psalms are Israel's book of praise and prayer. While the narrative books of the Old Testament relate what God has done and the prophetic books report what God has said, the Psalms express the response of God's people to his acts and words.

For Christians, too, they are a vital resource for worship. They offer us words with which we can come to God in a vast variety of human situations. Some are expressions of personal prayer and praise; others are meant to be used particularly when God's people meet together.

The following selection will help us to appreciate how they can speak to our condition, and can lift our hearts and minds to the God who meets us in our varying needs. One way of using each psalm is to study it with the comments, and then to read the psalm again, making it our own expression of prayer and praise to God.

Read Psalm 33

Call to worship (verses 1–5). The mention of musical instruments makes clear that this is a psalm to be used at an act of celebration in the temple. Praise of the Creator calls for the rich sound of a full orchestra!

As often in the Psalms, the hymn is called a 'new song' because it celebrates the 'new world' which God is creating through his powerful acts. God's actions are an expression of his faithfulness, righteousness, justice and unfailing love (verses 4–5). All four of these descriptions of God refer to his reliable and caring commitment to the people with whom he is in covenant relationship.

Praise for God's creation (verse 6–9). The psalmist speaks of God creating through his word, just as Genesis 1 describes how God spoke and different aspects of the universe came into being. What a God it must be who, like a householder storing up oil and grain, gathers up the water of the oceans ready to pour it out as rain upon the earth!

Some Eastern religions and some modern theologies believe that God and the world are identical, so that God is everything and everything is God. As we saw in Genesis 1, the Bible rejects this idea and views the world as distinct from God and dependent on him. This is the force of the claim that it was made through his word. While God is intimately involved with his world, he is distinct from it as the one who has called it into being.

Praise for God's power in history (verses 10–19). God acts not only in creation but in history. It has been Israel's experience that even mighty nations like Egypt, Assyria and Babylon ultimately serve God's purpose. Only one purpose lasts for ever, and that is God's. Therefore to be a nation living according to his purpose brings security and hope (verse 12). No amount of military fire-power will in the end bring security to a nation resisting his purpose (verses 16–17).

Twice the psalmist speaks of God 'keeping his eye on' all mankind (verses 13, 18). Though quite different from the world, God is utterly attentive to it. The implication in verse 13 is that human beings have a responsibility to live lives which are pleasing to God—by reflecting his character of justice and righteousness, faithfulness and love (verses 4–5). In verse 18 the watchfulness of God is a motive for confidence and trust in him. The God who acts in the great movements of history also has the needs of each one of his people in mind.

The response of the worshipping community (verses 20–22). This kind of God draws out from us a response of joyful trust and hope. To 'wait for the Lord' (verse 20) implies a confidence in God, a freedom from anxiety based on his character and his actions in the past.

> All my hope on God is founded;
> He doth still my trust renew.
> Me through change and chance he guideth,
> Only good and only true.
> God unknown,
> He alone
> Calls my heart to be his own.
>
> Robert Bridges

To think about

Look at the descriptions of God as 'help' and 'shield' (verse 20) and the reference to his 'unfailing love' (verse 22). What might these aspects of God's character mean for you today?

59
A song of thanksgiving
Psalm 34

Psalm 33 is a hymn for celebration by the worshipping community, but Psalm 34 is a more personal expression of thanks.

The heading relates the psalm to David's deliverance from an enemy (1 Samuel 21:10–15). But we can never be sure how reliable the headings of the Psalms are. They may simply be suggestions added by an ancient Hebrew scribe who copied the Psalms. However, it is important to recognize that the Psalmist is offering thanks for deliverance by God from a specific misfortune. He is not dealing in generalizations.

Incidentally, I wonder why I refer to the Psalmist as 'he'. If women wrote any parts of the Bible, they wrote songs (see the references to Miriam, Exodus 15:21; Deborah, Judges 5; Hannah, 1 Samuel 2:1–10; Mary, Luke 1:46–55). So maybe some of the Psalms were composed by women. But we simply can't know, so I will keep to the conventional 'he'.

Thanksgiving for deliverance (verses 1–7). Although we don't know what the problem was which caused distress to the Psalmist, words such as 'afflicted' (verse 2) and 'poor' (verse 6) suggest that he is one of those who live on the edge of society. He has no power or influence of his own to get his circumstances put right. Without God's help he is doomed to go on suffering.

Whatever his problem was, he prayed about it (verse 4). Now his prayer has been answered and he wants to offer thanks. He has learnt from experience that Yahweh listens to the cries of the distressed and the oppressed, the victims of injustice and neglect. He wants to offer his thanks in the presence of his fellow-believers (verse 3).

Why does he want to give thanks in public? First, because he wants his experience of God's activity to be an encouragement to others (verse 2). So he uses his own experience as an example to show how God is concerned and responsive to human need. And he also knows the infectious power of sharing stories. As individuals give testimony to their personal experiences of God, the whole community of worshippers grows together in its awareness of the living God.

Sometimes we express our puzzlement that Christians find it difficult to express their faith to their friends outside the church. But if there is no opportunity for people to share stories naturally in a supportive environment inside the church, as the Psalmist does, they will surely remain tongue-tied outside.

Invitation to share God's blessing (verses 8–10). The writer can't resist drawing some general implications from his experience. Already in verse 7 he declares that what has happened to him can happen to others. In that verse he pictures God in the form of his angel or messenger surrounding his people to protect them, as an army defends a city or a mother protects a baby in her arms.

Now he urges his companions to look to God for all the benefits he can give. Notice the words of exhortation: 'taste and see', 'take refuge', 'fear the Lord', 'seek the Lord'. (To 'fear' God means to honour him and, out of reverence for him, to live in obedience to his will.) And notice the results of such turning to God: 'the Lord is good', 'blessed', 'lack no good thing'.

'I will teach you the fear of the Lord' (verses 11–22). The shift from thanksgiving to instruction which has already begun in the previous few verses now becomes obvious. The Psalmist takes on the style of a teacher of wisdom, offering guidance which sounds very like the Book of Proverbs.

Though this change of tone is unusual in a psalm, it underlines the link between worship and life which is so central in biblical faith. The celebration in worship of God's blessings leads naturally to the concern that the character of this generous God should be reflected in daily life. If God has set us free for a new life we must learn how to live out the implications of that freedom.

Although at first sight the writer may seem to be offering a rather superficial understanding of morality and its rewards, it goes deeper than that. 'The righteous' here (verses 15, 17, 19, 21) means not simply observers of conventional morality. It means those who are seriously committed to obeying the demands of their covenant with God—and are probably suffering for it (as we saw in verses 2, 6). They are not spared suffering, but they are promised that suffering is not the last word (verse 19). Meanwhile they have the knowledge that God is 'close to the broken-hearted' (verse 18).

To think about

If you have a copy of it, read the hymn 'Through all the changing scenes of life', which is based on this psalm.

60

Where is God now?   *Psalm 44*

This psalm is one of those known as 'community laments', because in it we see the people 'lamenting' a national crisis and praying to God to deliver them from it. There is not here the joy of answered prayer (as in Psalm 34), but the agony of prayer as yet unanswered.

The believing community agonizes before God about a contradiction: he has done great wonders for them in the past, but now he appears to have let them down. But what matters is that they do hold the pain of this contradiction before God. They don't just shrug their shoulders and turn away.

The problem is that the nation has been defeated in battle (verse 10). Prisoners have been taken into exile (verse 11) and their cities left desolate (verse 19). They have become the laughing-stock of neighbouring countries (verses 13–16).

Reflection on what God has done in the past (verses 1–8). The people know their history. They have been brought up on stories of the Exodus and the conquest of the Promised Land. All this was the work of God, the expression of his love for Israel (verses 1–3). In verses 4–8 an individual speaks—perhaps the king, affirming that Israel owes its strength and security to God alone.

This kind of recital of 'where we have come from' is important both psychologically and spiritually. Many people try to trace their ancestry. Adopted children want to discover their real parents. Nations need a sense of history in order to understand their role in the world today. Worshippers need to see themselves as part of a continuing stream of faith rooted in what God did at Sinai and the Red Sea, in Bethlehem and in Jerusalem. Not only that, we need a sense of what has shaped us since New Testament times—the change from being a persecuted minority to being an influential force in the world, the monastic movement, the Reformation, the great times of spiritual awakening, the growth of the Church to become a worldwide movement, and so on.

Yet the whole problem of the Psalmist derives from his sure knowledge of what God has done in the past. Where now is the God we knew?

Grief over Israel's present plight (verses 9–22). As well as the actual experience of military defeat (verses 9–12) and the humiliation of being ridiculed by other nations (verses 13–16), there is the spiritual anguish of not knowing why things have turned out like this (verses 17–22).

If they could see this catastrophe as punishment for their sins, that would be a way of making sense of it. But, like Job, they can't rewrite their story to fit that theory. They have genuinely been seeking to live in submission to God's will (verses 17–18, 20–21). If they could see that God had somehow profited from abandoning his people, that too would be a way of making sense (verse 12). But no—they feel crushed and in despair (verses 19, 22).

129

Prayer for help (verses 23–26). They will not give up on God. In fact they want to shake him awake. There is a special irony about verse 23 when we compare it with the story of Elijah on Mount Carmel (passage 32). There Elijah taunted the prophets of Baal about Baal's inability to come to their aid: 'Maybe he is sleeping and must be wakened' (1 Kings 18:27). Now it is the God of Israel who needs waking up.

That is how it sometimes seems to the people of God. In our church life we see decline in membership, and as we look back at the past we say, 'Is God asleep?' Or in our personal experience we feel that God is not as real to us as he once was, and we ask, 'Is God asleep?' There may be many reasons for this. It is not necessarily that we have been unfaithful in our discipleship. The pain and the puzzlement may actually be because we are suffering 'for your sake' (verse 22)—out of faithfulness to God and for reasons which lie hidden in God.

When we feel crushed by circumstances, perplexed about where God is in our troubles, a Psalm such as this encourages us to pour out our distress before God, to pray and even to demand that he do something about it. The psalm invites us to hold before God the contradiction of his past activity and his present apparent inactivity. Recalling his love in the past (verse 3) we plead with him bluntly and insistently to reveal his unfailing love once again (verse 26). But, because he is a resourceful God who knows us better than we know ourselves, we may leave it to him to decide what form our deliverance shall take.

61

Why do the wicked prosper?   *Psalm 73*

This psalm is called a 'wisdom psalm' because, like some of the wisdom books which we have looked at, it explores the question of why good people suffer whilst bad people prosper. But it is also a powerful testimony to one person's growth in faith.

Verse 1 may sound smug—the kind of pious platitude with which you would expect someone to begin a religious poem. But then as you read the psalm you realize that verse 1 is in fact the conclusion to which the writer has struggled through bitter experience. And that gives it a very different 'feel'.

The Psalmist's faith challenged (verses 2–3). The words sound like a confession. The writer has been tempted to lose his faith and turn away from the believing community when he observed the prosperity of the wicked. He admits his envy.

The success of the wicked (verses 4–14). Who are these 'wicked'? The writer is not making a sweeping moral condemnation, but describing the kind of people who sit loose to the obligations of the covenant. They may be Gentiles, they may be Israelites whose connections with the worshipping community are merely nominal.

Life for them goes well. Good food and regular visits to the 'Living Well Club' make them fit and healthy. They are at the top of the social pile. They are full of ideas about how to 'get on'. In their affluence they have become arrogant. They have no qualms about using other people as ladders to their own progress. They have no shame about safeguarding their own interests at the expense of others. Their guiding principle is not, 'What is right?' but 'What will bring success?'

And the success of their self-interest brings them admirers. All the old values are being undermined (verse 10). The new values of every-man-for-himself and aggressive marketing take over. And there is no thunderbolt from heaven to give them second thoughts (verse 11).

The Psalmist's dilemma is that their approach to life works. His own tradition of faith seems to be in tatters. Is God tolerant after all of people who ignore his laws? Or has the success of their lifestyle shown God up to be powerless, or irrelevant? Either way, his attempt to be faithful to God seems a waste of time (verses 13–14). The detailed description of what the wicked are like betrays the Psalmist's fascination with them. He wishes he were like them.

Second thoughts (verses 15–17). But now another perspective comes in. If he were to give in to these thoughts and try to become like those whom he envies, he would be letting down those who are still trying to live as God requires (verse 15). He would be betraying the trust of those who, because of their faith in God, believe that right is more important than might and a caring society is more important than a wealthy one.

A visit to the temple provides the key to his new understanding (verse 17). It is in such a moment of distancing from the world that we are freed from the seductive fascination of affluence for long enough to see that God and his will are what matters above all else.

Rejection of the alluring alternative (verses 18–22). Though the wicked may flourish now, their prosperity is ultimately worthless. It is not clear whether the writer expects them to suffer a reversal of fortune before long, or is alluding to their fate after death. But he senses that in time their apparent prosperity will be as immaterial as a dream. The tycoon may be worth millions, he may be able to make thousands of people dance to his tune. He may even be given an honoured burial. But when he is dead and gone the rottenness of his business empire will be exposed and despised by all.

The new perspective of faith (verses 23–28). There is no tidy explanation for the prosperity of the wicked. But there is a solution of a different kind. Communion with God casts a new light on all experiences of inequality. It is not so much that the writer has a new hold on God as that he has a new sense of being held by God. The ground of his confidence is in God himself. That is the good news which breaks in on him at the climax of his journey of faith (verses 23–26).

It is impossible to tell whether verse 24 implies a belief that everything will finally be put right beyond death in God's eternal presence. Perhaps the writer cannot yet make that affirmation (which is in any case very rare in the Old Testament). But he knows that the faithful find well-being from God and with God. And he can't keep the secret to himself (verse 28).

62
Pilgrim song

Psalm 122

Singing meets many needs in human life. There are, for example, songs which keep us going when the going gets tough: 'We shall overcome...'. There are songs to honour special moments in our lives: 'Happy birthday to you...'. And every football club has its special songs for anticipating, and then for celebrating, its great victories.

Psalm 122 has a little of all these elements in it. It is one of a group of psalms (Psalms 120–134) which are thought to have been sung by pilgrims on their journey to Jerusalem to celebrate Israel's great festivals. Passover commemorated the Israelites' escape from Egypt. Pentecost marked the beginning of the wheat harvest. Tabernacles celebrated the fruit harvest in the autumn.

People from all parts of the country and beyond would travel in groups to the holy city, like busloads on the motorway on their way to the Cup Final. But such journeys were long and arduous. For some pilgrims they would take many days. Imagine their rising expectation as they began the final climb towards Jerusalem, and their shouts of joy as they reached the top of the hill and saw the temple glinting in the sunlight before them. They needed songs to express the emotions of the journey and the arrival!

This song perhaps captures the moment when a festival is over. The pilgrims are about to depart and they take a last careful look at the city in order to hold its precious memory when they go home. It is the special focus of Israel's hopes, the place where God rules through the earthly king (verse 5), and therefore a place which evokes the praise of his people (verse 4).

Verses 6–9 express prayer for Jerusalem's peace and security. We can imagine how much that mattered to the Hebrews for whom the temple was the place where God's presence was known. We can imagine how much it matters to Jewish people today, for whom Jerusalem symbolizes their history, their faith and their security as a people delivered from the Holocaust to live again in the Holy Land. We can pray as they do for the city of David.

But we must also recognize how difficult it is for Arabs—Muslims or Christians—to read this psalm and to join in its prayer for Jerusalem—if the prayer is read as an endorsement of Jewish hopes for the city. For Jerusalem is holy to them also. And too many people use this psalm deliberately or unconsciously to champion the national and political stance of the Israeli state.

To pray for the peace of Jerusalem involves praying for all its people, asking that God will lead them to a wholeness of relationships which joins their humanity rather than separates their races and nationalities.

A prayer for Jerusalem

God of peace,
you made Jerusalem the focus of your love for Israel;
in Jerusalem you made peace with all mankind
through the death and resurrection of Jesus.
We pray for all who live in this city, for whom in different ways
it is a place of memories and hopes, of faith and anxiety.
May they find a peace in which people of different races and faiths
may unite in trust and friendship.

May they find security based not on weapons
but on justice and acceptance of each other.
In the name of Christ, who wept in love over this city
and died in love outside its walls.

63

'Where can I flee from your presence?'

Psalm 139

This very personal psalm moves us with its description of the God who is always present, and shocks us with its cry for vengeance against the wicked. Let us take one thing at a time.

The God who knows everything (verses 1–6). The Psalmist reflects that everything he does, everything he even thinks about doing, is known to God. He is overwhelmed by the greatness of his Creator and his own smallness as God's creature (verse 6). This realization is rather threatening. It makes him feel hemmed in, like a criminal surrounded by police and unable to escape (verse 5).

The God who is everywhere (verses 7–12). There is no hiding away from God. Because he is Spirit he is not tied down by the 'rules' of space and time (verse 7). However high or low we go, however far east or west, he is there (verses 9–10). There is no sphere of life or of the universe which is not ruled by him and infused with his presence. Even the darkness—whose power must have seemed impenetrable in a world before electricity—is no darkness to him (verses 11–12).

But now the Psalmist can see God's presence as blessing rather than as threat (verse 10). Wherever I go I am not too far away for his care to reach me. Even though I may feel that God is far away, he is in fact 'closer than breathing, nearer than hand or foot'. I can rest in that knowledge.

The God who has made everything (verses 13–16). The writer expresses wonder about the delicate complexity of his own body and recognizes God as its origin. Each of us is a unique individual, a distinctive personality, with a fingerprint which distinguishes us from every other human being. Our lives have meaning only because we are made by God who values each individual.

The God to whom we come with awe (verses 17–18). This is the inevitable response of one who senses what the Psalmist has sensed. Awe is not a word in common use today. But we need it to express the breathtaking wonder which the Psalmist feels as he thinks about the God whom he has come to know.

In 1945 a nineteen-year-old German soldier was captured and later placed in a prisoner-of-war camp in Sherwood Forest. The horrors of the Second World War, and the shame they felt at what their nation had unleashed upon the world, caused many German prisoners to withdraw inside themselves and give up all hope. 'The same thing almost happened to me,' he wrote later, were it not for a 'rebirth to a new life... The experience of misery and forsakenness and daily humiliation gradually built up into an experience of God.'

He became fascinated by the Psalms, which helped him to find 'the experience of God's presence in the dark night of the soul: "If I make my bed in hell, behold, thou art there" [Psalm 139:8].' He adds that he does not so much want to say that this is how he found God, 'but I do know in my heart that it is there that he found me, and that I would otherwise have been lost.' He is Jürgen Moltmann, one of the great theologians of the twentieth century.

The cry for justice (verses 19–22). The first eighteen verses of this psalm often get used on their own, and these verses conveniently forgotten. But the words are there in the same psalm. Why?

The Psalmist's closeness to God and his awareness that nothing is hidden from God's view apparently bring to his mind the reality of evil and evildoers. He is struck by the contradiction between the all-knowing God and the existence of people who behave as if God counted for nothing. He sees, perhaps more clearly than we do, that God's will cannot triumph without the actual overthrow of evil.

He is not lashing out at his personal enemies. He is not saying to God, 'Make my enemies your enemies.' He is saying, 'I will recognize your enemies as mine. I will align myself with your view of evil, your opposition to all that conflicts with your will.'

The God who tests our hearts (verses 23–24). If we are really opposed to evil, we will resist it in our own hearts. So the psalm finally invites us to express our own inadequacy and to allow the ever-present God to keep us aligned with his purpose for us. Then we can discover that God's constant presence does not hem us in threateningly, but liberates us to walk the path of life.

64

By the rivers of Babylon

Psalm 137

Our final selection from the Psalms takes us back to the situation of the people of Judah in exile. The poignant beauty of verses 1–6 contrasts with the savagery of verses 7–8.

Verses 1–3. After years of exile the Psalmist reflects on his feelings for Jerusalem. He perhaps recalls a particular occasion when a group of exiles were pouring out their melancholy songs of lamentation over the destruction of the temple and their separation from home.

Their Babylonian masters, playing with their victims like a cat with a mouse, demanded to hear a happy song. They wanted exotic entertainment. They wanted to hear a 'song of Zion' (such as Psalm 122) so that they could sneer at their captives singing a confident song about the now desolate temple. They wanted to rub in the fact that the exiles were at their mercy. Such monstrous scenes were repeated in the concentration camp at Treblinka, where Jews were forced to dance and sing their Jewish songs.

Verses 4–6. To give in to such demands would be an act of extreme unfaithfulness. The exiles could not do it. To reduce holy words to the level of entertainment would be to betray their identity as God's people. It would destroy their dignity and their hope.

What is at stake here is the maintenance of Israel's vision of how life is to be lived and of the God before whom it is to be lived. By refusing to sing for their captors they are refusing to let their lives be controlled by Babylon. They are clinging to their hope of homecoming and renewal of their national life.

In his book, *An Evil Cradling*, Brian Keenan describes his imprisonment in Lebanon along with John McCarthy and other hostages. From February 1986 to August 1990 he was held by men who tortured him both physically and psychologically. He tells how through refusing to show weakness to their guards, through humour and constant mutual support, they kept their humanity, discovered hidden resources within themselves, and retained their hope of release to a new life.

It is the same kind of determination to survive that is expressed here, as the Psalmist keeps clear his vision of Jerusalem, more precious than health and even life itself.

Verses 7–9. Passionate longing for Jerusalem now turns into passionate anger against those who mock and humiliate the exiles. The Edomites, Judah's neighbours to the south-east of the Dead Sea, had taken political advantage of Judah's downfall. The Babylonians had no doubt been guilty of barbaric killing of babies in Jerusalem.

We are embarrassed and revolted by such expressions of hatred. Yet not to read them and grapple with them is too easy a way out. If we cannot excuse them or fully explain why they should be there in the Bible, we can try to listen to them and understand the mind from which they come.

We must be careful about feeling that we are somehow superior to such outbursts of anger if we have not suffered as much or lost as much as the Psalmist has suffered and lost. If we listened more carefully to black South Africans, Tibetan refugees, victims of child abuse or rainforest inhabitants bulldozed almost to extinction, we might understand more fully this cry of rage.

The presence of such words in Scripture is a sign that God listens to the anger of his people. We have permission to express our unacceptable feelings to God. Better to express them to God, as the Psalmist does, than to take it upon ourselves to wreak vengeance on our enemies. 'It is an act of profound faith to entrust one's most precious hatreds to God, knowing they will be taken seriously' (Walter Brueggemann).

But what of forgiveness? For us who are called to love our enemies and pray for those who persecute us (Matthew 5:44), forgiveness must be the goal. But is there a danger that forgiveness glides over a problem, treating it too lightly? Can there be real forgiveness before there has been real weighing of the hatred and the hurt which has been caused? Without excusing or explaining away the violence of this psalm, we may allow it to challenge our tendency to condone evil rather than to confront it, and to work through the hatred to a genuine and deep forgiveness.

The psalm raises sharply the question: How can such cries for vengeance be reconciled with the God whose love is revealed in Scripture? But it leaves us not with that question but with another: Am I hearing the cry of the refugee, the abused, the victimized, the forgotten people of our world? How, through my prayers and in other ways, can I support them in their search for hope?

4

EXILE AND AFTER

65

A new beginning

The magnificent poetry of Isaiah 40–55 addresses the situation of the exiles in Babylon in the sixth century BC. Some people believe that the whole of the book of Isaiah owes its origin to Isaiah of Jerusalem in the eighth century BC. But it seems more likely that the messages of hope which begin in Isaiah 40 were first addressed to people actually experiencing the despair of exile. If so, the author was a prophet whose own name we do not know, but who developed Isaiah of Jerusalem's understanding of God and his purpose.

It is not too fanciful as we read these chapters to think of the Church today as being in exile, in the sense that we live in a nation whose values and goals are sometimes hostile to the Christian gospel. We can read the prophet's message of homecoming to a more wholesome society as a word of hope to us also.

Read Isaiah 40

Whereas the message of Isaiah in the eighth century was mostly warnings of God's judgment for the sins of Judah, the prophet now brings words of comfort and hope. Once the judgment has come, in the form of exile, God's purpose is to open up for his people the possibility of repentance and renewal.

In a sense the key to this chapter is verse 27. The people now in exile feel abandoned by God. They are at the mercy of a foreign power. All hope is gone. The prophet's mission is to overturn that despair by announcing God's new plan.

Comfort for God's people (verses 1–11). Just as Isaiah of Jerusalem overheard God speaking to his heavenly servants (passage 38), so the prophet here pictures God instructing his heavenly servants to bring comfort to his dejected people (verses 1–2).

God, who had abandoned his people to exile because of their sins, is now making a fresh start with them. They have suffered more than enough for their sins (verse 2). God is making a new highway through the wilderness for a new exodus to the Promised Land (verses 3–5). Though the exiles feel that they have been tossed aside like grass, they have not reckoned with the power of God's word to bring permanent change (verses 6–8).

There is good news at last for Jerusalem: God who had withdrawn his presence is coming back! His power is demonstrated by his bringing his people as the prize of war. But he is also coming with great tenderness, like a shepherd lifting up lambs in his arms and taking special care of ewes at lambing time (verses 9–11).

Objection overruled (verses 12–31). In a series of questions God takes up the challenge of Israel's despair. Let us summarize what he says by putting it in a slightly different form.

'I know how you are feeling. I understand your despair (verse 27). But listen.

'You think that the gods of the Babylonians must be more powerful than I am. But don't you remember how I am spoken of in your psalms and in the prophets? I made the world, I needed no one else to tell me how to do it. These nations whose power impresses you so much—I am the Lord of their history, they are like a drop of water in a bucket to me (verses 12–17).

'Think again about these gods the Babylonians worship. They are just statues. It takes three men to create an idol, and one of them can't afford the expense! And yet you are overawed by them! (verses 18–20).

'These foreign rulers frighten you with their military power. But to me they are like grasshoppers, they are like tender plants blown over by a gale (verses 21–24).

'The star gods whom the Babylonians see as the controllers of their destiny—they are my creation. Every one of them has a name given by me. Every one of them has its place in the sky because of the forces which I created and control (verses 25–26).

'If I can do all this, do you think I'm too worn out to cope with you? My strength reaches to the ends of the universe. I'm ready and waiting to transform your weariness into vitality, your despair into hope (verses 28–31).'

The prophet, then, speaks to God's people in their time of need by reminding them who God is. That is the source to which we must return when bewildered by our own weakness or the hopelessness of our situation. Because God is the creator of all things, we can look to him to find meaning for our lives. We can resist the temptation to think that anything else can have a power over our lives greater than God's. We can wait in trust and hope for him to act.

66
The God who saves
Isaiah 45

The prophet now reveals how God will restore the exiles to their home. God, who used Babylon to bring his judgment on the people of Judah, will use the Persian ruler Cyrus to bring their release. Cyrus became ruler of Persia (roughly, modern Iran) in 559BC.

Since we do not know the date when this prophecy was uttered we cannot tell how much of the prophet's knowledge is due to specific divine revelation of the future. But we can see see him announcing with bold God-given insight how God is going to deliver his people.

Cyrus, God's anointed (verses 1–7). The remarkable thing here is that Cyrus is called God's 'anointed'. Israel's kings and priests were anointed with olive oil as a sign of their special role in carrying out God's will. The word 'anointed' is the Hebrew '*messiah*'—used later by Jews as a title of the expected deliverer-king descended from David. Here a foreign ruler is given this same title to indicate that he too is the agent of God's will.

Verses 1–3 speak of Cyrus' irresistible military progress against Babylon. God will use him to achieve his purpose for Israel (verse 4) and to demonstrate that he alone is God (verses 3–6). Even though Cyrus doesn't acknowledge him as Lord he is still the channel through whom God brings rebirth to his people (verses 4–5). Verse 7 asserts that nothing is ultimately outside the control of God. He brought darkness on his people through military conquest; he is bringing light through raising up Cyrus.

There is powerful encouragement here as we observe the activities of the nations' rulers today. Whether or not they acknowledge God personally, they are agents of his purpose for the world. It may seem often that he has left them on a long rein, so that they act oppressively and without any apparent restraint. Nevertheless, the rein in due course is pulled in and the justice of God is glimpsed again. The collapse of European communism in 1989, perhaps, or the ending of apartheid in South Africa, are examples of this truth at work.

Song of salvation (verse 8). The prophecy is interrupted by a hymn which uses two of the great words of this section of Isaiah. 'Righteousness' means God's putting things right, acting to maintain his covenant with Israel. 'Salvation' means his act of rescue. For the exiles it will be both physical—actual restoration to their homeland—and spiritual—renewal of hope in God and experience of his care.

God works in his own way (verses 9–13). Some of the exiles may say, 'But the pagan Cyrus cannot be an agent of God's salvation.' 'Yes, he can,' comes the reply. 'Who are you to question how God does his work (verses 9–10)? Do you know better that God himself (verse 11)? Cyrus is his chosen instrument to return the exiles and rebuild Jerusalem. It will bring no profit to him: the sole reason for this restoration is the gracious will of God (verse 13).'

The God who speaks tenderly of 'my city', 'my exiles', acts in gentle love towards his people. It is faithless ingratitude to complain if he chooses an unorthodox method to achieve his purpose. We should not be surprised if the creative God finds new and unexpected ways to do his work.

'There is no other god' (verses 14–25). Verse 14 depicts people coming from many nations to acknowledge Israel's God. But they will come in chains: released from Babylonian captivity, Israel will then take others captive. If understood literally this is not an uplifting thought. But the central theme is that they will bow before Israel's God rather than before its rulers. Verses 22–23 offer a more positive vision of the nations discovering that Israel's God is a saviour for them as well as for Israel.

Although God's way of working is mysterious (verse 15), he makes clear through the prophets all that we need to know to find him and to be sure of his love (verse 19). He has never promised to tell us everything we might want to know, but he has shown us enough of himself on which we may base our lives with confidence.

Verses 20–25 develop the theme of Yahweh as the only God, the only Saviour. He invites people of all nations to discover for themselves the scope of his love (verse 22). He warns of the danger of rejecting his invitation (verse 24). Finally he assures the exiles once more of the joy that is about to dawn (verse 25).

Coming from the lips of a captive prophet in a pagan land, this is a remarkable vision of the God who rules all nations and longs for them to know his saving love.

67

The suffering and glory of God's servant

Isaiah 52:13—53:12

Famous and yet mysterious, this passage takes us into depths which earlier parts of the Old Testament have not explored. It concerns God's servant. But who is he? Several times already the prophet of the exile has referred to Israel as God's servant (e.g., Isaiah 41:8–9; 49:3), whilst in 50:10 the prophet himself seems to be in view.

His identity here is altogether more elusive. It is as though the prophet is reporting a dream, a vision which has not come to him in a logical sequence, and which holds more meaning than he can himself detect. Before we can ask who the servant is, we must ask what the prophet sees.

It helps to see the shape of the passage. It begins and ends with words spoken by God about the suffering and glory of the servant (52:13–15; 53:11–12). In between (53:1–10) is a description of the servant spoken by a group of people ('our', verse 1; 'us', verse 2; 'we', verse 4). The identity of this 'we' and of the servant must be left open for the time being.

Despised and rejected by all (53:1–3). The prophet sees a man who is not at all impressive. He is tortured by suffering. His appearance is so disfigured that it is embarrassing to look at him. He is a social outcast.

Pierced for our transgressions (verses 4–6). Yet mysteriously his suffering does something for the watching group. Like many Israelites they thought that the servant's suffering was due to his sins (that is the meaning of 'we considered him stricken by God', verse 4). But no— somehow, they say, his suffering deals with our infirmities, our sorrows, our transgressions, our iniquities.

142

It reminds them of the ritual on the annual Day of Atonement, when the sins of the people were symbolically laid upon the head of a goat and the goat was then driven into the wilderness, taking away with it the people's sins (Leviticus 16:20–22). 'The Lord has laid on him the iniquity of us all' (verse 6).

But how can this be? Verses 7–11 repeat the story of the servant's suffering, but focus a little more clearly on the meaning of it.

For the transgression of my people he was stricken (verses 7–9). Here the servant's innocent purity is emphasized. He was like an unblemished lamb such as was used for sacrifice (verse 7). He had done no wrong (verse 9). Yet he was rejected and ultimately done to death, unjustly condemned to a criminal's grave (verses 8–9). If, then, he had no guilt of his own to suffer for, was it 'for the transgression of my people' that he was struck down (verse 8)?

Yet it was the Lord's will (verse 10). Here the new discovery of this passage occurs. God shows something of his purpose which has not been revealed before. The servant is not suffering for his own sins but for the sins of others. And this is somehow God's own idea. Just as, in Old Testament thought, an animal offered in sacrifice suffers to take away the sins of the people, so God uses the suffering of the servant to bring forgiveness and healing and new life to others.

The suffering and the glory (52:13–15; 53:11–12). In both the opening and the closing summaries God declares that because he has borne his suffering the servant is exalted or rewarded. 'Because he poured out his life unto death, and was numbered with the transgressors' (53:12), 'he will be raised and lifted up and highly exalted' (52:13). Through his servant God does for people what they cannot do for themselves. He has removed their sins. He has transformed suffering into a source of life and hope.

But who *is* the servant, and who are 'we'? Is the servant the prophet himself, suffering on behalf of the whole people? Is he the people of Judah in exile? But if so, who are the 'we' on whose behalf they suffer? Maybe the prophet himself pondered such questions.

But in the end suggestions such as these are inadequate because they don't do justice to the heavy emphasis on the innocence and purity of the suffering servant. The portrayal of the servant is like a job description with no applicants.

Until Jesus came. New Testament writers, and Jesus himself, see this passage of Isaiah as a description of how Jesus fulfilled his work of bringing forgiveness and new life from God to humanity. And 'we' means us—all who claim this Saviour as our own.

> *He himself bore our sins in his body on the cross, so that we might die to sins and live for righteousness; by his wounds you have been healed.*

1 Peter 2:24

68
True worship

Isaiah 56–66 speaks to the situation of exiles now returned to Judah. After his conquest of Babylon in 539BC, Cyrus allowed the Jews and other captive peoples to return to their own countries. They remained part of his empire, but were able to carry on their lives in their own way. So the prophecy of Isaiah 40 (passage 65) came true.

But the actual experience of returning to Judah did not match the great vision which had kept hope alive during the exile. Like many prisoners released after a long sentence, they were depressed and aimless. Economic life was in a mess and the temple lay in ruins. Without clear leadership, they became a nation divided against itself. There was need once again for a prophetic voice in the tradition of Amos, Hosea and Isaiah of Jerusalem.

Read Isaiah 58

The fasting which God requires (verses 1–7). Fasting—going without food and drink as an expression of religious devotion— was not common in the Old Testament. But it was practised on the Day of Atonement. And after the exile, four extra periods of fasting were appointed, when prayers of lamentation were offered for the destruction of Jerusalem (see Zechariah 8:19). Now the people are saying, 'We've fasted, we've sung our lamentations, we've given our whole selves to worship. And our national life remains in a mess. Why isn't God taking the slightest bit of notice?' (verse 3).

The reply is a devastating list of social sins. The fasting is self-centred rather than God-centred, because on the fast day itself the wealthier people keep their workforce hard at work (verse 3). They are irritable and their business haggling turns into violence (verse 4).

They have failed miserably to live up to God's expectations of them. They can please him only by releasing people unjustly enslaved, stopping the oppression of the powerless, responding to the needs of the destitute (verses 6–7). And they abuse the sabbath similarly (verse 13).

It is one of the strange ironies of human nature that people who have themselves been released from captivity should want to hold others captive to their power. Yet it happens often. An oppressed minority in a nation gains political power and begins to take it out on those who previously oppressed it. A person who was abused as a child becomes an abuser of his own children.

The attack is crowned by the argument that those whom the people neglect are 'your own flesh and blood' (verse 7). Although this is sometimes taken to mean 'close relatives' (as in REB), it probably means 'other human beings' (see Job 31:13–15, where Job recognizes that he must treat servants justly because they share with him a common humanity). Our obligation to those in need is based on the simple truth that they are human beings as we are, made and valued by God as we are.

There is a uncomfortable message here for Western Christians. When we wonder why our prayers aren't answered, the answer may not be because we haven't prayed enough or we haven't paid proper attention to religious activities. It may be that we have treated the care of the needy as an optional extra.

But the prophet offers no compromise. To fast, to attend all the worship services and to know all the right songs counts for nothing in God's eyes if we are not doing what is right and have in fact forsaken the commands of God (verse 2). The trouble is that most Christians observe the demands of God selectively. Some are rigorously pure in matters of personal and sexual behaviour, yet pay less attention to the social demands laid down in this passage. Others place proper emphasis on social action but leave their personal lives open to question. God calls such selectivity 'rebellion' (verse 1, NIV; the word is stronger than 'transgression' in REB would suggest).

The words of verses 6–7 are given added importance for us by Jesus' allusion to them in Luke 4:18 (passage 82) and especially in his teaching about the judgment of the sheep and the goats in Matthew 25:31–46.

God's promise to those who repent (verses 8–14). The people don't have to stay as they are. If they put their lives right as well as their worship they will experience all the blessings of God's presence and protection. A whole series of pictures expresses the completeness of what God longs to do for his people—light, healing (verse 8), a richly watered garden (verse 11). God will go before and behind them to protect them, as he did when they journeyed from Egypt to the Promised Land (verse 8). He will answer their prayers (verse 9). And Jerusalem will be rebuilt (verse 12).

69

New heavens and a new earth   *Isaiah 65:17–25*

Despite his uncompromising warnings of God's judgment on human wrongdoing, this prophet has a great vision of the future which God is going to create. Nothing less than the language of Genesis 1 is adequate to describe it. Three times in verses 17–18 he uses the word 'create' as if to say that the new thing which God is going to do is as momentous as his original act of creation.

So certain is this work of God that the prophet speaks of it as happening now. Despite the NIV translation, the verbs in verses 17–18 are present, not future: 'I *am creating* new heavens and a new earth', 'I *am creating* Jerusalem as a delight'. So complete is the transformation that the old order of things will be forgotten. There will be total renewal of heaven and earth (verse 17).

Although the language of 'new heavens and new earth' sounds as if it is speaking of a totally new order of existence to replace the old, the following verses make clear that this is not intended literally. It is a graphic way of insisting that God is doing something marvellous and radically new—'earth-shattering', as we might say, using a similar image.

The picture of the new era focuses on Jerusalem (verses 18–19, 25). Though Jerusalem later became a symbol of God's total transformation of human society at the end of history, the message here is for the people of Jerusalem and its neighbourhood in the sixth century BC.

Verses 19–25 describe what the new era will be like. The weeping which was once a familar sound in war-torn Jerusalem will be no more (verse 19). People will live to ripe old age, and if anyone dies young it must be for some quite exceptional reason (verse 20).

In contrast to the invasions of the past, there will now be peace and security, enabling people to build houses and develop crops without fear of losing them. Their work will never be pointless or fruitless (verses 21–22). Women who bring children into the world will no longer ask with anxiety, 'What kind of a world have my children been born into? What tragedy will strike them?' (verse 23). These references to the fruitfulness of work and the secure future for children are a reversal of the pains of human experience imposed on Adam and Eve in Genesis 3:16–19.

God's people will know his nearness. Their prayers will never be in vain (verse 24). And, like the vision of Isaiah 11 (passage 39), this passage ends with a picture of the natural world in total harmony.

It is a beautiful picture of the promised future. And the prophet speaks of it as if it lies just around the corner. But what happened in history? The story of Israel continued with its ups and downs—mostly downs, one is tempted to say. So what is the value of a passage like this? Is it just poetry without content? Is its vision as delightful, and as unrealistic, as Karl Marx's dream of a classless society when anyone may 'hunt in the morning, fish in the afternoon, breed cattle in the evening and be a critic after dinner'?

It is in the very nature of a prophet to speak of God's future acts as though they were almost present. Precisely because God gives him this vivid insight he tells what he sees. He speaks not of the *timescale* on which God achieves his purpose, but of the *certainty* that God's plan will reach its goal. To change the picture, the prophet is like a photographer who shows us a picture of a distant mountain, taken with a telephoto lens. What we see is the peak in all its magnificent attractiveness. But when we try to walk there, we find there are many smaller peaks and hidden valleys in between. And yet we keep on walking because we know, thanks to the photographer, that the peak is there.

So the promise of Isaiah 65, and others like it, are not to be dismissed because they offered to the Jews hopes which seemed not to be fulfilled. They are visions which keep expectation alive. They are signs of what God will ultimately achieve because he is the Lord of history's end as well as of its beginning. And every partial fulfilment, every small peak scaled, is a stage along the way towards the completion of his purpose for the world.

The new heaven and new earth and new Jerusalem described at the end of the Bible (Revelation 21) are the ultimate goal of all his activity in the world. In Isaiah 65 he is rekindling hope in his people so that they keep moving on their journey towards that goal.

70

The coming king

Haggai and Zechariah were two other prophets shortly after the return from exile. They stirred up the people's low morale and challenged their spiritual and moral carelessness. In particular they urged the importance of restoring the temple—a goal which was completed in 515BC.

The following passage foresees the promised king who will bring liberation to Israel and to the world.

Read Zechariah 9

Verses 1–8 depict God's judgment moving southwards from Syria to the land of the Philistines. The thought is similar to Ezekiel's prophecy against Tyre (passage 48). Zechariah may be describing what was to take place when Alexander the Great marched victoriously through the Middle East in 333BC. Or possibly he is not predicting a specific series of historical events, but is using this familar catalogue of places as a picture of final judgment. Just as powerful foreign armies have swept through Syria and Palestine, so finally God will bring every proud city to judgment.

But it is not all doom and destruction. God will transform the Philistines, taking away their habit of eating meat which is not 'kosher', and will join them to the people of Judah. Just as the original Jebusite inhabitants of Jerusalem were absorbed into Israel when David captured the city, the Philistines of Ekron will become part of God's people (verse 7).

Finally God's triumphant march will reach 'my house'—the land of Judah—which he will protect with a watchful eye (verse 8). If this passage *is* focussed particularly on the period of Alexander, it is worth noting that he spared Jerusalem when he came there in 332BC.

In verse 9 the keynote changes from war to peace. God announces the coming of his Messiah-king to Jerusalem and describes how he will exercise his rule.

His rule will be *peaceful*. As the bringer of peace he will arrive on a donkey, not on a war-horse (verse 9). He will banish weapons of war (verse 10).

His rule will be *universal* (verse 10). 'From sea to sea' means from the Red Sea to the Mediterranean. 'The River' is the Euphrates. The writer is portraying the king's control over the whole known world—in contrast to the tiny territory normally ruled by Judah's kings.

His rule will be *righteous* (verse 9). 'Righteous and having salvation' (NIV) repeats an aspect of Israel's ideal king familiar from earlier prophets (Isaiah 11, passage 39). He will see that right prevails and that those who might otherwise be victims of injustice will find their deliverance in him (compare REB, 'his cause won, his victory gained').

His rule will mean *security* for all his people (verses 11–12). These words are perhaps addressed to Jews still in exile in Babylon—for not all the exiles had returned in one group in 539BC. Because of God's covenant commitment to his people he will rescue them from exile and restore them generously to safety.

His rule will mean *the defeat of all the forces that oppose him* (verse 13). Judah and Ephraim—the Southern and Northern Kingdoms now reunited—will resist the onslaughts of their enemies. 'Javan' (REB) is 'Greece' (NIV)—though possibly the term is used here to denote enemies of Israel, and of God, in general.

Through his rule, *God's own presence* will be among his people (verses 14–17). Words are inadequate to express what this implies. Zechariah's extravagant language portrays the complete protection offered by God's presence and the unrestrained joy of his people.

So, finally, the king's coming will be a source of lasting *joy* among his people. The whole passage begins with the exhortation to Jerusalem to rejoice (verse 9) and reaches its climax in the exuberant celebrations of verse 15.

We face here a question similar to that of Isaiah 65. Is the prophet describing how things will ultimately be when God's rule or kingdom finally comes? Or is he thinking still in terms of the historical experience of Israel? He seems to envisage a situation where the Messiah's coming makes a radical difference to the world, yet conditions have not changed totally. He foresees the sure victory of Israel and its king in war, rather than the abolition of war. So, like Isaiah 65, his vision shows a step along the way to the final triumph of God's purpose. It is not the final victory itself.

By quoting Zechariah 9:9 in their accounts of Jesus' entry into Jerusalem (Matthew 21:5; John 12:15), New Testament writers point to Jesus as the Messiah who fulfils this prophecy. But in fulfilling it he transforms it. The day will come when his rule will have all the characteristics summarized above. But it will be by way of the cross, not the sword.

Worship renewed in Jerusalem

Two historical books which describe the return from exile and the rebuilding of life in Judah are Ezra and Nehemiah.

Ezra, who returned from Babylon to Jerusalem in 458BC, eighty years after the first exiles returned, was a scholar and teacher. He did much to organize the life of the people in accordance with the Law, and was probably responsible for the final collection and writing down of Israel's Law books (Genesis to Deuteronomy) in the form which is familiar to us. The following passages report events in 539BC and soon afterwards, before Ezra himself went back to Jerusalem.

Read Ezra 1 and 3

Cyrus' decree (chapter 1). Jeremiah had prophesied a seventy-year captivity (Jeremiah 25:1–12; 29:10) Cyrus' first year of control over Babylon and its empire was 539–538BC—roughly seventy years after the first deportation of leading men of Judah about 605BC (see 2 Kings 24:1–2; with Daniel 1:1–7).

It is interesting to compare the decree of Cyrus (1:2–4) with Cyrus' own account which survives on an inscription called the Cyrus Cylinder. Writing of the areas from which the Babylonians had brought conquered peoples into exile, though without mentioning the Jews in particular, he says: 'I gathered together all their inhabitants and restored them to their dwellings.' He also reports that he arranged for rebuilding of temples.

For the writer it is important to stress that Yahweh himself has 'moved the heart' of Cyrus to this act of liberation (verse 1)—thus fulfilling the promise of Isaiah 45 (passage 66). The reference to neighbours giving silver and gold and other supplies to help the returning exiles (verses 4, 6) echoes the help received from their Egyptian neighbours by Israelites at the exodus (Exodus 11:2; 12:35). The return from exile is to be like a new exodus, an equal demonstration of God's liberating power.

The list of sacred vessels (verse 9) indicates how lavishly supplied the temple was. The 5,400 total probably includes smaller items not individually specified in the inventory.

Temple worship restored (chapter 3). Jeshua (or Joshua) the high priest and Zerubbabel the civil leader take charge of things (verse 2).

Zerubbabel was the grandson of Judah's last king Jehoiachin and thus a legitimate national ruler.

The altar was rebuilt and sacrifices resumed before work began on the temple building itself. With great courage they got on with the work despite their fear of hostile peoples around them (verse 3).

The feast of tabernacles or booths (verse 4) is a harvest festival, at which the Jews also remember the tents they slept in on their journey through the wilderness after the exodus. Once again, we have an implied parallel between the exodus and the return from exile.

The start of the rebuilding was an occasion for great rejoicing, with a suitable psalm of celebration (verses 10–11). But old people who remembered the glory of Solomon's temple could only weep with sadness at the comparative poverty of the building now begun (verse 12).

Although this event is dated by Ezra immediately after the return from Babylon, we know from Haggai 1:1 that the temple remained in ruins in 520. It was not completed until 516. We can only presume that the opposition to the rebuilding described in Ezra 4, coupled with lack of resolve on the part of the people, led to the work being abandoned after the early enthusiasm.

What message is there for us in this account? Four points are worth reflecting on. First, 3:3 suggests that it is more important to worship as God requires than to lie low out of fear of enemies or cynics. Christians who are used to worshipping behind closed doors and stained glass windows may need to seek ways of making their worship more public, more visible to the world.

Secondly, the mention of names, no doubt based on careful records, is intriguing (3:9). All kinds of people, otherwise totally unknown, played their part in rebuilding the temple. Whether or not our name appears in the history books, each of us has a vital contribution to make to the work of God.

Thirdly, the people praised God more in anticipation of the future than in thanks for work completed (verses 10–11). Praise is itself an expression of trust in God's care and provision for the future.

Fourthly, there is something very moving about the mingling of tears and shouts of joy in verses 12–13. There are occasions in our experience when older people look to the past with longing, while the young look forward in hope. Rather than the one silencing the other, they should be allowed to mingle together. Both perspectives have value. They need each other.

Man of prayer, man of integrity

Nehemiah the Jew was cupbearer to the Persian king Artaxerxes I at his palace in Susa. His job was to taste the king's wine to make sure it wasn't poisoned. If they had had life insurance companies in those days his occupation would have attracted a 'high risk' premium.

He was concerned for the sad state of Jerusalem, defenceless against its enemies because its walls were still broken down. It was now 445BC, over seventy years after the first Jews returned from exile. So in Nehemiah 1 we find him praying that God will give him an opportunity to make his concern known to the king.

Read Nehemiah 2

Nehemiah waited four months for his chance. It came unexpectedly, when he momentarily dropped his official smile to reveal the distress beneath. The king noticed. Nehemiah was afraid because such a failure to be cheerful in the king's presence might be punished by dismissal, or worse (verses 1–2).

He told the king his concern (verse 3). He was not so tactless as to name the city or point out that Artaxerxes himself had stopped a previous attempt to rebuild the walls of Jerusalem (see Ezra 4:7–23)! Instead he appealed to an interest of many people in the ancient world, especially kings—the preservation of ancestral tombs. Nehemiah was a shrewd man who knew how to relate his concern for God's purpose to the interests and concerns of people.

When the king asked the question (verse 4) he gulped. He couldn't retreat now! So he offered a silent, split-second prayer and then asked for everything he wanted (verse 5). That prayer is not the prayer of last resort which people pray when they have tried everything else without success. It is the natural reaching out to God from a man whose life is bathed in prayer. Many prayers of Nehemiah are mentioned throughout his book. And if we wonder how it was that he could retain such devotion to the faith of his people and to the city of God amidst the opulent distractions of an Eastern court, the basic answer must be that he was a man of prayer.

Implicitly Nehemiah was asking to be made governor of Judah. Without such a position he would not have the authority to achieve what he hoped for. But he got permission and resources and an armed escort for his thousand-mile journey (verses 6–9). Nehemiah saw the providential hand of God in the king's generous arrangements for him (verse 8).

Not everyone was pleased at Nehemiah's arrival in Jerusalem. Sanballat was governor of the neighbouring province of Samaria. Tobiah probably had a similar position in Ammon, east of the Jordan (verse 10). They had prospered from the weakness of Judah and saw Nehemiah's appearance as a threat to their power. Geshem (who makes up a threesome in verse 19) controlled a huge area to the south occupied by Arabian tribes.

Verses 11–16 describe Nehemiah's secretive night survey of the city walls. No one yet knew that his plans include building fortifications to replace those recently destroyed by Artaxerxes himself! Reading this careful first-hand report, we can imagine the moon shining on the honey-coloured Jerusalem limestone, and Nehemiah and his aides picking their way carefully through piles of rubble.

Careful assessment led to decisive action. Appealing not to military or political motives but to the people's religious honour, he urged rebuilding of the walls (verse 17). Like many a church notice board and dowdy building, the state of the city reflected badly on the value they attached to their faith. And he encouraged them by showing how events were conspiring to show that God's moment had arrived (verse 18). The response was immediate and wholehearted.

When the seriousness of his intentions became clear, the opposition got sinister. To imply revolt or treason was a calculated way to unnerve the most determined of men (verse 19). But Nehemiah quietly assured his enemies that God would prosper the work and they had no business interfering with the Jews' right to their holy city (verse 20).

Nehemiah is a rewarding character to study. As a believer, he is a man of prayer (verse 4). He is a man of integrity who wins the confidence of a pagan king (verses 6, 8). He is sensitive to the influence of God on his life—the opposite of a self-made man (verses 8, 12, 18, 20).

As a leader, he puts concern for God's work above personal safety (verses 3–4). He knows how to relate to secular powers (verses 3, 5–9). He assesses situations carefully and forms a clear judgment (verses 11–17). He inspires people to action (verse 18). He is not thrown off course by opposition but trusts in the protection of God (verse 20).

Persistent opposition

Nehemiah's success in building the walls only intensified the opposition. We see in this chapter that the opposition comes in three forms.

First, the attempt is made to divert Nehemiah from his work and possibly to kill him. The plain of Ono is neutral territory twenty miles north-west of Jerusalem. Nehemiah suspects a plot to lure him away from Jerusalem and perhaps to do away with him permanently. Were his suspicions unfounded? Were Sanballat and his friends just wanting to normalize relations, to avoid the possibility that a higher authority would punish them all for provoking international instability? Possibly. But their obstinate persistence (verse 4) doesn't sound like the mark of constructive statesmen.

There is splendid irony in Nehemiah's reply (verse 3). He can't stop the job he is doing—which is precisely what they are hoping to achieve. His persistent refusal to be distracted is another mark of the man's greatness. He is clear about the task in hand, knows the importance of seeing it through, and won't let anything come in the way.

There is a disciplined stickability here which is in short supply among today's believers. In an age of instant coffee, instant soup, instant everything, people find it hard to stay with a task until it is finished. Distractions abound. Enthusiasm fails. But 'all God's things are grown things. He is never in the ready-made business' (Samuel Chadwick). To be in tune with God we need the perseverance which allows the growth to happen and refuses to be distracted when the outcome is delayed.

The second attack seeks to destroy Nehemiah by rumour (verses 5–7). Sanballat sends a letter reporting a rumour that Nehemiah's wall-building is part of a grand scheme to rebel against his Persian overlords and declare himself king. The letter is unsealed so that the rumour will spread. Modern tactics of leaked letters and personal attacks have added little to the art of political innuendo!

Rumours are hard to silence. Many a reputation is ruined by rumour which later turns out to be false. But by then it is too late. The damage has been done. This is why the Book of Proverbs and the New Testament letters take such a strong line on the evil of malicious gossip (Proverbs 4:24; 6:12–14; Romans 1:29–30; Galatians 5:15; Ephesians 4:29).

Nehemiah simply ridicules the lie and asserts his own integrity (verse 8). Who would you trust? If you were buying a second-hand car would you go to Sanballat or Nehemiah? Nehemiah understands his opponents' motives. His response is to pray for divine strength (verse 9).

The third attack on Nehemiah attempts to discredit him by making him break the Law of God (verse 9–10). The opponents hire a Jewish prophet (or so Nehemiah believes) who is more interested in money than truth. Claiming that there is a plot to kill Nehemiah, the prophet urges him to take refuge in the temple building—which was forbidden to a layman.

Nehemiah is wise to the deception (verses 11–13). He knows that God acts consistently. So a prophet who tells someone to break God's Law can't be a genuine spokesman of God.

As he writes his memoirs he prays that God will 'remember' all those who cause him trouble (verse 14). God who knows our hearts and motives can be relied on to deal justly and mercifully with all people. When we are attacked, abused and criticized by others the best thing we can do, after we have examined our own hearts, is to entrust them to God's merciful judgment and then get on with our job.

So the walls were completed (verse 15). Having lain in ruins for 150 years they were rebuilt (though with a smaller circumference) in fifty-two days. Such was the galvanizing effect of Nehemiah's leadership.

Now Jerusalem could lift up its head again. By the good hand of God its reputation among surrounding nations was restored (verse 15–16). But the opposition remained active (verses 17–19) and continuing vigilance was needed (7:1–3). There is some dispute as to precisely what is meant by verse 3, but clearly Nehemiah's intention was to ensure that no enemy made a surprise attack at a time when the city was not fully defended.

To think about

Am I under attack from people who misunderstand me or are deliberately trying to undermine my position? Or do I know someone in this position? If so, what can be learnt from Nehemiah's experience?

Am I too ready to criticize others? Do I need to put right a particular wrong I have done in this respect?

Reluctant prophet

The book of Jonah tells the story of an eighth-century prophet (mentioned in 2 Kings 14:25), a contemporary of Amos. We do not know whether it was written shortly after the events described or much later.

Many scholars think it was written after the exile to counter the protective nationalistic attitudes which stemmed from Ezra and Nehemiah's concern to preserve Israel's racial identity. On this view, the book is a story with a message, which uses a prophet of former times as its hero. To listen to its message is more important than to argue about whether the 'fish' was a whale and whether a man could survive three days inside one. As we read we shall see the writer using humour and irony to convey a challenging message.

Read Jonah 1 and 2

'Go and preach' (1:1–3). Jonah was a prophet. So it comes as no surprise to find God instructing him to proclaim destruction to the wicked city of Nineveh. This city summed up everything that opposed Yahweh and his people. As the capital of the feared Assyrians, the mere mention of it would send shudders down any Israelite spine.

Faced with this great commission, Jonah ran. Instead of going north-east to Nineveh he hurried south-west to Joppa (near Tel Aviv), paid his money and hopped on a ship to Spain. His intention was 'to flee from the Lord', but he was to find this more difficult than he imagined.

Man overboard! (1:4–16). When the storm arose the sailors prayed. They followed the sensible action of throwing out cargo to lighten the ship. They were pagans who did not know Israel's God, yet they did what was right. Jonah meanwhile was neither praying nor acting, but sleeping. It was not the sleep of simple trust in a heavenly Father but the sleep that wants to avoid all responsibility. It takes a pagan captain to urge an Israelite to pray (1:6).

When the drawing of lots identified Jonah as the apparent cause of the storm, his answer to the sailors' questions was thoroughly orthodox (1:9). 'I am a worshipper of Yahweh'. He didn't mouth the other half of the sentence: 'But I don't obey his instructions'.

But the sailors had gathered this by now (1:10). When Jonah told them to throw him overboard they did their best to avoid that by rowing for the shore. They were decent people, these pagans. They didn't fit the Israelite stereotype of how pagans behave.

But they went further than that. Though they threw Jonah overboard because no other option was left, they worshipped Yahweh ('the Lord', 1:14, 16)! So a reluctant prophet of Israel who couldn't stomach preaching to the pagans of Nineveh finished up in the sea and unknowingly converted a crew of pagan sailors! Isn't it just like God to arrange something like that?

Already the story is playing havoc with the expectations of the Jews who first heard it. To them, the people of Nineveh and the ship's crew (probably Phoenicians) are pagans. They know what kind of behaviour to expect from such people. Yet here are sailors doing their best to save the life of Jonah who put their lives in danger. To the Jews, Jonah is a prophet, so he can be relied on to be obedient to God. They can identify with him as the hero of the story. They know what should happen when a prophet encounters pagans and Israel ventures into the outside world. Their assumptions are turned upside down. And ours?

A prayer from inside a fish (1:17—2:10). But Jonah wasn't finished, because God hadn't finished with him. He 'provided' (REB 'ordained') a great fish to swallow him and keep him safe. That word 'provided' indicates God's control of Jonah's experience. We shall meet it again in chapter 4.

Inside the fish Jonah did what he hadn't done on land or in the ship. He prayed. Some people have to be *very* desperate before they will pray!

The prayer (2:2–9) is a psalm of thanksgiving, quite similar to Psalm 30. Jonah's position was still precarious, but he could thank God for saving him from drowning. Notice how the man who 'went down' to Joppa (1:3), then 'went below deck' (1:5) now speaks of 'sinking down' to the very depths (2:7). In each case the Hebrew word is the same, suggesting that his flight from God was a progressive descent, to the very brink of death.

But there is now an upward movement (2:6, 7). God can reverse every descent into disobedience or despair. This psalm is a word to readers of the story who are 'going under', whether through their own fault (like Jonah) or for reasons they cannot help.

157

Angry prophet

We left Jonah in prayer, promising to offer a sacrifice of thanksgiving (2:9). He had reached the same point as the sailors in 1:16. But for an Israelite, sacrifice can be offered only at the Jerusalem temple. Jonah was promising to go back there, but he wasn't promising to go as far as Nineveh.

The repentant city (chapter 3). Jonah got a second chance. Same command, different response (3:1–3; contrast 1:1–3). When he brought his message of judgment to this huge, evil city they abandoned their wickedness. The king spoke for all, urging genuine repentance in the hope that God would come in mercy rather than judgment (3:7–9). Even the cattle were organized for fasting, to make clear how seriously the people took the prophet's warnings!

And God relented (3:10). The God of the Bible is not unchangeable, unmoved by human response. His warnings of disaster are not inflexible predictions of unbending fate. Their very purpose is to warn people of the consequences of their actions *so that* they may change their ways and by God's mercy find a different future (see Jeremiah 18, passage 44). And that was Jonah's problem.

Angry with God's mercy (chapter 4). We now see more clearly why Jonah ran away from his commission in the first place. It comes out in his peculiar prayer (4:2–3).

The prayer begins and ends in the 'proper' way for a prayer: 'O Lord... Now, O Lord...'. Jonah is being correct with his religious language. But in between is a passionate outburst against the very character of God as declared in Israel's creeds: 'I ran away from preaching to Nineveh because I knew you would forgive them if they repented. That's the kind of God you are. I couldn't stand that. Being gracious and compassionate is all very well, but you've gone beyond the limits by acting like this to these degenerate pagans. So please leave me alone to die.'

Before we dismiss Jonah as narrow-minded, we should sympathize with his dilemma. The first readers of the book would certainly have sympathized with him. They had no soft spot for the Assyrians. To send Jonah to Nineveh is like asking a Jew who has lost a mother or a brother in the Holocaust to offer God's forgiveness to a Nazi. It is risky, painful. Human nature recoils against it.

God asked a question: 'Do you think anger is the right reaction, Jonah?' (4:4). Jonah's reply was to walk out. He made himself a shelter and sat down waiting to see what would happen (4:5). Was he still hoping that disaster would strike after all?

In the rest of the story God 'provided' (REB 'ordained') three things to make his point to Jonah (4:6, 7, 8; see also 1:17). His emotions fluctuated wildly—joy at the shade offered by the plant, fury when the plant was killed, exposing him to the hot sun and scorching wind.

Now he was cornered. 'You are sorry about the plant,' said God, 'though it lasted only a moment. How much more should I be sorry for all the people of Nineveh, who are like children without a parent to guide them?' (verses 10–11). The writer wants us to see that this is God's answer to Jonah's outburst in 4:2–3. In Hebrew, Jonah's prayer to God and God's message to Jonah balance each other exactly, each taking up thirty-nine words.

Nineveh, God and Jonah—these are the actors in the story. Nineveh is the pagan world, feared for its hostility to God's people. God is 'gracious and compassionate, slow to anger and abounding in love'. He will not be boxed in by human assumptions about the limits of his mercy. Jonah is the believer, whose belief-system is blown open by God's surprising grace.

The minister was explaining to his congregation what changes would be necessary in order to cater for more worshippers. 'But we don't want to grow, do we?' interrupted someone. 'We're fine as we are.'

'We must cut back this year on what we give to support Christian mission overseas. The refurbishing of our church will take all our spare cash.'

'Turkey is a great place for a holiday. Oh, I'd no idea how tough it is being a Christian there.'

In these and a thousand other ways the spirit of Jonah stalks the church today.

The writer doesn't tell us how Jonah replied to God's question, 'Shouldn't I be sorry for Nineveh?' He wants to leave it as a question for his readers. Jonah is not only the prophet, he is also Israel. He is the Church of Christ. He is me?

76

Faithfulness under pressure

Daniel was one of the first group of Jews taken away to Babylon by Nebuchadnezzar in 605BC. Chapters 1–6 of his book record stories of Jewish faithfulness in a hostile world. Chapters 7–12 are detailed visions of the future.

The whole book is presented in a way which would have been particularly helpful in the mid-second century BC, when Jews were fighting for the survival of their faith against the brutal oppression of the Syrian ruler Antiochus Epiphanes. This was the time of Judas Maccabaeus and the Maccabaean Revolt (167BC). It is likely, therefore, that the book was written to encourage persecuted Jews in the second century BC. It does so by retelling old stories of Jews under pressure during the exile in Babylon.

Read Daniel 3

The statue (verses 1–12). The story doesn't make clear whether it was a statue of the king himself or—more likely—of a Babylonian god. As is the way with totalitarian governments, the dedication ceremony became a test of loyalty to the régime (verses 4–7). With mocking detail (repeated in verses 5, 7, 10, 15), the writer describes how all the officials present were to bow down to the statue when they heard the band strike up.

Shadrach, Meshach and Abednego were friends of Daniel who, like him, had been given responsible positions by Nebuchadnezzar (1:7; 2:49). Their refusal to comply with the decree is viewed as disloyalty to the king and an insult to his god (verse 12). For the three men there was a higher loyalty to a different God.

The issue was idolatry. The three men were utterly faithful to the first two commandments of Exodus 20—loyalty to the one God and refusal to worship any man-made image. Idolatry means giving one's energy and devotion, 'selling one's soul', to a part of God's creation rather than to God himself.

In the modern world there are a thousand idolatries. In some places still the state claims a power over people's lives which belongs to God alone. But elsewhere people surrender willingly to idols of money, success and peace at any price. Even job security or 'a stable future for my family', which are proper goals in themselves, can become for some people obsessions which cloud their moral judgment and their openness to God's guidance for their lives.

This story challenges us to reflect: am I a genuine and wholehearted servant of God, even when the pressures are hard against me?

The fiery furnace (verses 13–30). The centre of the story is in verses 15–18. In his question (verse 15) the king imagines himself to be greater than any god—and therein lie the seeds of his own destruction.

The three men's reply shows their confidence that God's power can overrule the king's power. Then comes the revealing part. 'Even if our God doesn't deliver us from the furnace, we want you to know, Nebuchadnezzar, we're going to remain faithful to God anyway.' They will obey God not because they have any guarantee of deliverance but simply *because it is right to obey him*.

There is serious reckoning here with the demands of discipleship in a hostile environment. It reminds us of the obedience of Peter who told the high priest, 'We must obey God rather than men' (Acts 5:29), and of Jesus before Pilate (Luke 23:1–25). What price discipleship when there is no miraculous deliverance, as in the case of Christian martyrs and Jews in the Nazi concentration camps?

For genuine disciples the big question is, 'What does the Lord require of me?', rather than, 'What do I get out of it?' Having glimpsed the greatness and the love of God they will respond to his demand and trust the consequences to him.

The mysterious fourth man in the furnace (verse 25) is called an angel of God by Nebuchadnezzar (verse 28). He is a God-given presence with the men in their ordeal. God is present with his people in their deepest need.

The story illustrates the truth of words spoken to the Babylonian exiles in Isaiah 43:2–3: 'When you walk through the fire, you will not be burned; the flames will not set you ablaze. For I am the Lord, your God, the Holy One of Israel, your Saviour.'

A minor figure of the Reformation in England in the sixteenth century was Thomas Bilney, who was burnt at the stake for his Protestant faith. In his Bible, which survives in the library of Corpus Christi College, Cambridge, those words from Isaiah are heavily marked in ink. For him there was no miraculous rescue from the flames. But there was the faith, fed by the promise of Scripture, that in this ultimate test God would not abandon him.

77

Four beasts and 'one like a son of man'

The visions of Daniel 7–12 have been a happy hunting-ground for people looking for precise predictions of events within their own lifetimes. Such interpreters see a sequence of events in Daniel, identify these events with moments or periods in human history, declare that the last such event mentioned by Daniel has just happened or is just about to happen, and thus predict confidently when human history will be brought to its end.

But probably the writer's intention is pastoral rather than simply predictive. His main purpose is not to give a detailed catalogue of future events, but to assure persecuted Jews that God hasn't lost control of human affairs and to strengthen their faith in his final victory.

Read Daniel 7

Four beasts (verses 1–8). We are familiar enough with animals standing for nations or their sports teams (the British Lion, the American Eagle, the South African Springbok). In Daniel's dream, four beasts stand for powerful nations engaged one after another in conflict with the Jews. (Verses 17–25 show that the beasts represent specific nations, though without naming the nations concerned.)

There is some disagreement about which nation each of these beasts represents, but comparison with a further vision in chapter 8 suggests that the lion is Babylon, the bear is Media, the leopard is Persia, and the frighteningly powerful beast is the Greek empire set up by Alexander the Great.

The ten horns of this fourth beast (verse 7) express its all-pervasive power. The 'little horn' (verse 8) is Antiochus Epiphanes, who in Daniel's dream is the ultimate expression of the tyrannizing power of the Greek empire. When Alexander died in 323BC his huge empire was divided between four of his generals. Antiochus, ruling from Syria, was descended from one of these generals. Towards the middle of the second century BC he certainly 'spoke boastfully', by his arrogant introduction of pagan worship and suppression of Jewish religious practice.

In a sense, it doesn't matter whether we have got the significance of each of these beasts exactly right. There are times throughout history when evil régimes oppress the people of God and seek to replace godly living with demonic abuse of power. But all such régimes in due course meet with divine judgment.

The Ancient of Days (verses 9–12). There follows a picture of God in a divine court-room. The books recording human deeds are opened, and the final beast is brought to judgment.

The idea that all human deeds are recorded so that one day precise judgments may be made on every person is a powerful and frightening symbol. Its purpose here is not to intimidate sensitive people with the thought that God keeps a score of all their little failures, but to assure the persecuted that their oppressors will not escape his judgment. Those who defy God and abuse other human beings do not get away with it for ever.

'One like a son of man' (verses 13–14). This peculiar phrase, translated literally in NIV, means 'one like a human being' (REB). Daniel sees a human-like being who approaches God and receives authority and a kingdom that will never be destroyed. But is he human? Or is he perhaps an angel? And what does the vision mean?

The dream interpreted (verses 15–28). The 'little horn' (Antiochus) persecutes 'the saints' (NIV; REB has 'the holy ones') until God passes judgment in favour of the saints and grants them 'the kingdom' (verses 21–22; compare verses 26–27). In the context of the Jewish experience of oppressive empires, 'the saints' must mean God's faithful people who experience the pains of persecution. Since both the 'one like a son of man' in verses 14 and 'the saints' in verse 22 receive from God 'the kingdom', it seems that the one must be a symbol or representative of the other. The 'man-like figure' symbolizes or stands for the suffering saints of God.

And this whole passage is designed to assure them that God has set a limit on the ravages of their oppressor. Antiochus—*or any other tyrant*—may oppress the saints and defy God's shaping of history ('change the set times', verse 25 NIV), but he has them at his mercy only for a limited period ('a time, times and half a time').

We can see the point of this message to its original readers. But in the Gospels another dimension is added because there Jesus calls himself 'the son of man'. He sees in Daniel's description of how suffering leads to glory and to an everlasting kingdom a pattern for his own ministry. He is 'that son of man' who suffers at the hands of his enemies in order to receive a kingdom which he will open up to the world. To that story we now turn.

163

5

GOOD NEWS

The first Christians were Jews for whom the Hebrew Scriptures—available to them also in a Greek translation—were the word of God. But gradually they found the need to produce their own documents. First there were letters such as those of Paul, written to guide the young churches when he could not be present with them. Later came Gospels, telling the story of Jesus' life, death and resurrection. Eventually, after these documents had long proved their value in the Church's life and mission, they were collected as the New Testament which we know today.

Although they are among the latest of the New Testament documents (written probably between AD60 and 90), the four Gospels contain in written form stories about Jesus and accounts of his teaching which had been used in preaching and worship from the very beginning.

Although they tell the life of Jesus, they are not biographies in the modern sense. They report very little about Jesus' birth and upbringing. They don't tell us what he looked like. They record little of his inner feelings. They tell the story not simply to satisfy curiosity but to proclaim the significance of Jesus for their readers. So when we read a Gospel we are meant to ask not only, 'What is this passage reporting about what happened?', but also, 'What does it mean for me and for other people today?'

The four Gospels, and especially the first three, have much in common. They often tell the same incident in very similar ways. But each has a distinct 'slant' on the significance of Jesus, like portrait painters observing him from different angles.

Luke, whose Gospel we shall look at, is unique in that he adds a second volume telling the story of the Church after Jesus' resurrection (the Acts of the Apostles). As we shall see, he wants to show how the Church of Jesus continues the mission of Jesus, and how the Holy Spirit who empowered Jesus empowers the Church today.

78

New beginning

Empires came and went. After the Babylonians came the Persians, then the Greeks. Then a few decades of Jewish independence after the success of the Maccabean revolt. But from 63BC Palestine was under the control of a new power—Rome.

Through constant political change and uncertainty, there were Jews who continued to cherish the hope of God's deliverance. The first two chapters of Luke's Gospel introduce us to such people— Zechariah and Elizabeth, parents of John the Baptist, and Simeon and the old prophetess Anna who rejoice at the birth of Jesus. And a teenage girl called Mary.

Read Luke 1:26–38

God sends a messenger to announce that his time has come at last. An ordinary girl in an unremarkable village called Nazareth is the one chosen to bear the coming Saviour. Like Moses and Jeremiah and many of God's servants before and after her, her reaction is, 'Why me?' (verse 29). Like them, she is reassured with a promise that God has chosen her as a vessel of his love for humanity (verses 30–33). She is to have a baby whose special role is described in verses 31–33.

He is to be called Jesus. That is the Greek form of the Hebrew Joshua, meaning 'The Lord saves'. His role will be to bring deliverance, freedom, new life.

He is to be the Son of God. Only as the story of Jesus unfolds shall we see how special is the relation of this baby to the Creator of the universe. But he is announced from the beginning as 'Son of the Most High'.

He fulfils the promises to David. As a descendant of David, he is qualified to be the deliverer, the Messiah promised in 2 Samuel 7 (passage 26). God is now doing a new thing, and its impact will last for ever.

The girl who asked 'Why?' now—not surprisingly!—asks 'How?' (verse 34). The answer announces the virginal conception, or virgin birth, of Jesus. Many are sceptical about this part of the story, because the New Testament only mentions it explicitly here and in Matthew 1, or because they find the whole idea of miracles difficult. Or they have heard it suggested that the story was invented in order to demonstrate in the Greek world—where myths of divine–human intercourse were common—that Jesus really was divine.

It is certainly not an easy story to come to terms with. But no one has come up with a satisfactory explanation of how or why it should have been invented. It is, for example, totally unlike those Greek myths. For there is no suggestion here of a mating between Mary and the Holy Spirit, but a much more mysterious 'overshadowing' of the Spirit. And the story must have been first told not in the Greek world but in Palestine, since Luke shares it not with those New Testament documents addressed to the Greek world (Paul's letters) but with Matthew's Gospel, which is more concerned with Jewish ideas.

The virgin birth marks a new beginning in God's plan. Just as the Holy Spirit was active in the original creation (Genesis 1:2), so now he brings about the new creation. Jesus is blessed with special powers not because of his own human merits but because a generous God is entering into human experience in a new creative act. The salvation of the world depends not on human achievement but on God's action.

Mary's reaction was one of humble acceptance of God's plan and God's way (verse 38). She was, in a sense, the first of countless millions to say 'yes' to Jesus.

79
The birth of Jesus

Luke 2:1–10

In his familiar story of the birth, Luke emphasizes three things about Jesus.

First, in verses 1–3 he sets the birth of Jesus in the context of world history. His story is set on a public stage, a story which concerns the world.

Augustus ruled as Roman emperor from 31BC to AD14. He controlled all the countries around the Mediterranean as well as Switzerland, Germany and much of central Europe. Some of his subjects called him 'saviour' because he had brought peace and stability after a period of civil wars. But Luke is announcing a different kind of ruler, a different kind of Saviour. The subject of his story will affect millions of people who have never heard of the all-conquering Augustus.

There is a problem about the date of the census. We know from the Jewish historian Josephus that Quirinius conducted a census (for taxation purposes) while governor of Syria in AD6–7. But there is no other evidence that Quirinius was governor, or that a census was taken, in the period around Jesus' birth. But Luke may have had access to reliable information which has simply not come down to us in other sources.

The year of Jesus' birth causes confusion too. We know from Luke 1:5 and Matthew 2:1–19 that Jesus was born before Herod the Great died. But we know from ancient historians that Herod died in 4BC. So Jesus must have been born about 5BC. In the sixth century AD a monk named Denys the Little began the practice of dating events from the year of Jesus' birth, which he named AD1. But we now know that he was a few years out in his calculations!

Secondly, verses 4–7 report the actual birth of Jesus. The census caused Joseph to return with Mary to Bethlehem, his family home. So, thanks to the decree of a pagan emperor, Jesus was born in the town of his ancestor King David.

This underlines his role as the *Messiah* (Greek *Christos*, Christ, meaning 'the anointed one'). Many Jews expected a ruler descended from David to deliver them from their enemies and bring in 'the kingdom of God'. As we shall see, Jesus did bring the kingdom of God, but not quite in the sense that many of the Jews hoped for.

The location of Jesus' birth has been assumed, because of the manger, to be a stable—perhaps a cave used to shelter animals at night. But Luke probably means that he was born in the main room of a house, 'because there was no room for them in the guest-room'. An ordinary village house would have one living-room, with an area at one end where the family goat and donkey and a few chickens would rest at night. Some would also have a guest-room above (an 'upper room'). We can imagine that Joseph and Mary would naturally go to relatives in Bethlehem. But the guest-room was already allocated to other relatives there for the census.

Thirdly, in verses 8–20, Jesus' birth is announced to the world. The receivers of the announcement are not national and religious leaders, but shepherds. Why shepherds? Just because they are ordinary people. The good news of Jesus comes first to people who have no religious qualifications, but are open to being surprised by God.

But why should the birth of Jesus be 'good news of great joy for all the people' (verse 10)? Every birth brings joy. This birth is special because of who Jesus is and what he will do. He is a *Saviour*—he is to set people free. He is the *Messiah*, on whom the hopes of Israel rest. He is *the Lord*—the Old Testament name of God. Jesus' relationship to God is here left undefined, but Luke is giving a signpost to where his story will lead. This small bundle of human flesh will carry humanity back to God.

His birth is a cause for praise to God and a source of peace for humanity (verse 14). Augustus had brought peace, and it was worth having. But his peace remained a transient thing which did not touch people's deepest needs. 'Peace' in its biblical sense means health and harmony at every level of human experience—peace within myself, peace with my neighbour, peace healing divisions in society, peace restoring friendship between humanity and God. Peace at all those levels was to be the concern of Jesus.

And who would experience this peace? 'People on whom his favour rests.' Again the message is about the grace of God, God showering his generosity on undeserving people. This is good news for shepherds, and for us all.

80
John the baptizer

Luke 3:1–23

The story moves on about thirty years. The date implied by Luke's careful listing of rulers (verses 1–2) is about AD28.

The significance of John the Baptist is expressed in four ways.

First, he prepared the way for the Messiah by arousing repentance and expectation in the people (verses 2–9). The word of God came to him as to prophets of the Old Testament (verse 2). Baptizing and preaching in the Judean wilderness, John was fulfilling the prophecy of Isaiah 40:3–5. He was straightening the road for the Messiah's arrival (verses 4–6).

John's approach was not taken from manuals about 'how to win friends and influence people'. Everything about him was disturbing.

When Gentiles converted to Judaism they expressed their conversion in baptism—immersing themselves in water. By challenging Jews to be baptized John was saying that they too needed to be converted! Only by a radical change of life, symbolized in baptism, could they hope to escape from God's judgment (verse 3). Those who seek baptism merely as an admission ticket or a safety precaution get no comfort from him (verses 7–9).

Secondly, John's preaching showed what repentance involves (verses 10–14). To 'repent' means not just to feel sorry but to change one's life. To 'love your neighbour' is practical and costly. All but the most basic possessions are surplus to requirements: someone else's need is greater (verse 11). Tax-collectors, well known for taking more money than was required, must deal honestly (verses 12–13).

Jewish soldiers, who acted as policemen and guards, must not use their power to extort money by intimidation (verse 14). 'Be content with your wages' is a specific word to them: it is not a message for employees in other places at other times whose wages are unjustly low.

But the key demands in this passage—costly love for the neighbour, honesty and integrity at work—are a message for all time. John's examples of what true repentance involves cut people to the heart. And he paid the price for his fearless exposing of evil (verses 19–20).

Thirdly, John witnessed to the nature of the Messiah's mission (verses 15–16). Having raising people's expectation, he diverted it from himself to Jesus. Taking off a man's sandals was a slave's job. 'I'm not even good enough to do that for him,' said John. 'You've seen me immerse people with water. The day will come when he will immerse people in the Holy Spirit and the fire of purifying judgment.' The fulfilment of this prophecy lay beyond Jesus' earthly ministry, in the event of Pentecost (passage 98).

In another way this passage points to the character of Jesus' mission. Verse 6 says that 'all mankind shall see God's salvation'. The deliverance which the Messiah will bring goes far beyond the Jewish people. This is a theme which Luke's story will constantly emphasize.

Fourthly, John's baptism of Jesus marked the beginning of his ministry (verses 21–23). These verses backtrack to the period before John's imprisonment. By being baptized Jesus identified with the people he came to rescue. He received assurance from God about who he was and what he was called to do.

169

The words of the voice from heaven are important echoes of Old Testament Scripture. 'My Son' (Psalm 2:7) identifies Jesus as the Messiah. That is what 'son of God' would have meant to a Jew of his time. But the phrase 'whom I love' or 'beloved' suggests a more personal intimacy between Jesus and God. 'With you I am well pleased', or 'In you I delight' alludes to Isaiah 42:1, one of the passages in Isaiah about the suffering servant (see passage 67). Jesus is God's unique Son who fulfils his mission by living in total obedience to the Father's will.

At his baptism Jesus was empowered for this demanding ministry. Why the Holy Spirit came upon him 'like a dove' has been the subject of much fruitless speculation. 'In bodily form' is Luke's way of stressing the reality of the Spirit's presence to Jesus.

It was as Jesus was praying that the Spirit came to him. Luke delights in drawing attention to the fact Jesus was a person who prayed. In response to prayer the Spirit came to empower him for God's service. And not only to Jesus, but to all God's people, the Spirit is given when we pray. 'If you, bad as you are, know how to give good things to your children, how much more will the heavenly Father give the Holy Spirit to those who ask him!' (Luke 11:13).

To think about

John the Baptist came to clear the way for Jesus. How may I, by my lifestyle and my words, clear the way for others to find him?

81

The testing of God's Son
Luke 4:1–13

After the divine reassurance of the voice from heaven at his baptism, Jesus now faced the testing of his call. It is not reported whether Jesus sensed the devil's presence as though he were standing beside him, or in the form of an 'inner voice'. Did he actually, or in his imagination, go to the temple in Jerusalem?

Whatever the answer to those questions, Jesus was aware of an intense challenge to his obedience as Son of God. The forces of evil were trying to drag him off course even before he had begun. But he was not simply abandoned to the power of evil. He was 'led by the

Spirit' during his testing (verse 1). He was in a battle, but faced it with divine resources.

The question confronting Jesus was, 'What does it mean to live as the obedient Son of God?'

The testing is in three stages. At each stage Jesus responds to the devil's challenge by quoting from the Book of Deuteronomy. A comparison is being made between his experience and the wilderness experience of the Israelites travelling to the Promised Land. Whereas they failed when their obedience to God was tested, he will be true to his calling—even though there may be no certain proof that he is doing the right thing.

Verses 3–4. The devil suggests that Jesus can relieve his hunger by a miracle. The attraction of listening to this seductive voice was that at a stroke he would make life easy for himself and reassure himself that he had God's power at his immediate command. But to do so would be to place his own comfort before his commitment to live by God's word.

Verses 5–8. Playing on a suspicion which grips all of us some of the time, the devil claims that the whole world is in his hands. Jesus is tempted to imagine that he can win the world, not by obedience to his Father, but by compromise with another master, another strategy. 'The end justifies the means' is always the devil's tactic. But Jesus refuses to compromise his loyalty to God's will.

Verses 9–12. 'Why not jump off the top of the temple in the ultimate hang-gliding stunt? Doesn't Scripture promise that the angels will be there to catch you?' The idea is attractive to Jesus. It will remove once and for all any lingering doubts about his relationship to God. But no—God is not to be played with like that. God's Son must live by trust which demands no proof.

It is hard sometimes to see the difference between 'the prayer of faith', which asks boldly for God to act decisively in a crisis, and 'putting God to the test', which is essentially an attitude of mistrust. But the difference is that the devil here is proposing an artificially created crisis just to prove a point. He is not advocating trust in God in an emergency which results from obedient service.

Verse 13. Here it is clear that temptation was Jesus' constant companion, not just a once-for-all experience at the beginning of his ministry.

The story helps us to see that, though God doesn't lead us into sin, he does allow our faith to be tested ('He was led by the Spirit', verse 1). Without testing our faith doesn't grow. A football team which plays no matches keeps an unbeaten record, but it doesn't improve its football. The challenge to faith is a normal part of our experience, and the power of God's Spirit is given to help us in the battle.

And we can learn from Jesus' use of the Bible in facing temptation. He knew the Bible well enough to find guidance in it for his obedience to God. He had thought about it carefully enough not to be misled by a quotation out of context. One of the things we are doing in working through this book together is storing away insights which are shaping our attitudes and actions. We are glimpsing the mind of God on a whole range of vital issues.

Many people go through periods when their faith is under strain and they long for God's reassurance. 'Wilderness experiences', we sometimes call them. I once stood gazing at the Judean wilderness in the area where Jesus was tested. A young Jewish boy came alongside me and said, 'It's beautiful, isn't it?' I had never thought of the wilderness as beautiful before. For it is a barren place, where we are without all the 'props' which normally hold our lives together. But his exclamation helped me to see that the wilderness can be a place where God comes close to us in a new way and leads us deeper into loving obedience to him as our Father.

8 2

Drama in Nazareth
Luke 4:14–30

Strengthened by testing ('in the power of the Spirit', verse 14), Jesus began in Galilee his public ministry of teaching. In his home town of Nazareth there occurred one of the most dramatic incidents in the New Testament.

Jesus is invited to read from the Scriptures at the synagogue service. He reads from Isaiah 61—a passage which speaks of how God would bring new hope to his people. Then he makes the startling announcement: 'Today this scripture is fulfilled in your hearing' (verse 21). What prophets glimpsed from a distance, what God's people longed for, is in your midst! The kingdom of God has dawned because Jesus is here!

The passage from Isaiah lists several signs which Jews associated with the arrival of God's kingdom. When those things began to happen they would know that the longed-for 'new age' of God's rule and God's liberation had dawned.

'Today,' says Jesus, 'those things are happening through my ministry. The kingdom of God is no longer something you hope for in the future. It is something you can experience and be part of now. God has come close to you.'

A closer look at Luke 4:18–19 will suggest to us what the Isaiah passage meant to Jesus.

'He has anointed me' speaks of his role as Messiah ('the anointed one'), confirmed at his baptism by the giving of God's Spirit.

'To preach good news to the poor' sums up what Jesus was most concerned about. 'The poor' means the people who are powerless, the people written off by the political and religious establishment, the people who don't count for much in the world's eyes.

In Jesus' time they would include not only people who were short of money but also widows, orphans, refugees, the disabled. And people who were despised because they did dirty jobs or because they benefited from the Roman occupation of Palestine. To such no-hopers Jesus came to offer hope.

'Prisoners', 'blind', 'oppressed' (REB 'broken victims') are variant ways of referring to the same kind of people. The different images speak powerfully of the shackles which prevent people from experiencing the liberation which God intended for them.

'The year of the Lord's favour' is a further picture of the revolution which Jesus brings. The Isaiah passage was alluding to the Year of Jubilee described in Leviticus 25:8–55. The law laid down that every fifty years slaves were to be freed, debts cancelled and property returned to its original owner. For Isaiah this law of revolutionary freedom and equality was a picture of the return from Babylonian exile. For Jesus it becomes a picture of the larger liberation brought by the Messiah.

Jesus brings this liberation not through political revolution nor through wielding power in society. He did not, for example, free John the Baptist from prison. But neither is the freedom he brings a merely inner, spiritual freedom.

For the rest of Luke's Gospel shows how, when people respond to him, he welcomes them into a new community. Among his disciples, those who have been battered by society or by circumstances are accepted and valued in a new way. Those who have been gripped by evil habits are set free by the power of his love. 'Nobodies' become 'somebodies'. Their world is turned upside down. They become part of an 'alternative society' which shows a new way of human caring, a new pattern of human society.

In verses 24–30 Jesus went on to remind his hearers how it had always been God's plan to show his favour to Gentiles, not just to Jews. Old Testament prophets like Elijah and Elisha were sent to show God's care to people outside Palestine.

'The kingdom of God has dawned in your midst,' Jesus is saying. 'You can know its blessings—but only if you'll share them with others.'

This is more than the audience can take. They rise in hostility against Jesus, because he has threatened to disturb their cosy assumption that God is more concerned about them than about anyone else.

This story sums up the pattern of Jesus' whole ministry as Luke portrays it. His mission is especially to bring good news of deliverance and new hope to the poor. The rest of his Gospel will give examples of Jesus showing God's generosity to all kinds of people who were looked down on by many of his contemporaries—lepers, Samaritans, tax-collectors and those whose sins shocked society.

Luke's second book, the Acts of the Apostles, will report how the early Church reflected Jesus' concern for all such despised groups. And it will show especially how the Church fulfilled God's plan that his love should be made known to Gentiles.

To think about

What does this passage suggest about priorities for the Church's mission today?

83
The first disciples

Luke 5:1–11

Villages around the Sea of Galilee (or Lake of Gennesaret, verse 1) were the centre of Jesus' ministry. Thirteen miles long and eight miles across at its widest point, it supported a thriving fishing industry, and still teems with fish today.

Teaching and healing in various villages, Jesus was attracting a lot of attention (4:31–44). So on this occasion, as always, a crowd gathered round him. Quick to seize an opportunity, Jesus commandeered a boat belonging to Simon. (He asked permission *after* getting on board, and disturbed Simon from his net-cleaning, verses 2–3!). From there he taught the crowd gathered on the beach.

The centre of the story is the encounter between Jesus and Simon (later nicknamed Peter, 'the Rock', 6:14). Here is the expert fisherman who has been out all night and caught nothing. And the ex-carpenter from Nazareth, who knows nothing about fishing, is telling him to throw out his net in the deep water. What tone of voice does that suggest for Simon's reply, 'Because you say so, I will let down the nets' (verse 5)?

It sounds more like a sceptic's compliance than expectant faith. Or is it? Simon calls Jesus 'master'—a term used elsewhere in Luke's Gospel only by people who are committed to Jesus as his disciples. And he has already seen his mother-in-law healed of a fever (4:38–39). So maybe this preacher knows something that Simon doesn't know. He had better play along with him . . .

Jesus responds with a miracle (verses 6–7). Not a miracle like turning water into wine or healing a blind man. For large shoals of fish do occur in the lake, and sometimes you find them all around your boat. But the timing of it! Just when Simon is thoroughly depressed with business and beginning to think that all the fish in the lake have fallen through the plug-hole. Catches like this don't just 'happen'. God is at work!

When something amazing like this happens, we feel a mixture of excitement and utter inadequacy. So Simon feels he is totally unworthy to be in the presence of someone whom he now recognizes as a very special man of God (verse 8).

But Jesus has other ideas (verse 10). For him, the miracle is a picture of where Simon's future lies. Jesus won't go away from Peter—he'll take him with him. The fisherman will now be joining Jesus in 'catching' people for God, bringing them under his rule. For the 'call' of Simon is at the same time his 'commissioning' to share in the task of bringing others to know Christ.

There is no half-way house between the call to discipleship and the commission to service. Everyone who has begun to follow Jesus is involved in his mission to make other disciples. Not that we are all spectacular evangelists. But we have a vital part to play.

In the other Gospels, the call of the first disciples comes right at the beginning, before any details are given about Jesus' public preaching and people's reaction to it. Luke's ordering of events is probably closer to what actually happened. People hear Jesus and are attracted by the freshness of his message. They see his acts of healing as signs that God is at work amongst them. So when he addresses them personally he is calling for a commitment based on what they have already seen and heard.

Even so, there is a bluntness about this story which takes us by surprise. Jesus seems to *assume* that Simon will join him, rather than invite him to do so. And Simon and his two friends 'left everything and followed him' (verse 11). Perhaps Luke doesn't really intend to say that they immediately and totally abandoned their trade. But he wants to leave us in no doubt about what came first in their lives from now on.

This is the first appearance in Luke's Gospel of the word 'follow', so often used by the Gospel-writers to describe the response of those who commit themselves to Jesus. It means that they quite literally went with him on his travels. But it also describes an inner attitude which is true of disciples, then and now, who cannot literally follow his physical presence around. As a picture of discipleship it suggests movement, not stagnation; obedience, not self-will; humility, not self-importance. It suggests relationship with a living Lord.

8 4

New teaching for a new people   *Luke 6:12–26*

From a wider circle of 'disciples' Jesus chose a group of twelve to share closely in his ministry. He named them 'apostles'—'sent ones' (verses 13–14). The number twelve stood for the twelve tribes of Israel. In appointing twelve, Jesus was deliberately making the point that God's people was being renewed. It was receiving a new focus around him. Because it was that important, no wonder he spent the previous night in prayer (verse 12).

The teaching which follows from 6:20 is a shorter version of Matthew's more famous 'Sermon on the Mount' (Matthew 5–7). No one can respond to Jesus and become part of this 'new people of God' without being changed.

176

Blessings and woes (verses 20–26). Jesus speaks to his disciples (not just the Twelve) of the joy promised to them in God's kingdom in contrast to their present experience of poverty and hostility from society. And he warns the rich and self-satisfied of the poverty which will be theirs in the end.

Verse 20 makes the key statement. Despite appearances, congratulations are due to the disciples. They may be poor, powerless and part of the underclass of society. But in reality they are rich! Why? Because 'yours is the kingdom of God'.

God's kingdom, or rule, is the centre of Jesus' teaching. He is not saying, 'You may be having a tough time now, but it will all be put right in heaven when you die.' He means, 'The rule of God—the new time of salvation which Israel longed for and the prophets pointed to—has dawned in my ministry. It hasn't yet come in its completeness. But so certain is its coming, so central is it to God's purpose, that you may rejoice in its blessings. The day is coming when it will be clear at last that it is God's values, not the world's values, which endure, because they alone are true.'

There is not always a sharp conflict between God's will and popular values in the world at large. But often there is, and Jesus highlights that contrast in the following verses.

Our society values *wealth* (verse 24). Jesus looks for *dependence on God* and openness to his grace (verse 20). When Jesus says 'woe' to the rich he isn't uttering threats. He is saying 'alas' (REB), expressing sadness for people who can't see beyond their possessions and have no room left for what God longs to give them.

Our society values *security* and self-sufficiency (verse 25, first part). Jesus offers a *feast to the hungry* (verse 21, first part). We have an instinct to protect ourselves, to make ourselves secure, *before* we feel free to look beyond ourselves to other people's situations. Such concern for self-preservation may sound like common sense. Jesus suggests that it is the way of self-destruction.

In contrast, he assures disciples, for whom nothing is secure, that all their real needs will be met. His promise, 'you will be satisfied' (verse 21), pictures God's coming kingdom as a banquet. When God's kingdom comes in its fulness, it will be like a party where there is celebration without limit and food to meet everyone's need!

Our society values *pleasure* (verse 25, second part). Jesus looks for *sorrow* on behalf of the world (verse 21, second part). Of course there's nothing wrong with entertainment and enjoyment. But the search for pleasure has become one of the great goals of Western society, a way of escaping from the harsher realities of life.

Many say, 'Let's get away from the problems of life, let's enjoy ourselves while we can.' But Jesus says, 'Get stuck into the demands and sorrows of people! You will only find lasting happiness if you weep, if you take on yourself a share in the world's anguish.'

We are doing that when we pray for the world, or when we give time to listen to a confused teenager, or when we visit a lonely old person down the street.

Our society expects us to *go with the crowd*, to gain people's approval (verse 26). Jesus promises suffering for standing out *against the crowd* (verse 22). People often talk about being different from the crowd, but they don't like being different. We follow fashion, in attitudes and behaviour as well as in clothes. We want to be accepted, to feel safe, with others.

Jesus doesn't promise that kind of security. It can be tough, even in a tolerant, civilized society, to be known as a Christian at school or at work. Jesus' promise is not that being Christians will make us popular, but that we shall be on the side of truth and of God. And we shall discover the closeness of Jesus himself, who has gone the way of suffering before us.

85

The meaning of love

Luke 6:27–49

Love for enemies (verses 27–36). Jesus' teaching is at its most demanding when he speaks of love for enemies. His command goes beyond passive acceptance of hatred and abuse—though that can be difficult enough—to positive action and prayer for the enemy (verses 27–28). He gives examples of what such action will mean in specific situations (verses 29–30).

Precisely because these are examples, they are not rules to be applied mechanically in all situations. In our experience, for example, there are occasions when to give to a beggar only enables him to get more drunk than he already is. And there are ways of 'turning the other cheek' which will provoke further abuse rather than defuse the situation and create the possibility of healed relationships. Jesus' examples are chosen to shock his hearers into thinking that a different reaction is possible than the 'getting our own back' which is our usual reaction in such situations.

The so-called 'golden rule' (verse 31) sums it up. If we always acted towards others as we hope they would act towards us, relationships would be transformed.

Conventional love responds to those who love us. That is natural, safe, mutual care. Jesus' followers are called to go beyond that, to take risks in caring for the unloved, the despised, the hated. Those who have entered the kingdom of God are called to be like God. And *he* is generous to those who hate him as well as to those who love him (verses 32–36).

To get the full force of what Jesus is driving at we must ask, 'Who did Jesus mean by "enemies"?' To his first hearers one answer would spring to mind: the Romans! How could anyone be more hated than the foreign dictator and his armies who are never far away?

So we can imagine the shock and the anger when Jesus tells people to love the Romans. 'You mean love the people who take our taxes and arrest our brothers?' they say. 'That's outrageous. That's the last thing you'll find me doing.'

'No,' Jesus replies. 'Unless we dare to do good to our enemies instead of matching hate with hate, there will never be a new world of peace and trust. We shall destroy ourselves.'

Probably when Luke's readers heard the word 'enemies' they would think of people who hate and cause trouble for the Christian community. When we hear it we may think of people who persecute us at work or make fun of our Christian beliefs. To all of us Jesus says: 'Love them, do good to them, pray God's blessing on them. Dare to break the cycle of hatred, and you will be acting as children of God himself.'

That of course is what Jesus did himself. And where did it get him? To the cross, apparently destroyed and his ideals destroyed with him. But the resurrection which followed his death shows that self-giving love always wins in the end.

Judging others (verses 37–42). In the examples of verses 29–30 Jesus envisaged situations where his followers were the underdogs, the people being abused. He turns now to situations where they have power over others—perhaps as leaders and teachers. Their criticism can ruin another person's confidence.

Jesus does not mean that it is always wrong to point out the weaknesses of others. But through this whole passage he is saying that his followers cannot be true teachers and leaders unless they pay attention to their own weaknesses and their own spiritual growth. And if they fail to show mercy to others they short-circuit God's mercy to them (verses 37–38).

Actions speak louder than words (verses 43–49). Jesus was famous for his parables—short stories or word-pictures which drove home his message in an arresting way. These two bring the sermon to an end.

In the light of what has just been said in verses 37–42, the message of the tree and its fruit is that we cannot bring about growth in others through criticism alone. The fruit of goodness in our own lives is a much more powerful incentive.

The parable of the wise and foolish builders is a word to all who have been exposed to Jesus' teaching. We are accountable not for what we have heard, but for how we allow that hearing to determine the direction of our lives.

A prayer

Lord, enable me today to love rather than to retaliate, to encourage rather than to criticize, so that I may be not merely a hearer but a doer of your life-giving word.

86

A Gentile soldier's faith   *Luke 7:1–10*

A Gentile army officer shows a willingness to trust in Jesus which goes beyond the faith of his Jewish contemporaries. As the 'outsider' who understands Jesus better than the 'insider', his story challenges the faith of all who claim to be Christians.

In Galilee at this time there were no Roman legions, since the area was not governed directly by Rome, but was ruled by Herod Antipas. So the centurion was a Gentile officer controlling forces which served Herod for police and tax enforcement purposes.

He had heard of Jesus' reputation as a healer and in his desperation—his slave is 'about to die' (verse 2)—sent for him.

Luke draws out the contrast between the attitude of the Jewish community leaders who act as go-betweens and the attitude of the centurion himself. The elders are keen to impress Jesus by reporting the soldier's good works and his positive attitude to Judaism (verse 4–5). He '*deserves* to have you do this'. Incidentally, remains of a first-century synagogue—presumably the one financed by this centurion—have been found below the third-century synagogue which dominates the site of Capernaum today.

The centurion, on the other hand, speaks for himself through the friends in verses 6–8. He is full of humility—'*I do not deserve...*'. His humility arises from a dawning awareness that Jesus' power comes from God—as his next words show.

'Say the word, and my servant shall be healed' (verse 7). His confidence in the authority of Jesus is based on his own experience of authority. 'I know from personal experience,' he says, 'what the word of a person in authority can do. A word from my superiors makes me act. And because of the authority over me, when I give an order my subordinates obey. In the same way I can see you are a man under God's authority. So when you speak, what God wants gets done.' Here, like Jeremiah at the potter's house (passage 44), is another example of God using life-experiences to reveal his truth to people.

Humility and faith in Jesus' authority, then, are the centurion's attitude. This provokes the reaction of Jesus which is the high point of the story (verse 9). Twice in the Gospels we read of Jesus' amazement. In Mark 6:6 he is amazed at the lack of faith in his home town of Nazareth. Here he is amazed at the bold faith of a Gentile.

This story vividly portrays a Gentile grasping the truth about Jesus while those who might have known better struggle to come to terms with him. What is more, the soldier never actually meets Jesus: the whole 'conversation' happens through go-betweens. This point is not lost on Luke, writing as he is for people in the Roman world a generation later. They never saw Jesus personally, yet they believed in him. For them and for us, distance in time and space is no barrier to our being among those to whom Peter could write: 'Though you have not seen him, you love him' (1 Peter 1:8).

And what of the poor sick slave, whose healing is mentioned almost as an afterthought (verse 10)? He is healed, we must presume, by the authoritative word of Jesus which the centurion asks for in verses 7–8.

There are many examples of God healing today in answer to prayer, just as Jesus acted in response to the centurion's urgent request. Sometimes when the doctors are puzzled, God manages without them. I remember once meeting a nun for whom prayer had brought healing from a chronic back problem. She spoke with a wonderful mixture of thankfulness and humour of how awesome it was, after reading and hearing so many stories of God's healing, suddenly to find God acting like this within her own body.

But we are wise not to look for tidy formulas which will ensure healing in all cases. These are pastorally disastrous, as when they lead someone to say, 'You haven't been healed because you didn't have enough faith.'

The slave in the story, after all, played no part in his own healing. All depended on the faith of his master and the commanding word of grace from Jesus.

It is a miracle when some who are prayed for are healed. It is a mystery why some who are prayed for are not healed. The anguish when healing does not take place must be expressed honestly and handed over to God. To do so is no less an act of trust than the prayer for healing itself.

87

The truth about Jesus, and about discipleship
Luke 9:18–27

Again a crucial moment had been reached, and again Jesus was praying (verse 18). He had been teaching, working miracles, calling disciples and sometimes worrying the religious authorities by his liberated view of the sabbath and other laws. The time had now come to assess the impact of his ministry.

Jesus was commissioned at his baptism for his work as the Messiah. But he didn't go around proclaiming, 'I am the Messiah'. He had to do the work of the Messiah (as described in passage 82) and leave people to reach their conclusions about him. The results so far were not encouraging. There was a widespread feeling that Jesus was quite out of the ordinary, but no commonly agreed conclusion (verse 19).

But what about those who had responded to his call? How did they see him? Peter spoke for them: 'You are God's Messiah' (verse 20). He'd got the message!

Why did Jesus strictly warn the disciples to keep quiet about this (verse 21)? Surely they should be proclaiming it as clearly as possible? The problem was that the popular expectation was of a Messiah who would bring political deliverance. To declare Jesus' messiahship against that background would be to court misunderstanding. Jesus had to be the Messiah—in the way God intended—before the label could be attached to him.

And the disciples themselves had hardly begun to understand what his messiahship involved. So from this point on Jesus taught them carefully about his suffering. As Son of Man (here an echo of Daniel 7—see passage 77) he is destined to share in God's triumph only through suffering and death (verse 22). In human terms, Jesus knew he was on a collision course with the Jewish authorities which would put his life at risk. On a deeper level he saw his death as God's way of 'absorbing' the effects of human sin and restoring friendship between humanity and God. 'The Son of Man *must* suffer' is the 'must' not of resignation to fate but of self-giving to God's plan of salvation.

The cost to Jesus of his self-giving for the sake of the world is reflected in the cost of discipleship (verses 23–27). The suffering Messiah means also a suffering messianic community. The response of discipleship has three aspects (verse 23):

'Deny self'. This is not merely the 'self-denial' of going without chocolates during Lent. It means refusing to put self at the centre of my concerns. It means allowing Christ to take control of my ambitions, my priorities, my self-concern.

'Take up the cross daily'. This involves a willingness to face hostility and all its possible consquences, for the sake of Christ. A follower of Jesus is, in a sense, continually travelling with him on the journey to Jerusalem.

'Follow me'. Followers cannot at the same time be leaders. They accept the leadership of Jesus, and move forward under his direction and in his company.

Jesus then suggests a motivation for such costly discipleship (verses 24–25). Many voices tell us today that we should never deny ourselves anything that feels good; the essence of life is to express ourselves, to fulfil our potential by gaining possessions or power over people. But Jesus says: The only way to find your true self is to deny yourself, to give yourself in obedience to God and for the sake of others. That is real freedom, because that is how God made humans beings to live. To be obsessed with yourself and with satisfying your desires is to cut yourself off from the source of life.

The same theme is expressed negatively in verse 26. At the final judgment those who have not acknowledged Jesus will not be acknowledged by him. He will respect the choice they have made.

In contrast, there are disciples standing around Jesus who within their lifetime will see the dramatic presence of God's kingdom (verse 27). The allusion is probably to events such as Jesus' resurrection and Pentecost. As Luke will report later, these are powerful expressions of God's rule at work in human experience.

So Jesus sets before people two ways of living and two destinies. There is the way which is focussed on self and which leads to death. There is the way of self-giving which leads to real life under the rule of the liberating God.

To think about

Jim Elliot, a young American missionary who was killed by Auca Indians in Ecuador in 1956, commented on Jesus' saying in verses 23–25: 'He is no fool who gives what he cannot keep to gain what he cannot lose.'

88

'Lord, teach us to pray'   *Luke 11:1–13*

Jesus' practice of prayer provokes the disciples to ask for guidance about prayer (verse 1). The form of the 'Lord's Prayer' which follows is briefer than the more familiar version in Matthew 6:9–13. It offers a pattern of *what to pray for*.

'Father'. Underlying this way of addressing God is the Aramaic word *Abba,* which seems to have been the starting-point of all his prayers. It is a family word—'dear Father'. But it is not sentimental. As we see from his use of it in Gethsemane before his arrest and crucifixion (Mark 14:36), it implies both an intimacy with God and submission to his will, costly though that may be—'Yet not my will but yours'. Jesus invites his followers to share in that intimacy and to live in that costly obedience.

Longing for God's kingdom. The next two phrases are a prayer for God to act. 'Hallowed be your name' does not mean, as is often assumed, 'I wish people would take more notice of you and pay you more respect.' It is asking God so to act in the world, to demonstrate his character as Father, that he is held in awe by people.

He will do that supremely by bringing his kingdom in its fulness. When people who believe that God's kingdom has already dawned in the coming of Jesus pray, 'Your kingdom come', they are saying that their chief longing is for God to complete what he began in Bethlehem and in Galilee. They are praying that what they now

184

experience in part will come in its completeness. They are looking for God's kingdom of justice and peace, when pain and death will be no more. They pray because they know that only God himself can do this.

Requests for ourselves. After the prayer for the coming of God's rule there are three requests about things which hinder his rule in us—our anxiety about the basic needs of life, our sins which needs forgiveness and the temptation to give up when the going gets tough.

Some of us find it easy to take our 'daily bread' for granted. Others, perhaps, have reason to worry about how we are going to 'make ends meet'. All of us need to express our dependence on God's daily care.

We ask forgiveness, and commit ourselves to forgiving others. This does not mean that God forgives us *because* we forgive others, as a kind of transaction. It expresses the terms on which we are able to to receive forgiveness. Unless we see forgiveness as central to our relationship with others we are never going to see it as central to our relationship with God. If you don't practise forgiveness you don't believe in it, and therefore you can't experience it.

When the young John Wesley was a missionary in America he was chaplain to General Oglethorpe. The general once said to him with great pride, 'I never forgive.' 'Then I hope, sir,' replied Wesley, 'you never sin.'

Finally we pray that God will guard us when our faith is put to the test. Whether under the pressure of persecution or of affluence, we face the temptation to compromise our faith. Just as God's Spirit enabled Jesus to stand firm when he was tested, so he can enable us.

Verses 1–4 suggest *how* to pray; verses 5–13 answer the question, '*Why* pray?' The parable of verses 5–8 envisages, with some humour, a situation where a man's shameless persistence gets his neighbour out of bed to supply his need. The point is: if one man will respond to another's request out of sheer exasperation at his boldness, *how much more* will your heavenly Father answer your prayers?

Verses 9–10 underline the point. Jesus says, 'Make a habit of praying! Keep at it, not so much because God is reluctant to answer as because he keeps answering.' There *is* the problem of prayer which apparently goes unanswered, but this passage is not about that. It is about the generous giving of a loving Father in response to prayer.

Verses 11–13 add one more point: God's greatest gift is not things, but himself. He gives his Spirit to all who ask. As we have begun to see, Luke's Gospel and Acts are full of what the Holy Spirit can do when he is at work among God's people.

89

The rich fool

Luke 12:13–21

Not only does Luke show Jesus' concern for the poor, he also has much to say about wealth. He doesn't say making money is wrong. But he does say it can be extremely dangerous.

Sometimes perhaps we imagine Jesus preaching sermon after sermon—set-pieces which people solemnly listened to just as they mostly do in churches today. Here we catch a glimpse of what it must often have been like. Someone in the crowd asks a question on an issue which always provokes argument: money (verse 13). It is no theoretical question. He and his brother are at daggers drawn about sharing an inheritance which has come to them. If sermons in church more often came as direct responses to such burning questions they might get more attention!

Jesus refuses to get embroiled in this particular dispute. He picks up the underlying issue—greed or covetousness. So much misdirected energy, so much stress in marriage, so many arguments over wills occur because people do not believe one truth: that 'even when someone has more than enough, his possessions do not give him life' (verse 15, REB).

One person who was certainly looking for life was Kriss Akabusi, Britain's champion 400 metre hurdler. 'At an early age I decided that the purpose of life was to see who could die with the most toys. I decided to get as much as I could for myself.' He aimed at fame, fortune, a Mercedes, an Olympic medal—and got them.

But 'no sooner than I'd got something, there was something else I wanted. I began to think there had to be another meaning to life.' Through reading the Bible he discovered life in Christ, and all his values began to be transformed.

The parable of verses 16–20 is blunt and powerful. It needs no explanation. Jesus doesn't need to show the sinfulness of greed. He simply shows how futile it is. 'How much did he leave?', they asked about a man who had died. 'All of it,' came the reply.

Finally Jesus points up a contrast (verse 21). It is simply not possible, he argues, to be both greedy about possessions and rich towards God. When people build around themselves the security of possessions, they do so at the expense of concern for God and neighbour. That is why Paul calls greed 'idolatry' (Colossians 3:5). It sets up an alternative object of worship, to which people devote their lives.

In the experience of many Christians the problem of greed or covetousness is not one that is settled once and for all. It keeps coming back. At different stages in life we become more comfortable—perhaps when we land a new job, or when the children have left home and cease to be a major demand on our resources. So we have once more to face the question, 'How am I now to put into practice my claim that a person's life does not consist in the abundance of his possessions?'

Luke has learnt from Jesus that wealth is for sharing. He tells of wealthy women who helped to support Jesus and the Twelve (Luke 8:1–3), about Zacchaeus the transformed tax-collector who gave half his possessions to the poor (Luke 19:1–10), about Barnabas who sold a field and gave the money to the needy (Acts 4:36–37).

There is no simple answer to what we should do with our money. The rich ruler should give it all away, because he is in love with it (Luke 18:18–25). But the same requirement is not made of Zacchaeus (Luke 19:1–10). And Luke later mentions Christians in Thessalonica and Corinth whose large houses were not sold so that the money could be given away but were used as bases for hospitality, worship and Christian witness (Acts 17:7; 18:7).

A prayer

Lord, my possessions are not my own, but are held in trust for you. Show me how to use them generously, so that I may be truly rich towards you.

90

The lost son and the generous father

Luke 15:11–32

Part of the appeal of this story is that we can identify with the emotions of the characters. We know people who have left home, to get away from their parents or to make their fortune elsewhere. We sympathize with the elder brother, faithfully plodding on with his unexciting duties. We have experienced the exasperation of parents with their children.

The story's first hearers wouldn't have been surprised at the young man wanting to leave home. Palestine was short of work opportunities, and many in those days went off to try to make their fortune in the cities of the Roman empire.

But they would be shocked at the younger son's attitude to his father. The law permitted children to receive their inheritance from their father during his lifetime, but not to spend it. So the son is behaving as though his father were already dead. He is squandering the money which should be kept safe to care for his parents in their old age. He is violating the commandment to honour his father and mother (verses 12–14).

What is more, he tries to rescue the situation by looking after pigs— a job which was sinful in Jewish eyes (verses 15–16). So Jesus' hearers would be filled with righteous indignation against the boy. 'He deserves everything he gets,' they would be thinking.

Then to their surprise comes Jesus' portrayal of the father. It might be a reasonable response, they think, for the son to be engaged as a hired servant. Then perhaps he can pay back some of the money he has wasted. But no—at first sight of the boy the father runs to meet him—a totally undignified act for a middle-aged man. He hugs him, gives him a kiss of forgiveness, and showers him with signs of welcome. The robe is a sign of honour, the ring a sign of authority. Sandals are the mark of a free man, the feast is a celebration of joy.

But why this joy over a good-for-nothing boy? What kind of a father is this? The hearers are confused. Their predictable world has been disturbed.

Then the elder son appears. They can sympathize with him. But he too shows no respect for his father. He launches into an attack without even a respectful 'father' to introduce his appeal (verse 29). He accuses his father of favouritism (verses 29–30). He distances himself from the family—'this son of yours'. He thinks the worst of his brother: the 'prostitutes' (verse 30) are in his mind, not in the earlier part of the story.

In other words, he has done his duty, but he has done it resentfully, unlovingly. He too is a man who needs to be set free from his self-concern. He needs to catch his father's generous spirit. He needs to discover that joyful celebration is the only proper response to a prodigal's repentance (verses 31–32).

Why did Jesus tell this story? Look back to verses 1–3 of this chapter. Religious people were criticizing him for his warm relations with people whom they despised. Tax-collectors were notoriously dishonest. 'Sinners' were all kinds of people whose lifestyle flouted the law. 'Riffraff', 'social outcasts', 'vermin' was the language used by respectable people to describe them. To eat with such people was a betrayal of religion and morality.

The elder brother's complaint (verses 29–30) echoes that of the critics in verse 2. And the whole story is Jesus' response to their attitude. The attitude is understandable. But it is out of step with the generosity of God.

So this parable is good news. It points to a Father who welcomes back a wayward child with extravagant rejoicing. It shows how the lost are found and the dead restored to life when they return to the Father's love.

But it is also a warning. The elder brother is the Pharisee, the person whose secure religious system is disturbed by God's generosity to sinners. He is the unsympathetic church which will not have its peace disturbed by noisy teenagers, by homosexuals and by unmarried mothers.

And the parable is left open-ended. We aren't told the elder son's reply to his father, because the story is addressed to its hearers and readers. It is not the son's response which matters, but ours. Will I rejoice when a 'sinner' comes to faith, even though it may disturb my peace? Or will I be out of step with God's generosity?

91
The fall of Jerusalem
Luke 21:5–24

Jesus and his disciples have now travelled south to Jerusalem. We find here a very different atmosphere from what we have met so far. A chance remark about the beauty of the temple leads to a prophecy of its destruction and of world-shattering events beyond that.

The disciples' question (verses 5–7). Just as Old Testament prophets had warned of Jerusalem's destruction because of Israel's sins, Jesus foretold that catastrophe awaited the temple. This was to be fulfilled in AD70, when the Romans crushed the Jewish Revolt and destroyed Jerusalem and its temple.

The disciples' question (verse 7) reflects the fact that there were Jews and Christians, as there are people today, who thought they could calculate when the great acts of God would happen. Jesus' reply refuses to play that game. What matters is not that his followers should be able to calculate God's timing, but that they should be warned about what to expect and given clues about the meaning of such events. So he sets Jerusalem's destruction in the broad context of God's purpose in history as a whole.

False messiahs and upheavals in the world (verses 8–11). Jesus' words assume that he is soon to be taken away from them. One day he will reappear—his 'second coming' at the end of history.

In the meantime his followers are not to be misled by self-styled messiahs with exaggerated ideas about their own importance. One such figure was David Koresh, who gathered around him a community of disciples in Waco, Texas. In 1993 he was charged with firearms offences and besieged in his compound by police and soldiers. He set the buildings alight, bringing death by fire on himself and seventy-six followers. Maybe he thought his action would spark off the end of the world itself and glory for his community. But that was not to be.

The truth is that all such 'messiahs' are false, because when Christ comes again he will come not as a man among humans, but in majesty and glory. There will be no mistaking him because of the *contrast* between the humility and ambiguity of his first coming and the public splendour of his final coming.

Jesus also warns that natural disasters and wars between nations are not a sign that history's timetable has almost reached its end (verse 9). They are part of the turmoil of historical experience, part of the ongoing conflict between good and evil.

Persecution for Jesus' followers (verses 12–19). God's people will experience the world's hostility against Christ. Since verse 16 warns of the real possibility of martyrdom, verse 18 cannot be a promise of physical safety. But Jesus does promise divine guidance for Christians put on trial for their faith (verse 15), and ultimate security in him (verses 18–19).

The destruction of Jerusalem (verses 20–24). Jesus now warns of the horrors which will befall the city. Like an Old Testament prophet, he interprets the fall of Jerusalem as divine judgment for the people's unfaithfulness. But he does not specify the nature of that unfaithfulness. The later Christian tendency to accuse the whole Jewish race of being 'murderers of Christ' goes beyond any New Testament evidence.

There has been much speculation about the meaning of 'until the times of the Gentiles are fulfilled' (verse 24). Did their time end in 1948 when the state of Israel once again had control over part of Jerusalem? Or in 1967 when they captured East Jerusalem as well? Or was Jesus not interested in Israel as a political state? Does 'the times of the Gentiles' mean the whole period from AD70 to Christ's return, when human control over disputed territory will become a thing of the past?

The difficulty of interpreting this should again make people wary of thinking that they can look at events in recent history and say, 'Now it is clear that Christ will come and the world will end by the year whenever.' Jesus is concerned that the upheavals of history should not take his followers by surprise. They don't mean that God's purpose has been thrown off course. But they have more important things to do than spend their time guessing about dates.

9 2
The coming of the Son of Man   Luke 21:25–36

Jesus now looks beyond the fall of Jerusalem—an event within history—to his final appearance at the end of history.

The coming of the Son of Man (verses 25–28). The language is poetic, and it would be wrong to interpret every detail as though it were a photographic record of an event already past. The words about heavenly bodies and the roar of the sea (verses 25–26) may in fact refer to *political* events. Similar imagery is used, for example, by Isaiah to prophesy the destruction of Babylon's political power (Isaiah 13:10). If so, such events will not be obvious signs of the end to any casual observer. For it will remain possible—even for the unwary disciple, let alone for the world at large—to be taken by surprise when the end finally comes (verses 34–35).

But the use of such vivid picture-language points to the victorious completion of Christ's work on earth. He who suffered as Son of Man to bring people to God will come again in glory to reveal the triumph of God's purpose (verse 27). When the cosmic signs of verses 25–26 occur, then at last we know that our prayer, 'Your kingdom come', is about to be answered in full (verse 28).

The kingdom of God is near (verses 29–33). A parable (verses 29–31) reinforces the message of verse 28. Verse 32 appears to say that the end of all things will take place within the lifetime of Jesus' contemporaries. But Luke who recorded this saying belonged to the next generation, and therefore could not himself have understood it literally. Probably it is a vivid way of expressing the *certainty* of Christ's coming rather than a statement about *calendar time*.

Sometimes we sing:

> This day the noise of battle,
> the next the victor's song.

But we don't understand it literally. We don't say it's misguided because day after day the 'tomorrow' of Christ's victory never comes. We recognize it as a poetic statement of faith, that the victory of Christ is assured, however much its calendar date may be delayed.

The fall of Jerusalem, however, *did* occur within a generation, and was for Jesus and for Luke a *stage* in God's bringing history towards its climax. The high points of history and of our personal lives are signs and foretastes of the final salvation and judgment at the end of time.

'Be on your guard' (verses 34–36). Jesus speaks finally of what this expectation implies for Christian lifestyle. Verse 34 makes clear that, despite the talk of signs, Christ's coming remains a sudden and unpredictable future event. It will involve judgment on people's lives (verse 36). Therefore we are to be always alert, expectant and free from distractions (verse 34).

But what does this mean in practice? As every child discovers who has spent weeks waiting for Christmas to come, you cannot live in a state of high excitement all the time. Look at it like this. Suppose I am expecting an important visitor. He has asked for certain things to be made ready for his arrival, though he cannot say when he will be coming. What do I do? I don't stand on the doorstep all the time looking for him. But I make sure that his instructions are carried out, so that when he does come I am not caught unawares.

To live in the light of Jesus' coming, then, means to take his teaching as a serious guide for my life. It means, for instance, sharing God's joy at the repentance of society's outcasts (passage 90), being generous with my wealth rather than possessive of it (passage 89), praying for God's kingdom to come (passage 88), accepting the radical demands of discipleship (passage 87), loving my enemies (passage 85). And that's only a start!

To think about

In the New Testament the important questions are not, 'When and how will Christ come?' They are, 'Who will come and why will he come?' And, above all, 'In the light of this hope, what kind of person should I be?'

93

The last supper

Luke 22:1–23

Ever since the Israelites' escape from Egypt the Passover had celebrated God's deliverance of his people. Now, about AD30, Passover was to be the time when an even greater act of rescue would take place.

Verses 1–6. The Jewish authorities wanted to be rid of Jesus because he challenged their traditions. And his popularity with ordinary people threatened to arouse the attention of the Romans. Any suspicion of unrest and revolution might provoke Pilate to act with a heavy hand and take more powers away from Jewish leaders.

The Gospels don't report Judas's motive for betrayal. Perhaps he was too attached to money. Perhaps he was disillusioned because Jesus' messiahship had turned out to be non-political?

Verses 7–13. Jesus was to share one last meal with the Twelve. The instructions seem to be part of a pre-arranged plan. Perhaps Jesus was concerned not to disclose the plan to Judas, lest he should be arrested before this final meeting was finished. The sight of a man (rather than a woman) carrying a water jar would be very unusual.

Verses 14–18. At the meal Jesus speaks about his death. He has seen it coming and he accepts it as God's will. This is the last time he will share in a Passover until the final coming of God's kingdom. Then he will share the 'messianic banquet' with all God's people (we saw in Luke 6:21, passage 84, that Jesus often pictured God's coming kingdom as a feast or a party). So Jesus points forward to the freedom which his dying will achieve.

Verses 19–20. Some translations, such as REB, omit part of these verses, since some ancient manuscripts have a shorter version. But the longer version is in the oldest Greek manuscripts, and most scholars accept it as what Luke wrote (as in NIV. If you are using REB or RSV, the longer text is in the footnotes).

When Jews eat the Passover meal they follow a liturgy which explains how different aspects of the meal symbolize the various parts of the exodus story. Jesus here takes the bread and one of the cups of wine used in the Passover celebration and gives them new meaning. They speak of his 'exodus' by which he will deliver the world from death to life.

The unleavened bread, broken and shared, represents Jesus' body, 'given for you' (verse 19). It achieves something for their benefit and for ours.

The cup of wine represents 'the new covenant in my blood, poured out for you' (verse 20). This is rich with Old Testament allusions. In the new covenant foretold by Jeremiah (passage 46) God was to take responsibility for enabling people to respond faithfully to him. Now, says Jesus, my death will open the way for that new relationship. Like the covenant which God made with Moses at Sinai, it is a covenant sealed with sacrificial blood (Exodus 24:8).

'Poured out' probably alludes to Isaiah 53:12—'he poured out his life unto death'. So it suggests that Jesus is offering himself up to death as the Suffering Servant, dying so that others may find life.

The instruction to 'do this in remembrance of me' (verse 19) relates to the whole ceremony. Every time the disciples celebrate Passover they are to remember Jesus' death and its significance. The Lord's Supper (Holy Communion or Eucharist) soon became established in the Church not simply as an annual event at Passover but as a regular form of worship. The four actions of Jesus in verse 19—took, gave thanks, broke, gave—came to be repeated, as they are today, at each celebration.

In the Lord's Supper we look back to the death of Jesus and its significance for our salvation. We look forward to the messianic banquet in God's kingdom. We look up to the living Lord who meets with us now. We look around to our fellow-worshippers, bound in covenant to God with us. And we look out to the world which we are called to serve in obedience to Jesus the Servant.

Obedience, betrayal, denial

Luke 22:39–62

The story now moves swiftly towards its climax. We see Jesus wrestling with, and accepting, the will of God. And we see him becoming more and more alone.

Jesus' prayer (verses 39–46). Jesus and his disciples slipped out of the city in the darkness to a quiet place on the slopes of the Mount of Olives. Mark says it was called Gethsemane, and John describes it as an olive grove. The issue was 'temptation' (verse 40). Jesus had faced the testing of his obedience to God before (passage 81), and had taught his followers to pray, 'Lead us not into temptation' (passage 88). Now they faced the ultimate test of their obedience.

In his prayer (verse 42) Jesus was not going through a routine or mouthing pious thoughts. He was wrestling with a real choice. Would he allow himself to be arrested and accept the consequences, or would he run away? For a man knowing that he had been betrayed, the natural reaction was to run. In ten minutes a fit man could get from Gethsemane to the top of the Mount of Olives. Then he would be quickly down the other side and far away into the desolate Judean wilderness by dawn.

But Jesus fought through that temptation to an acceptance of death. The agony of choosing had physical effects (verse 44). He did not rush to embrace martyrdom with a lust for self-destruction. But he surrendered himself to his Father's will. If that was to mean death, so be it.

Luke is presenting Jesus as an example to his followers when *they* face extreme testing. He shows them that prayer is the weapon with which to fight it, that divine strength is available, that faithfulness to God's will is what matters above all.

But while he was winning this great battle, they were asleep. Like so many disciples down the centuries, those who were instructed to 'be always on the watch' (Luke 21:36) were asleep when it mattered most.

The arrest (verses 47–53). Jesus here rejects violence as a way of escaping from death. The kingdom of God does not come by force of arms. His non-violence points up the irony of his arrest, the utter darkness which it expresses. Why should a man whose way is peace be arrested at all? Why should he be arrested by men armed to the teeth as though sent out to catch a gang of terrorists?

Jesus is isolated by the sleep of his friends, by the kiss of Judas, and now by Peter's denial.

Peter disowns Jesus (verses 54–62). The darkness of night adds to the tenseness of the atmosphere. The disciples disappear into the shadows. Peter alone, it seems, is brave enough to follow where Jesus is taken. But he has overestimated his own courage. The 'Rock' crumbles.

Recognized by his face and his northern accent, he denies any link with Jesus. The word 'deny' has two levels of meaning. Peter rejects the charge that he has any knowledge of Jesus. But in so doing he distances himself from Jesus, he refuses to follow his master.

Jesus had warned that Peter would let him down in this way (Luke 22:31–34). So no scene in the Gospel is more charged with emotion than the climax of this episode (verses 61–62). There is a 'magical' moment in Bach's *St Matthew Passion* when Peter's utter despair at his failure is captured in a series of descending notes.

What is the difference between Judas's betrayal and Peter's denial? Why does history judge one so harshly and the other so gently? Judas's crime is calculated, premeditated. Peter's spirit is willing, but it breaks at the crucial moment. His failure arises from fear. As his immediate reaction shows, he is open to God's forgiving grace. There is a way back for him, and for others who repeat his failure.

A prayer

Father, I am often like Peter and the other disciples—wanting to follow, yet prone to let you down when my faith is under pressure. As I think of Jesus surrendering himself to your costly will, strengthen me to stand firm in times of testing, to offer myself in love and obedience to your will for me. Amen.

9 5
Jesus on trial
Luke 22:66—23:25

Jesus before the Sanhedrin (22:66–71). The trial of Jesus is in four stages. He is brought first before the Sanhedrin, Judaism's highest legal and administrative council.

'Are you the Messiah?' 'Are you the Son of God?', they ask, picking up phrases which have been used about Jesus during his ministry. Jesus's replies are non-committal. (The reply in verse 70 should probably be translated as in REB, 'It is you who say I am'.)

Why is Jesus so evasive? Partly, perhaps, because he has no longing for death. If it comes he will accept it, but he will not provide the nails for the cross himself. Partly also because he knows the inadequacy of these titles. People—both friends and enemies—think that when they have pinned a label on him they have understood him. But no one can be reduced to labels. A label can conceal meaning as well as reveal it, as when 'Messiah' is understood as a political leader or military freedom-fighter.

Yet, when understood properly, Jesus is rightly called by these titles. As the one who sets people free for a new life in relationship to God, he does fulfil Israel's messianic hopes. As the person whose whole life suggests a unique oneness with God, he is the Son of God. He himself prefers the more ambiguous term 'Son of Man', but is in no doubt that beyond his coming death lies his welcome at God's right hand (verse 69).

For the Sanhedrin this is enough to condemn him. It is blasphemy to claim such status alongside God (verse 71).

Jesus before Pilate (23:1–7). The Sanhedrin can condemn Jesus but it has no authority to order his execution. Only Pontius Pilate, the Roman governor of Judea, can do that.

Pilate is not concerned about theological arguments. His job is to keep the peace. So the Jewish leaders change the charge of blasphemy to a charge of political rebellion (verse 2). It is the question of kingship which would most concern a Roman ruler. So Pilate asks, 'Are you the king of the Jews?' He, like the Sanhedrin, gets an evasive reply: 'The words are yours' (verse 3, REB).

Pilate finds no firm evidence to condemn Jesus (verse 4). At this the Jewish leaders introduce another attempt to blacken his character (verse 5). Galilee was well known as a hot-bed of unrest. Mention of it suggests to Pilate another way of getting information about Jesus (verses 6–7).

Jesus is brought to Herod Antipas (23:8–12). Herod, who is in Jerusalem for Passover, is ruler of Galilee and therefore a rival of Pilate. But even rivals can be useful sometimes (verse 12).

Herod is curious. But when he doesn't get his miracle he resorts to playing games at Jesus' expense. Jesus, Israel's true king, is rejected.

197

Jesus is condemned to die (23:13–25). Three times Pilate declares Jesus innocent (verses 14, 20, 22). He sees the whole affair as a religious squabble and cannot imagine that Jesus is a political theat. But he is too weak, too frightened of losing his job, to hold out against the Jewish leaders.

And the crowds, who hover round the edge of each scene, are easily swayed by the leaders. Perhaps they feel let down precisely because Jesus has turned out *not* to be a political threat and a freedom-fighter. In their disappointment they can sympathize with the Sanhedrin's complaint that Jesus is guilty of blasphemy.

Ironically, Jesus' accusers call for the release of a real terrorist, Barabbas, in order to secure the condemnation of a supposed terrorist, Jesus (verse 18). And Pilate, to save his own skin, allows himself to be bullied into their demand.

Luke deals gently with Pilate's guilt. Perhaps he wants his Roman readers to understand that Roman authorities have always found Jesus and his followers innocent of rebellion, and there is therefore no reason for them to think differently in Luke's own day.

But Pilate's cowardice still comes over in Luke's account. People contribute to the condemnation of Jesus in many different ways. Jewish religious leaders want him out of the way to preserve their own position. Pilate goes along with them for the sake of a quiet life. Herod treats Jesus as a curiosity, and has no genuine concern for truth. The crowd are easily manipulated and turn their anger on a Messiah who fails to fulfil their nationalistic dreams. In such ways do people express their preference for darkness rather than light (Luke 22:53).

96

Crucifixion and burial
Luke 23:26–56

Jesus is led away to one of the most painful forms of execution ever devised by man. It was reserved by the Romans for slaves, foreigners and particularly violent criminals.

On the way to the cross (verses 26–31). From the place of judgment to the place of execution a condemned man would carry the horizontal bar of his cross. But Jesus, exhausted by ill-treatment and a sleepless night, cannot do it. So Simon is drafted in.

The fact that his name is known, and that Mark names him as the father of Alexander and Rufus (Mark 15:21), suggests that this enforced duty led to Simon and his family becoming Christians. Luke says Simon was made to 'carry the cross behind Jesus'. Does he intend this as a picture of someone who has responded to Jesus' word that a would-be follower of his must 'take up his cross and follow me' (Luke 9:23)?

In response to the women's laments, Jesus utters his last prophecy about the fate of Jerusalem. If the innocent Messiah suffers this fate, what hope for the guilty city (verses 28–31)?

The crucifixion (verses 32–43). The actual crucifixion of Jesus is recorded in three words (verse 33). But its impact on others fills the surrounding narrative.

The soldiers who carry out the execution are to some extent the victims of circumstances. But their 'ignorance' (verse 34) does not mean they are guiltless—otherwise there would be no need to pray for their forgiveness. Jesus prays for them as he has taught others to pray for their enemies and persecutors (Luke 6:27–28, passage 85).

Religious leaders, soldiers and one of the criminals crucified with Jesus mock and insult him. Those who mock speak the truth without knowing it (verse 35). It is because Jesus refuses to save himself that he is able to save others. Through his life poured out in self-giving, God's love draws people to himself.

Perhaps Pilate mocks too, with the notice stating the cause of condemnation (verse 38). But is he mocking Jesus, whose pretensions to a throne have come to nothing? Or is he mocking the Jewish leaders by giving Jesus the title they could never agree to?

The story of the repentant criminal shows that it is never too late to ask for God's forgiveness. To the criminal's request to be remembered, Jesus promises immediate security in the presence of God (verses 40–43). On this incident Martin Luther commented that a criminal was forgiven so that no one need ever give up hope—but only one so that no one should take God's mercy for granted.

Jesus' death (verses 44–49). At the sixth hour (that is, midday) darkness came over the land. This might have been caused by the sirocco wind whipping up dust storms. But for Luke it symbolizes the spiritual darkness of this day.

The curtain of the temple is probably that which shut off the 'holy of holies'—the place of God's presence which no one entered except the high priest on the annual Day of Atonement. Its tearing signifies that through Christ's death the way into God's presence is open for all—including the repentant criminal.

Jesus' dying words express trust in God. Matthew and Mark record Jesus' agonized cry, 'My God, my God, why have you forsaken me?' But Luke chooses to emphasize his trustful offering of himself to his Father (verse 46).

The centurion responsible for Jesus' execution sees the manner of his dying and is convinced of his innocence (verse 47). His reaction foreshadows the conversion of Gentiles which will be a main theme of the Acts of the Apostles.

The burial (verses 50–56). Executed criminals were normally buried without honour in a public field. But even in the Sanhedrin there is someone who sympathizes with Jesus and his mission. Joseph, probably at some risk to himself, gets permission to bury Jesus' body in a tomb he originally intended for himself and his family. The long day of darkness draws to a close.

To think about

No day was ever so dark, or so loaded with hope, as Good Friday.

Blaise Pascal

97

Jesus is raised from death
Luke 24:1–12, 36–53

Jesus' death was like thousands of other cruel deaths in those times. But on the Sunday morning after he died, the shock-waves began.

Verses 1–8. Imagine the women's bewilderment at finding the tomb's entrance open, and the huge stone rolled to one side (verse 2). Imagine their horror when they discovered that Jesus' body wasn't there (verse 3). And then there were two angels gleaming with heavenly glory, proclaiming the news which was too good to be true (verse 6). Their message has two aspects.

'Why do you seek the living among the dead? He is not here, he has been raised!' (verses 5–6; REB omits the second part, without

200

sufficient reason). The tomb is empty because Jesus is no longer dead. God has raised him from death into the life of eternity.

It is important to stress two things here. First, the New Testament usually—as here—speaks not of Jesus 'rising' from death but of his 'being raised'. New Testament writers do not see Jesus as performing a miracle upon himself in the resurrection. New life—for Jesus himself as for us—is always a gift of God's grace, an act of his creative power.

The second thing is that Jesus' resurrection was not a restoration to physical life, like the miracles which he himself performed on a special handful of people. They were *restored*, only to die again later. Jesus was *transformed* to the life of the world to come—for ever!

These two facts help to demolish the theory which is revived from time to time, that Jesus never really died but merely swooned, and gradually recovered in the coolness of the tomb. Such a theory fails to explain how he could move away the huge stone which blocked his exit, or how after the battering of torture and crucifixion he could give an impression of vibrant aliveness, or how the Christian faith continued when he eventually died.

The second part of the angels' message is that Christ's resurrection was in line with his own promise (verse 7)—which we saw, for example in Luke 9:22 (passage 87). His followers had not known what to make of it at the time, but after the event it all began to fit into place (verse 8). Our understanding of God's involvement in our lives is often like that. Life has to be lived forwards, but it can only be understood backwards.

Verses 9–12. On hearing the story, the Eleven react in different ways. Most of them dismiss it as the tale of 'hysterical women'. Men have a habit of missing out on good things because of such prejudice! But their scepticism gives permission for our honest doubt as we search for the truth about Jesus. And it underlines the fact that when belief in the resurrection came to them it was not a piece of wish-fulfilment. It took them entirely by surprise.

Peter, perhaps hoping against hope for a chance to make good after his denial of Jesus in the high priest's courtyard, ran to see for himself (verse 12; REB has it in a footnote). His reaction shows another important aspect of the resurrection: the empty tomb alone did not create faith in the risen Jesus. An empty tomb can be explained in various ways—for example, by suggesting that someone stole the body. It took appearances of the risen Lord himself to the disciples to persuade them that he really was alive for ever.

Verses 36–53. On the same evening Jesus appeared to the Eleven in Jerusalem. Luke's account is particularly concerned to stress that it is not the appearance of a ghost, or a hallucination, but a real appearance by the risen Christ.

Now they are overcome with joy (verse 41). An empty tomb is no proof of resurrection. An 'appearance' without an empty tomb might be a ghost or a hallucination. Empty tomb and appearance *together* demonstrate that death has been conquered and the risen Christ will stay with them for ever and share his life with theirs.

Christ also stresses that his resurrection, as well as his life and death, fulfil Old Testament promise (verses 44–46, referring particularly perhaps to Isaiah 53:10–12). He explains that the time is now ripe for taking the good news to the Gentile world, once the promised Holy Spirit has empowered his followers for that work (verses 47–49).

Finally he parts from them in his 'ascension'. This event, retold more fully in Acts 1, marks the end of his appearances to various groups of disciples. It is the beginning of his reign as Lord over the Church and the world.

To think about

He takes his place in glory. And as he does so, he draws our world with him into his.

Andrew Knowles

6

FOR ALL THE
WORLD

98
Pentecost

Luke's second volume, the Acts of the Apostles, picks up the story where the Gospel left off. Before moving on to our selection of readings we shall take note of two verses in Acts 1.

Acts 1:1, like Luke 1:1–4, addresses Theophilus, who is covering the cost of producing Luke's books. And it speaks of 'all that Jesus *began* to do and to teach ...'. In this way Luke underlines the connection between his two volumes. The Gospel has described the action and teaching of Jesus during his earthly ministry. Acts is about to describe what Jesus *continues* to do as the Holy Spirit works through the Church.

So we shall not be surprised to see the Church in Acts reflecting the concerns which Jesus showed in the Gospel account. And we shall be challenged to ask whether the Church today shares the same concerns.

Secondly, Acts 1:8 is a key verse for understanding the shape of Acts. Here, before his ascension, Jesus summarizes the pattern of the Church's missionary expansion, which Acts is going to describe. And he makes clear that it all depends on the coming of the Holy Spirit.

Read Acts 2:1–13

Pentecost, the Jewish festival celebrating the grain harvest, was seven weeks after Passover. All that time the Eleven and other followers of

203

Jesus in Jerusalem—about 120 of them (Acts 1:15)—had stuck close to each other, waiting. Then it happened. The promised Holy Spirit came to them with power. Several things are important in Luke's account.

First, what happened was the *coming of God himself.* The references to wind and fire (verses 2–3) echo such big events as the presence of God at Mount Sinai when the Law was given to Moses (Exodus 19:18), and the filling of the temple with God's presence in the vision of Isaiah (Isaiah 6, passage 38).

Notice that Luke doesn't describe the event too precisely. He says there was a sound *like* a wind blowing and what *seemed* to be tongues of fire. Experience of God is too awesome to be contained in a neat description.

Secondly, this experience was God's *fulfilment of the promise* of John the Baptist (Luke 3:16), repeated by the risen Jesus in Acts 1:5: 'In a few days you will be baptized with the Holy Spirit'. But in Acts 2:4, Luke calls it being 'filled with the Holy Spirit'. It means being filled with the life and power of God.

Some Christians speak of 'baptism with the Spirit' as an experience of God's presence and power which comes to them at a later time than their first response of faith in Jesus. But for Luke 'being baptized in the Spirit' describes the *beginning* of Christian experience. The phrase 'filled with the Spirit' refers not only to that beginning (as here) but also to moments at various points in the Christian life when people receive a fresh awareness of God's power and presence (for example, Acts 4:8, 31). And Luke can describe people's continual spiritual experience and Christian character by saying they are 'full of the Spirit' (Acts 6:3, 5; 11:24; 13:52).

Thirdly, the Spirit enabled the believers to '*speak in tongues*' (verse 4). This is a form of speech experienced by many Christians today, sometimes in private prayer, sometimes in public worship. It enables them to express their love for God without the struggle to find appropriate human words. Sometimes it is ecstatic speech corresponding to no known language. But sometimes it uses a real human language not known to the speaker. There are modern examples of people hearing their own language spoken by people with the gift of tongues.

So what seems to have happened at Pentecost was that people from various parts of the world who had come to Jerusalem for the festival heard snatches of praise to God ('the wonders of God', verse 11) in their own local languages as those 120 believers moved out into the crowd. It was not just the commotion, but the praise of God, which drew people's attention. Perhaps there is a message here for a modern Church whose excessive use of words on matters of secondary importance generates more heat than light.

Fourthly, the Spirit is the *basis of the church's life and mission*. Until Pentecost had happened, nothing else of significance could happen. The Church isn't simply a human organization. It exists because of what happened in Jerusalem that early morning. The rest of Acts will work out the implications of that.

99
Peter's message
Acts 2:14–36

Here is the first evidence of the reality of the risen Christ and the gift of God's Spirit. Peter, who a few weeks before had denied that he ever knew Jesus, now stood just a few hundred yards away from the place of his execution and burial, proclaiming his resurrection!

Peter's sermon interprets to the puzzled and excited crowd what God has done, and provides an example of how the first Christians told the good news about Jesus. He began with the question which some people had expressed (verses 13, 15). Having shown why the charge of drunkenness wouldn't do as an explanation of what had happened, he had got their attention for a better explanation.

God's promise is fulfilled. In verses 16–21 Peter quotes the prophecy of Joel 2:28–32, with its wonderful vision of how God would pour out his Spirit 'in the last days'. In the New Testament this phrase means the period between Christ's first coming and his final coming, the time when God's final act of salvation has begun to take place. Now, says Peter, what has happened today is what Joel was looking forward to (verse 16). This outpouring of the Spirit shows that the age of the Messiah has come and God's new day has dawned.

In Jesus, God has visited the world (verses 22–24). Peter's preaching of the good news is different from much modern preaching. It is not primarily an argument about people's need of God, or a little talk about people's spiritual lives. It tells the story of Jesus and what God has done through him.

It draws attention to Jesus' ministry, including the miracles which he did through the power of God. It speaks of his death—an act of wicked men but at the same time an event willed by God. And it announces that Jesus is risen from death—proving that from God's perspective Jesus was in the right, and those who put him to death were in the wrong.

Jesus's resurrection is supported by witness both divine and human (verses 25–32). With hindsight, he says, we can see that the resurrection was foretold in Scripture. Appealing to this common ground between himself and his Jewish audience and using a method of biblical interpetation which was normal to them, he quotes from Psalm 16. This was generally accepted as a Psalm of David. It cannot refer to David himself, says Peter, because David died and his body 'saw decay', as we all know because his tomb is near where we stand right now in Jerusalem! So David must have been speaking under God's inspiration, pointing forward to his descendant, the Messiah (verses 29–31).

Not only God, but the apostles also bear witness to the resurrection (verse 32). Peter's sermon is a telling of Jesus' story much more than it is a telling of his own story. But he does not hold back from sharing his personal experience to add conviction to his message and to show that God is really at work in human lives. The chief qualification of an apostle was that he had seen the risen Lord. And his chief role was to bear witness to the Lord whom he had seen (Acts 1:21–22).

The resurrection shows Jesus to be 'Lord and Christ' (verses 33–36). Peter now draws together what he has said about the outpouring of the Spirit and the significance of Jesus' resurrection. It is Jesus, exalted to the right hand of God, who has given the Holy Spirit to his people as the sign that the new age of God's blessing has come. It is Jesus, rejected by his contemporaries, whom God has marked out as Lord and Messiah.

In the New Testament the risen Jesus frequently bears the title 'Lord'. It means 'master' and signifies his authority over the church and the world. It implies that we are his servants, called to carry out the will of our master. But it is also the title of God himself. As we saw in the Old Testament, in most English versions it translates the Hebrew name of God, Yahweh. So when the first Christians called Jesus Lord, they were already implying that it was inadequate to describe him in anything less than the language they used to describe God.

100

Pentecostal harvest

Pentecost was a harvest festival, and there was certainly a surprising harvest that year! This passage describes how Peter's message bore fruit in the response of three thousand people. In verses 38–39 he sums up the response which God calls for and the promise that he makes.

'Repent'. This means to change the direction of my life, to turn from what is wrong towards God and his will. But for repentance to be effective I need the power of God in my life. So it is linked with a further demand, and then the promise.

'Be baptized'. For John the Baptist, baptism was a sign of repentance (passage 80). Christians took it over but enlarged its meaning. If we looked at all the references to baptism in Acts, we could summarize its meaning in three stages. Apart from repentance, it involves *faith in Jesus*, a commitment of one's life to the risen Lord. This is implied by baptism 'in the name of Jesus'.

It involves *welcome into the Church*. Baptism is performed by a representative of the Church and marks a person's entry into the Christian community. For all its imperfections, the Church is the place where God's love is celebrated and the growth of Christians is encouraged.

'You will receive the gift of the Holy Spirit'. This third element is God's promise. All who turn to Jesus receive the life of God within them, to forgive and renew them. The Spirit who has already made such a difference to Peter is given to all Christians—not only to those listening to him on the day of Pentecost, but to later generations and to 'all who are far off'. Here the promise of God's salvation for the Gentiles is foreshadowed.

Among the first Christians baptism was performed as soon as people expressed repentance and faith in Jesus (verse 41). Few churches follow this practice today. In churches of the 'believers' baptism' tradition, people are baptized after—and often quite some time after—they have put their faith in Jesus. This is to ensure that their faith is genuine and that they understand the implications of baptism.

On the other hand, since the late second century many churches have practised 'infant baptism'. They argue that the most important thing in baptism is not the response of faith (which infants cannot express for themselves) but the grace of God, and therefore it is right to baptize infants as a visible sign of that grace. The personal response of faith can come later.

It is not our business here to settle this issue in favour of one view or the other. But it is right to reflect on our own understanding of baptism in the light of New Testament practice. Do I share Luke's vivid awareness that coming to Christ involves redirecting my life, trusting in him, commitment to the life of the Christian community and receiving the life and power of his Spirit?

For the three thousand who responded to Peter's message an effective 'support system' was quickly developed (verses 42–47).

The apostles' teaching would involve telling the stories about Jesus which were eventually written in the Gospels. It might also include explanation of how the Old Testament found its fulfilment in Jesus, and guidance about new problems faced by the Church.

Fellowship probably went further than simply having meetings together. It meant sharing meals as an expression of commitment to each other, and probably also sharing possessions as need arose (verses 44–45). Those who shared the same life-blood, the Spirit of God, found it natural to share everything else.

The breaking of bread refers also to shared meals (as in verse 46), but specifically to the sharing of the Lord's Supper, when they recalled the dying of Jesus on which their faith and life depended.

The prayers (plural here, according to Luke, rather than 'prayer' in general) refers perhaps to the regular Jewish hours of prayer, in which the Christians continued to share. But Acts is full of examples of Christians praying, individually and together, in all sorts of circumstances.

In each of these activities we see the Church in Acts 'mirroring' Jesus and his followers in Luke's Gospel. Like Jesus' first followers, the Church in Acts followed the Lord's teaching, they welcomed the poor and provided for their needs, they shared meals, they received the command to observe the Lord's Supper, they learnt to pray. Luke does not expect the Church slavishly to do all the same things as Jesus did. But he does suggest that a Church which no longer pursues the same goals as Jesus has given up the right to be called Christian.

To think about

How do the activities of my church compare with those described in verses 42–47? Does it matter?

101
Saul's conversion

Through preaching, miracles, suffering and practical Christian living the church in Jerusalem grew quickly (Acts 2–6). It spread wider into Judea and then north to Samaria (Acts 8). Christian groups began to appear further afield, for example two hundred miles away in Damascus, Syria.

Such success provoked vigorous persecution from the Jewish authorities. Stephen became the first Christian martyr (Acts 7). An approving bystander at his death was Saul, a man determined to make his mark as a defender of Judaism against the new faith (Acts 8:1).

Read Acts 9:1–22

The first Christians were Jews who saw no reason to stop going to the synagogue. The only difference between them and other Jews was their belief that the expected Messiah had already come, and his name was Jesus. This of course provoked argument within the synagogues, and led many Jews to fear that this 'heretical' belief in Jesus would undermine their traditions. So Saul got permission from the high priest to arrest, under the discipline of the synagogues, followers of Jesus in Damascus (verses 1–2).

The appearance of Christ to Saul (verses 3–9). On the Golan Heights Saul himself was 'arrested' by the risen Christ. The language of verse 3 indicates the overwhelming nature of this experience. Christ appeared to him in an experience similar to that of the first apostles after the resurrection. It was something more intense than the vision given to Ananias (verse 10) and to other Christians in later times.

The words spoken by the risen Lord are striking. Not, 'Why do you persecute my Church?', but 'Why do you persecute *me*?' Those who attack his people are attacking him. And those who suffer for his sake know that he is with them in the heat of suffering, sharing the pain with them.

Immediately the zealous Saul became dependent and obedient to the risen Lord (verses 6–9). His blindness was perhaps the physical effect of shock at the experience which had begun to turn his world upside down.

The vision of Ananias (verses 10–16). Ananias is one of those minor characters in the Bible whose obedience to God's call plays a major role in carrying forward God's plan. Out of this man's obedience flowed the mission to the Gentiles which is Luke's major theme in Acts. God's work depends as much on the faithfulness of 'ordinary Christians' as on the achievements of 'big names'.

Luke emphasizes God's involvement in the whole episode with the 'double vision' of verses 10–12, in which Ananias was told that Saul had seen Ananias in a vision. Neither knew the other, and Ananias had every reason to fear Saul—unless God showed him that he is in control.

The reason why God's involvement was so crucial becomes clear in verses 15–16. Saul was to be God's chosen instrument to bear witness not only to Jews but to Gentiles. Nothing must prevent the revealing of God's love to the wider world. But there was a price to be paid: the persecutor would become the persecuted.

Saul is healed and baptized (verses 17–19). Ananias put aside his fear of Saul and welcomed him as a fellow-Christian: his first word to him was 'Brother'. Saul's turning to Christ had begun on the road to Damascus. It was now completed by the healing of his blindness, his baptism and receiving of the Holy Spirit, and his welcome into the Christian community which he had hoped to destroy.

Persecutor turned preacher (verses 20–22). All the urgency which Saul had put into uprooting the Christian Church he now put into proclaiming his new-found faith in Jesus the Messiah.

Looking at how Saul turned immediately to such demanding work, I wonder whether one reason why the Church in the West today so often looks unattractive to people—especially men—is because we fail to show that following Christ will take every ounce of energy and imagination. The only faith worth listening to is one which is worth living and dying for.

Saul's conversion has many dramatic and unusual features. But it is also a challenging picture of what every person's commitment to Christ is meant to involve. His *mind* was illuminated with the truth about Jesus. His *conscience* was challenged as he saw the wrongness of persecuting the Church. His *emotions* were stirred and his *will* was redirected into energetic service of the risen Lord.

102
Peter's 'conversion'

Before Saul's mission to the Gentiles developed, God still had work to do in bringing Jesus' original disciples into line with his purpose for the world.

Read Acts 10:1–23

It is easy from our viewpoint to think Peter was too attached to ancient traditions, too slow to realize the new things that God was doing since Jesus came. But let us look at things from his viewpoint.

Long ago God had given the Law which marked the Jews out as different from other nations. Many Gentiles despised them for their 'exclusiveness', but others admired them for sticking to the clear standards which the Law laid down.

This Law included instructions about what to eat and what not to eat. Jesus had displayed a certain freedom towards the Law. But he had not actually said that the laws about food no longer mattered. So Jews who believed in Jesus continued to observe them, and Peter was no exception. There was no reason to change their view, unless something happened to challenge it.

God had such a challenge in mind. As in chapter 9, the story involves a 'double vision', to show that God really was involved in what happened.

Verses 1–8. Cornelius was a Roman army officer stationed at Caesarea on the coast, capital of the province of Judea. His devotion to God was evident through his attachment to Judaism. As a result of his vision he sent for Peter.

Verses 9–16. In Peter's vision he was instructed to eat meat, including that of animals which the Law forbade Jews to eat. Peter's reply (verse 14) is understandable. He had always obeyed the Law, and he wouldn't dream of disobeying now.

But there was a built-in contradiction in his opening words: 'Surely not, Lord!' He called God Lord—master—yet refused to obey his directions. That is not a logical option for a disciple, but how often we try to take it.

But God persisted. 'Do not call anything impure that God has made clean' (verse 15). From now on traditional distinctions between 'pure' and 'impure' food were finished.

Three times the voice spoke. Would Peter say 'No' three times, as when he denied his Lord (passage 94)? The question—like the cloth!—was still hanging in the air when Cornelius' messengers arrived (verse 17).

Verses 17–23. Peter was nudged by the inner voice of God's Spirit to welcome the messengers (verse 19). The issue at stake was too important to be left to chance, and God was lovingly reassuring Peter that a bold step forward would be an act of obedience, not a betrayal of God's will.

Verse 23 is a key moment. For a Jew to eat only meat permitted by the Law of Moses cut him off from close social contact with Gentiles. By welcoming the men into the house and providing lodging, Peter was accepting that rules about food were no longer to create barriers between Jews and Gentiles. His 'conversion' to a new openness towards Gentiles was under way.

The rest of the chapter reports Peter's preaching to Cornelius and his family, which led to their receiving the Holy Spirit and being baptized. Thus God confirmed that Peter's revolutionary step was within the will of God.

For Luke the real issue in this story is that it shows Peter—representing traditional Jewish Christianity—endorsing the mission to Gentiles. If God no longer makes a distinction between 'pure' and 'impure' foods, then he no longer makes a distinction between Jew and Gentile. All may come to know him through Jesus. So significant is this that in Acts 11 Luke tells the story all over again by reporting Peter's explanation of the event to other Christians in Jerusalem!

For us, the story asks whether God is calling us to take risks, to break with tradition, in order to keep up with where he is leading in mission.

Ray Bakke tells of a Pentecostal businessman in Indonesia who took his family to live in a slum inhabited mostly by devout Muslims. He asked his well-off friends for donations and told the Muslim leaders: 'My Christian friends want you to have this money to build your mosque.' He helped them build it, at the same time running a Bible study for the men with whom he worked. Eventually thirty adult believers had been baptized, with thirty teenagers coming to afternoon classes (*The Urban Christian*, 1987, page 134). Many missionary societies would have called him home for a psychiatric examination. But his story invites us to think what bold steps are called for in *our* locality, if people are to hear the good news.

103
Missionary journey

Acts 13:1–12

This is just one glimpse into the 'missionary journeys' of Paul. It is now about AD 46, a dozen years after his conversion. We find him in Antioch in Syria—the third largest city in the world at that time.

The church at worship (verses 1–3). To judge by Jewish and Roman names in verse 1, the Christian community at Antioch reflected the racial mix of the city. The role of teachers is to instruct people in the faith, to explain the Bible, to pass on the teaching of Jesus. Prophets, like those in the Old Testament, are inspired to speak words of warning and encouragement and to give insight into the future.

While the whole church was at worship 'the Holy Spirit said'— presumably through one of the prophets—that Barnabas and Saul were to be commissioned for a special task. It is God's Spirit who directs the Church's missionary growth. He chooses people for specific tasks and guides them where to go.

We also see here that he calls people in the context of worship. Seriously to seek God in worship can be a dangerous thing! Just when you are enjoying a time of praise and the company of your friends, God may disturb you with a demanding call.

The church at Antioch was a church open to the world, already engaged in ground-breaking missionary activity (Acts 11:19–26). They were open to where God might direct them next. And when the challenge came they didn't say, as we might be tempted to say, 'But

these are our best people. We can't possibly let them go elsewhere.'
They commissioned Barnabas and Saul and sent them off.

Witness in Cyprus (verses 4–12). Again Luke stresses the direction of the Holy Spirit (verse 4). But why Cyprus? There had already been some Christian witness there (11:19), and Barnabas had relatives there (4:36).

Sometimes we think that what seems attractive or natural to us cannot be God's will. We imagine that God's will must always be difficult or exotic. But the direction of the Spirit and 'human' or 'commonsense' reasons for a particular decision are not necessarily in conflict. God uses us as the people we are. Our gifts, our interests and our friendships are his natural lines of communication.

For Luke, what happened in Cyprus illustrates four key issues. First, the story shows the strategy of preaching first in the synagogue—a pattern repeated by Paul in many places. In the synagogue were not only Jews but Gentiles who were already committed to belief in the God of Israel. To go first to the synagogue honoured God's continuing commitment to his covenant people. But it is a wise strategy in any case to share our faith first with people who are close to us—our family, our friends, those who already have some link with the Church—before going to people of very different cultures.

Secondly, it depicts a leading Gentile—the Roman governor of Cyprus—showing sympathy for the Christian message (verses 6–12). This shows the power of God to bring influential people to faith in Jesus. It encourages Christians to take a positive attitude towards the rich and powerful, in Rome or elsewhere, and not to write them off as 'beyond redemption'.

Thirdly, it shows that the power of the gospel is stronger than the power of pagan magic. Elymas, the 'court astrologer' of Sergius Paulus, engaged in occult practices. Armed with the power of God, Christians have nothing to fear from such people. Those who are gripped by the fascination of the occult, those who are agents of evil, can be liberated for service to Christ. People hooked by the idea that their lives and futures are controlled by an impersonal fate can be set free to know the personal love of God.

Fourthly, Saul the junior partner becomes Paul the leader. In verses 2 and 7 we read of 'Barnabas and Saul'. Verse 9 marks the turning-point where Saul steps forward into the prominence which he retains to the end of Acts. From now on Luke calls him Paul, and mentions him before Barnabas (except in 15:12). Now that his mission is firmly in the Gentile world, it is natural to use his Roman name Paul rather than his Jewish name Saul. Contrary to popular mythology, Saul's name was not changed to Paul at his conversion. He always had both names. And for the good missionary reason of building bridges in the Gentile world, he now prefers to use his Roman name.

104
The Council at Jerusalem

Acts 15:1–35

The mission to Gentiles threw up a major dilemma which threatened to tear the Church apart: on what basis are Gentiles to be included in the people of God? *God's* will in this matter became clear through Peter's vision in Acts 10 (passage 102). But would *the Church* come into line with God's decision?

The council convened (verses 1–5). In Antioch and churches established by Paul, Jewish and Gentile believers apparently accepted each other without conflict. But now some Jewish believers from Judea came to Antioch arguing that, according to the Law of Moses, no man could belong to God's people unless he was circumcised. So by not requiring circumcision Paul and Barnabas were being unfaithful to God.

Such a dispute called for a careful discussion among representatives of the various viewpoints. The Council of Jerusalem thus provides a model for Christian debate and resolution of disagreements over key issues.

Peter's argument from experience (verses 6–11). Peter told the story of Cornelius' conversion. 'If God has blessed Gentiles with the same experience of the Holy Spirit without circumcision, who are you to impose such requirements on them? For Jew and for Gentile alike, the way to God is by his grace, received through faith. He has no favourites.'

This argument from experience is the same type of argument which I might use in a dispute about the ordination of women. 'In my experience many of the most important insights and growth points in my Christian life have come through the ministry of women teachers, women preachers, ordained women. Deny the validity of that ministry and you are saying that my Christian experience is an illusion.'

James' argument from scripture (verses 12–19). James was the brother of Jesus. As the leading figure of the Jerusalem church he might be expected to support the traditionalist line. Rather, he confirmed the argument from experience with an argument from biblical prophecy. 'The coming of Gentiles into the church fulfils the expectation of Amos 9:11–12. It is part of God's plan. So we must accept that God is doing a new thing and not impose unreasonable demands on Gentile believers.'

The compromise proposal and the letter to Gentile believers (verses 20–35). James' proposal (verse 20) is that Gentile Christians should be asked to respect certain ritual or technical matters which are important for Jews.

'Food polluted by idols' means meat which has been offered in sacrifice to pagan gods and then eaten in a pagan temple or sold in shops.

'Sexual immorality' (REB, 'fornication') probably denotes marriage to close relatives, which was forbidden by Jewish law (Leviticus 18). But sexual immorality in its general moral sense was often a problem among Paul's converts from paganism. So possibly this requirement has a general ethical sense rather than the ritual or technical sense of the other three demands.

'Meat of strangled animals' and 'blood' refer to meat slaughtered in such a way that the blood remains in the animal. It is not 'kosher', according to Leviticus 17:10–13. If we think that such strict regulations about meat must have made things very difficult for Gentile Christians, we should remember that meat played a much smaller part in the diet of ordinary people then than it does today.

These proposals were attempting to safeguard table-fellowship between Jewish and Gentile believers. If they had not found a way of meeting Jewish scruples about kosher food they would have sealed division in the Church for good.

So the letter was sent reporting this agreement to the various Gentile churches in Antioch and the surrounding regions.

Luke's account of the Council:

◆ shows us the Church grappling with a question thrown up by 'what God had done' (verses 4, 12). They had to think through a way of understanding something new in their experience which seemed to conflict with their tradition.

◆ attributes the crossing of frontiers in mission to the Holy Spirit (verse 8).

- sees the coming of Gentiles into the Church as fulfilment of prophecy and therefore as the will of God
  (verses 16–18).

- insists that in the decision taken, the Church was coming
  into line with God's decision: 'it seemed good to the
  Holy Spirit and to us' (verse 28).

- shows the Church on an international scale coming to
  agreement for the sake of unity. Many things in Church
  life should be decided locally and should reflect local
  culture. But some issues are such important matters of
  principle that national and even international agreement
  is vital.

- shows that compromise need not be 'fudging the issue'
  and can be a positive way forward in preserving the unity
  of the Church (verses 20, 28–29).

- makes clear that the unity of God's people cannot be a
  matter of indifference.

105

Paul at the heart of Greek culture

Within a year of the Council of Jerusalem Paul's journeys had taken
him as far as Athens. Although not now the powerful city which it once
was, Athens retained its position as the leader of Greek thought and
culture. How could the gospel be preached there?

Read Acts 17:16–34

Paul perhaps did not at first intend to preach in Athens. He was there
on his own, waiting for friends to catch up before moving on to
Corinth, the capital of southern Greece. But once he looked around
he couldn't stop himself sharing the good news! Jews, sympathetic
Gentiles, philosophers, ordinary people in the city square all found
themselves engaged in conversation with him (verses 16–18).

Paul's talk of 'Jesus and resurrection' sounded to some like a new
god and goddess to add to their already large collection. But this led to

an opportunity to explain his message to leading citizens in the council of the Areopagus (verses 18–19).

Luke wants his readers to see the speech which follows as a model of how to win a hearing for the gospel with educated Gentiles. There are similarities between beliefs of the Athenians and 'New Age' thinking today. But whether we are wanting to express our faith to 'New Age' people or to teenagers in the youth club or to anyone who doesn't share our Christian standpoint, we can learn from Paul's method.

Paul's method:

◆ He started from what people were interested in: 'you are very religious' (verse 22).

◆ He understood what mattered to them. He had spent time listening to what they really thought. Verses 24–28 refer to several specific beliefs of Stoic and Epicurean philosophy.

◆ He aimed to move them step by step from where they were to an awareness of the living God (verse 23). He was referring here to the Greek practice of dedicating altars to unnamed gods who might be offended if they were accidentally omitted from the range of gods to be worshipped.

◆ He spoke their language. In speaking to Jews he naturally used the Bible to make out his case. To Gentiles with no biblical background it was better at this stage to quote their own authors where their thoughts were in line with God's truth (verse 28).

◆ Underlying this is the conviction that all truth is God's truth. The beliefs of a non-Christian are not to be written off just because they are held by someone who doesn't share my faith. If Stoics believe that God can't be contained in human temples, Paul will affirm it. If 'New Agers' believe that rain-forests are precious and not to be exploited, I will affirm it. All people have some insights, some convictions which overlap with the truth revealed in Jesus. Through them we can build bridges to the true God.

◆ To people who felt God was unknown, and perhaps unknowable, he showed how the risen Jesus makes him known (verse 31).

Paul's message:

Despite the unfamiliar language, a distinctive message shines through Paul's words:

◆ There is one God, not many (as ordinary Athenians thought), and not none (as some people think today).

◆ He stands outside the created world. He is not part of it, as Stoics and many 'New Agers' believe.

◆ Everything owes its existence to God, not to chance. The whole human race lives under his watchful eye.

◆ God wants people to seek him and find him. Personal knowledge of God is possible. It is what we are made for. We see signs of it in every longing for 'something better', every expression of inner emptiness, every moment when we sense that reality is greater than what we see and touch.

◆ Since God is distinct from the world, we should abandon worship of idols and of everything that is less than God himself.

◆ God takes us so seriously that he holds us to account for our attitudes and actions.

◆ In Jesus God has entered our world so that the unknown God becomes knowable. The God who is distinct from the world enters into relationship with human beings. He has proved that Jesus is 'his man' by raising him from death.

◆ In the end, truth is not a matter of personal preference. There is one Truth against which all other 'truths' must be measured.

Paul didn't try to say everything on one occasion. But he built a bridge on which people could start walking. We can do the same. Not perhaps by understanding the details of a particular philosophy—though it is important that some Christians do that. But by understanding what is important to our friends, affirming their beliefs and longings where we can, and saying how those those longings can lead to a knowledge of God through Christ.

106

The end of the beginning

Paul continued for several more years to travel in countries around the Eastern Mediterranean, sharing the good news and planting churches. On a visit to Jerusalem he was arrested on a charge of having taken a Gentile into the area of the temple where only Jews were allowed (Acts 21:27–36). When Jewish accusations against him increased he appealed to be tried in Rome by the emperor Nero himself (Acts 25:10–12).

The ship taking Paul to Rome was shipwrecked off Malta, but all the passengers survived. Luke then brings his story to its close.

Read Acts 28:11–31

Luke himself accompanied Paul on this journey and experienced the shipwreck with him. Notice the 'we' in verses 11–16. Since Paul was a Roman citizen and was not accused of a serious crime, he was allowed more freedom than we might expect while he awaited trial (verse 16).

It is surprising to us that Luke doesn't report what happened at Paul's trial. Possibly he was condemned and executed, but more likely he was acquitted and continued his ministry for two or three more years before his eventual martyrdom.

Luke doesn't tell us this probably because his readers know already what happened. And Luke's own concern is to finish his story on a note of triumph. He shows us his hero at the centre of the empire, sharing Christ with all kinds of people even though he is under house arrest. The very last words of the book in Greek are 'quite openly and without hindrance' (verse 31).

In this final scene we see Paul trying once more to show his fellow-Jews that Jesus was their Messiah. Notice how he addressed them as 'brothers' (verse 17). He retained a deep bond with them and longed for them to share his joy that God's kingdom had arrived in Jesus. But there was resistance, provoking him to quote those tough words from Isaiah (verses 26–27; the reference is to Isaiah 6, passage 38). The Messiah's own people had heard the good news. Now the Gentiles must have their opportunity (verse 28).

By the time he puts his pen down Luke has written what amounts to a quarter of the New Testament. He has shown how the story of a Galilean carpenter has made its impact on the Roman world, penetrating within thirty years to the heart of the empire itself.

Acts is above all a book about the Church's mission and growth in the power of God's Spirit. But in the process it illustrates what I call the 'both... and' of Christian faith. So often we talk about our faith in terms of 'either... or'. For instance, some say, 'our priority must be evangelism,' while others say, 'No, we must show Christ's love for people without trying to make them share our point of view.' Some say, 'We must hold on to our traditions,' while others say, 'No, we must ditch tradition and accept wholesale change as the only way forward.'

Luke's vision of God's purpose for the Church and the world is wider than these one-sided views. He has shown us:

◆ People are won to faith in Jesus not by miracles or by preaching alone, but by the activity of God's Spirit and the preaching of the word together.

◆ The gospel is not for Jews or Gentiles alone, but for both. It is not only for the poor and the ordinary but also for the rich and powerful.

◆ The Church's calling is not only to bring people to a living faith but also to care for the poor and needy and to create a community of love and acceptance.

◆ If the Church is to grow there needs to be both faithful prayer and bold, imaginative action.

◆ It is right to respect tradition—the early Christians valued the Old Testament and did not abandon the temple. But it is important to be open to change in response to a God who keeps moving—Peter must learn to eat with Gentiles, and Jewish Christians must learn not to demand that Gentiles be circumcised.

◆ Worship includes regular 'liturgical' elements such as the Lord's Supper. But it also is open to the unexpected, such as a word from God through a prophet.

◆ The work of God requires its great figures such as Paul. But it needs equally the 'ordinary' people like Ananias.

To think about

Do any of these 'both... and' statements pose difficulties in your church or your personal experience? Does your reading of Acts suggest a way forward?

7

LETTERS TO
YOUNG CHURCHES

107
The foolishness of the cross

From reading Luke's account of Paul we turn now to listen to Paul himself.

He wrote letters to churches when he could not be present with them personally. Sometimes they are a bit puzzling because we don't have the churches' letters to Paul—we only hear one end of the conversation. But that's part of the fun of reading them! It's exciting to realize that they come straight out of the lives and arguments of the early Christian communities. They are real letters to real people needing pastoral help or teaching.

We begin with a selection from 1 Corinthians, which Paul wrote to one of his most troublesome churches. Anyone who thinks the early church was an oasis of love and peace should read the New Testament!

Read 1 *Corinthians* 1:18—2:5

People tend to be impressed by power. Political power, the power of the media, the power of money, the power of a dynamic personality— grudgingly or wholeheartedly, we acknowledge their impact.

Christians at Corinth were impressed by the power of skilful orators. They lived in a world where the ability to talk cleverly and persuasively was admired above almost anything else. They brought this attitude with them into the church. 'Wisdom' was their buzzword. Like Christians in every age they faced the temptation to allow their Christianity to be moulded by the surrounding culture. And they caved into that temptation. Paul challenges them with three arguments.

The gospel message is not 'wisdom' but 'foolishness' (1:18–25). Contrary to all human reasoning, God's greatest act is not an act of overwhelming power but of apparent weakness. Through a criminal's death he has brought forgiveness and new life to the world. Who but God would be so wise as to be so foolish!

God's way goes against how we humans would have arranged things (verse 22). Jews look for a powerful demonstration of God's deliverance, a bigger and better exodus. They cannot tolerate a crucified Messiah. Gentiles ('Greeks') want God to conform to their idea of wisdom and reason.

Paul is not belittling human knowledge or thoughtful use of our God-given minds. But human cleverness cannot bring us into knowledge of God (verse 21). If knowledge of God depended on our intelligence, how unfair that would be! As it is, the message of the cross declares that we owe everything to God's grace. To know and love God is possible for all of us, because it depends on what he has done, not on us.

In about AD200 one of the emperor's page-boys drew on the wall of their school in Rome a boy worshipping a crucified man with an ass's head. Underneath he scribbled, with a misspelling: 'ALEXAMENOS WURSHIPS GOD'. That is how crazy most Gentiles thought the Christian message of the cross was. But nearby someone else— Alexamenos himself?—wrote: 'ALEXAMENOS IS FAITHFUL'. And long after the Roman empire crumbled, the story of the man on the cross continues to bring life and hope to the world.

God's people themselves are a sign of God's wisdom (1:26–31). 'Look at yourselves,' says Paul. 'If human wisdom were what counts, who would have chosen *you* to be God's people?' The ordinariness of Christian people was, and is, their glory. The poor, the slaves, the unimportant people of society were drawn together into a community which overturned normal assumptions about what matters in the world.

Why? 'So that no one may boast' (verse 29). To show that it is always dangerous to claim too much for human achievement. To show that every benefit we enjoy from God is his gift to us through Christ (verse 30).

Paul's own preaching shows that everything depends on God (2:1–5). 'Look at my ministry among you,' Paul continues. 'My weakness, my fear of opposition, my preaching of Christ the crucified one. They are the very opposite of the flashy oratory which impresses you so much. Yet you know what has happened. Out of nothing a church has been born in Corinth. You are established as Christians by God's power, not by mine.'

Paul's message here brings to us both encouragement and warning. Encouragement, because it means that God loves and accepts us as we are, not because we are clever or successful. Warning, because it is so easy for the Church to rely on techniques, polished preaching and powerful organization, and to squeeze out the power of God's Spirit.

A prayer

Forbid it, Lord, that I should boast,
Save in the death of Christ my God.
All the vain things that charm me most
I sacrifice them to his blood.

Isaac Watts

108

The limits of Christian freedom

Another slogan at Corinth was 'freedom'. Influenced by the so-called 'liberated' Corinthian society, some Christians claimed that Christ had set them free to do anything they liked.

One thing that they liked was to go to special dinners which were occasionally laid on at one or other of Corinth's pagan temples. These were a normal part of city life, and it seemed as natural to go to them as it would be for us to attend a wedding reception in a hotel. But at such meals the meat had been dedicated to the temple's god before being eaten. Paul's words to these free-thinking Corinthians say something important for our understanding of the freedom which Christ brings.

Read 1 Corinthians 8

'Knowledge puffs up' (verses 1–6). 'Knowledge' was yet another 'in' word at Corinth. 'We all possess knowledge' (verse 1) was their catchphrase. By 'knowledge' they meant some special spiritual insight which entitled them to behave with unrestricted freedom.

To their catchphrase Paul's reply is, 'Yes, but...'. They have knowledge, but it is not true knowledge of Christ because it makes them full of their own importance. They don't have true insight into Christ's will for his people (verses 2–3).

People at Corinth were saying, 'We know that there is only one God and these pagan gods, or idols, don't really exist' (verse 4). Paul of course agrees with that, and offers a remarkable summary of what God is like (verses 5–6). God the Father is the source of all things and the purpose of our lives is to serve him. It is through Jesus Christ that he has brought the world—and us—into being. It is striking that in the same breath Paul can insist on the oneness of God *and* call Jesus 'Lord', the Old Testament name of God.

In contrast to the reality of *this* God, the 'gods' and 'lords' who dominate peoples' lives in pagan Corinth are non-existent.

Love builds up (verses 7–13). The trouble is that for some Christians the power of these pagan gods is not yet broken. They are recent converts, for whom pagan rituals and practices still have a powerful attraction (verse 7). The 'liberated' Christians of Corinth may call them 'weak' and despise their lack of robust faith. But such an attitude is disastrous for three reasons.

First, it makes food more important than it is (verse 8). Our spiritual lives won't suffer if we don't eat meat for a while!

Secondly, it may bring disaster to the Christian of tender conscience (verses 9–11). A visit to the temple may feel OK to you, says Paul. But what if a young Christian who hasn't got pagan worship out of his system sees you going there? He may go himself and then be full of guilt because his conscience doesn't allow him to go there freely.

Thirdly, such thoughtless behaviour is a sin against Christ, because it fails to care for the brother or sister for whom Christ died (verses 11–12).

So Paul draws his conclusion (verse 13). My behaviour cannot be decided only by what feels right for me, even if I claim to be acting in the light of my knowledge of Christ. If what I feel free to do may damage the faith of someone else, love requires me not to do it.

Paul has more to say about this issue in chapters 9–10, where he gives other reasons why attendance at temple meals cannot be squared with commitment to Christ. But chapter 8 already says much to Christians who live, as we do, in a society which attaches great value to 'being free', 'expressing yourself', 'doing your own thing'.

Jane fancies going to a Hallowe'en party at a local night club. What will she say to her husband Tim, who until quite recently was addicted to various occult practices? Richard wants to see an 'adult' film which everyone seems to be talking about. But what if members of his youth group see him going? Graham has been invited to join the Masons and is keen to do so. He can't understand his wife's worries about him joining what she has heard is 'a secret society whose understanding of God waters down Christian beliefs about Jesus'.

Truly free people are not those who proclaim their rights and insist on them, but those who are willing to forgo their rights for the sake of others.

109
Spiritual gifts

The church at Corinth was sometimes chaotic, but never dull! Another cause of conflict was the over-excitement of 'liberated' Christians at certain kinds of 'charismatic gifts', particularly 'speaking in tongues'. In contrast with the abuses at Corinth, Paul provides guidance on the right use of gifts in Christian experience and ministry.

Read 1 Corinthians 12

Genuine spiritual gifts express the Lordship of Christ (verses 2– 3). Ecstatic speech was known in pagan cults to which many of Paul's readers had previously belonged. Therefore the mere fact that a person speaks in tongues is no guarantee of spiritual maturity or even of genuine Christian commitment. The real evidence of being 'led by the Spirit' is obedience to Christ as Lord.

The one God gives a variety of gifts (verses 4–6). Some people may concentrate on a few gifts, the more spectacular ones. But God gives a great variety. Several are mentioned in this chapter (verses 8–10, 28). But they are examples, not a complete list.

There are different kinds of gifts. There are, for instance, gifts of spiritual insight. Several are mentioned in verses 8–10, though it is difficult to know exactly how Paul understood the differences between them. There are gifts of healing and power to work miracles (verses 9–10), and gifts of leadership, church-planting and teaching (verse 28). There are gifts of practical service (verse 28, though NIV's 'administration' here probably means 'giving guidance or counsel' to individuals or to a church).

God gives his gifts for the the health of his whole church (verse 7). Gifts are not for private enjoyment, but for the benefit of all. Paul goes on to describe the Church as 'the body of Christ', in which every member has a vital part to play (verses 12–27). Worship, service, evangelism—none of these essential tasks of the Church is to be left to a few 'experts'. It is the life of the whole body, working together, which bears witness to the reality of the risen Christ, whose 'body' we are.

Every Christian has a gift (verses 6–7, 11). Paul takes it for granted that spiritual gifts are not the peculiar possession of a few special people, but are given to all God's people. All have been 'baptized by the Spirit' (verse 13) and therefore all share in the Spirit's gifts. Not all have one of the gifts mentioned in this chapter. Some have more than one gift. But each one has an important role to play.

Not all have the same gift. This is clear from what we have already seen, and is clearly the answer to the questions which Paul poses in verses 29–30. But from this truth he draws two vital conclusions. Most of the unhappiness and conflict associated with charismatic gifts in recent years comes from ignoring these two convictions.

First, no one need feel inferior to those who have other gifts (verses 12–20). Probably people at Corinth who didn't have the more spectacular gifts felt overshadowed by those who did. Paul's picture of the local church as a body shows how wrong they are. Without the smaller, unseen parts the body can't function. The Church is no less dependent on those who are tempted to feel that their simple gift makes no difference. God needs people with the gift of encouraging others, or people who can organize a Bible study rota, just as he needs his evangelists and pastors.

Secondly, no one may feel superior because of his particular gift (verses 21–26). People with certain gifts sometimes throw their weight around. They look down on those who don't have the same gifts. Or they say everyone ought to have the same gift as they do. But they are arguing against God. For the picture of the body again suggests that every part is dependent on every other part. Without the tiny blood vessel, the brain cannot function.

Gifts are to be desired and developed (verse 31). Although these gifts are given by God, not chosen by us, we are encouraged to long for the 'greater gifts'. Although every gift is valuable because it comes from God, Paul seems to regard some gifts as more significant. This is partly because people at Corinth were overvaluing some gifts. As Paul will make clear in chapter 14, the real test of a gift's importance is not how 'miraculous' it seems, but how much it builds up the Church.

If we long for the Church to be healthy and full of the life of God, our response is to discover the gifts which God is giving to us—through prayer, and through asking one or two people we trust what strengths they believe we have. And to develop the gifts we have—through study and through use of those gifts.

110

The way of love

1 Corinthians 13

Not many starry-eyed couples who hear this passage read at their wedding realize the context in which Paul wrote it. In chapter 12 he has set out the basic principles for healthy use of spiritual gifts. In chapter 14 he will develop this with some firm practical advice—though we haven't the space to include that as a reading here. In this chapter he sets the whole discussion of gifts in a wider framework.

It is important to see what Paul is *not* saying here. He is not saying that love is a better gift than all those mentioned in chapter 12. People sometimes say, 'What matters is that we love each other. If we get that right then it doesn't matter much whether we use charismatic gifts. Love is far more important than all those gifts.' But they completely misunderstand Paul.

He does not call love a 'gift' or compare it as a gift with those listed in chapter 12. He calls it a 'way'—an attitude, a way of living. Love is the attitude with which all gifts are to be used. It is the atmosphere in which gifts can contribute to the Church's life and growth. Without it, gifts are pointless. Among the Corinthians there is pride and competitiveness. If they continue on this way they will destroy themselves. They need to find again the way of love.

How much love matters (verses 1–3). Paul pricks the bubble of all who are full of the importance of their gift, their spiritual experience, their achievements, their self-sacrifice. The test of any gift, any service for God, is: Does it express genuine love? Does it genuinely build up and serve the needs of other people? Do they meet the risen Lord through the gift, or do they only meet the person using the gift?

How far love goes (verses 4–7). Love is 'patient': it isn't easily offended, it can absorb all kinds of ill-treatment without itching to get its own back. It is 'kind': it is full of positive goodness towards others. Paul then refers to eight actions which love does not do, and five which it does do. Love is not matter of talk or feelings. It is known by what it does.

You can see immediately the force of some of these descriptions for the situation in Corinth. They speak directly to those who who are feeling superior, and those who are feeling inferior, in this matter of spiritual gifts (see 12:14–26). But once we start to think about them, they speak to many other situations too, and challenge us at many levels of our lives.

How long loves lasts (verses 8–13). Here Paul contrasts the present time with the future time when God's kingdom comes in its perfection. Now the gifts are given so that we may know God better. Then we shall know God with full and true insight, as he knows us now. Just as children finish with childish activities once they are grown up, the gifts which are rightly important now will not be needed when we stand in the very presence of God.

Faith, hope and love last for ever. Faith is the hand by which we receive the love of God. Hope is the confidence that God's love will always be there. But love is greater even than these because it is the heart of God's own character. His love holds us and draws from us the response of love.

Great passage that it is, 1 Corinthians 13 speaks to people in many other situations as well as guiding in the use of spiritual gifts. It has often been noticed that in verses 4–7 Paul seems to capture the character of Christ, so that we might write 'Christ' where Paul has written 'love'.

But Paul's purpose is not simply to describe Christ, but to encourage Christ-like behaviour. So should we then write in our own name, and use the passage for a spiritual health check-up? If God calls me to be patient, kind, etc., how far is this reflected in my marriage, my friendships, my relationships in church, at work...?

A prayer

*Give me such love for God and for other people
as will blot out all hatred and bitterness.*

Dietrich Bonhoeffer

1 1 1

Christ's resurrection and ours

We cannot truly come to terms with life unless we have come to terms with death. Yet through the embarrassed silence about it we hear conflicting voices.

Some agree with Bertrand Russell: 'When I die, I rot.' Others— about 30 per cent of people in Britain, according to opinion polls— believe in reincarnation. To others, death is just a fact without a meaning. The playwright J.B. Priestley wrote, 'We know the processes of birth and death, the *how* of them; we have entrances and exits without meaning, as if compelled to take part in a bad play.'

Amid this confusion the Christian hope of resurrection may sound, as it sounded to some of Paul's readers, like a message too good to be true.

Christians at Corinth were influenced by their non-Christian contemporaries not only in their behaviour but also in their beliefs. They found Paul's teaching about life after death difficult to accept. They didn't believe that death led to nothing. But they couldn't understand Paul's confidence that God's people would rise to a new life more real and vivid than this life. So Paul takes them back to basics.

Read 1 Corinthians 15:1–20

The resurrection of Jesus (verses 1–11). 'If you have doubts about your own future,' says Paul, 'look at what happened to Jesus.' He recites here what is in fact the earliest record we have of Christian preaching of Jesus' resurrection. 'What I received' (verse 3) means 'the message which I received from other Christians when I first believed'. And that was within three or four years of the resurrection itself.

The message proclaimed the Christ who died, was buried and was raised bodily from the tomb on the third day. When Jews used the word 'resurrection' they meant the raising up of the whole person, including the body. They did not mean merely that the person's 'spirit' or 'soul' lived on.

This death and resurrection was 'for our sins' and 'according to the Scriptures' (verses 3–4). In other words, it was not just something which happened. It was an event which God planned, in which God was involved and which brought forgiveness and new life to humanity.

And there are a whole range of key witnesses to the risen Jesus— including Paul himself, dramatically changed by his encounter on the Damascus road (verses 5–8). Paul's experience was later than the others ('abnormally born', verse 8), but just as real.

This message of Christ crucified and risen is shared by all the early preachers. It is this message through which the church at Corinth has been born, the message on which all Christian stake their lives (verses 9–11).

Christ's resurrection and ours (verses 12–19). Paul now drives home the logic of this message. 'If you believe that Christ rose from death, and your lives have been changed by that, can't you see that you also will be raised from death like him? It doesn't make sense to believe one thing and not the other. The fact that Christ has been raised is the sure sign that God intends to raise also those who belong to Christ. Deny your own resurrection, and you deny Christ's resurrection. Affirm Christ's resurrection, and your own resurrection follows from it.'

Without the resurrection of Christ (verses 13–19):

◆ We are wasting our time.

◆ We are lying about what God can do for you.

◆ Christian faith is a fantasy.

◆ There is no forgiveness for human failure and wrongdoing.

◆ There is no life in God's presence beyond death.

◆ Our hope is a miserable illusion.

But because Christ has in fact been raised—and the evidence for that is early, varied and reliable—then all those negatives can be turned into positives!

- ◆ Our life and ministry have a purpose grounded in Christ the Lord.

- ◆ Our message is life-changing truth.

- ◆ Christian faith is trust in the living God, who brings life out of death.

- ◆ God offers forgiveness to all.

- ◆ God's people are promised life in his presence for ever.

- ◆ Christian hope is not wishful thinking but expectation based on what God has already done.

Verse 20 offers a further way of linking our destiny with Christ's. The 'firstfruits' was the first sheaf of the grain harvest, which was dedicated to God, and served as a guarantee that the full harvest was to follow. So the resurrection of Jesus is God's guarantee that those who have died in faith will be raised to eternal life with Christ.

112

Living in hope

When does this resurrection of God's people take place? What is it like? Does it make any difference to how we live now? In an earlier letter Paul responded to such questions. During his brief stay at Thessalonica he had emphasized the hope of Christ's future return from heaven. But he didn't have time to explain how believers who died before this event could take part in it. So the Thessalonians Christians were worried that some of their members who had died would miss the blessings that Christ's return would bring.

Read 1 Thessalonians 4:13—5:11

Paul offers first a specific answer to their question, then draws out some implications.

Always with the Lord (4:13–18). In contrast to the uncertainty and hopelessness of the pagan world, Jesus' resurrection guarantees eternal life for his people who have died (verses 13–14). They will not be at a disadvantage compared with those who remain alive when Jesus comes (verse 15). The 'word of the Lord' is probably a word of the risen Lord given through a Christian prophet.

When the Lord descends, dead believers will be raised to life and will be joined by the living to 'meet him in the air'—between heaven and earth. Paul doesn't make clear whether all then return to heaven, or to earth, because his concern is not to give a detailed description of an indescribable event, but to reassure his readers that Christians who have died do not miss out. But even if the *manner* of Christ's coming is hard to understand, its *result* is that 'we will be with the Lord for ever' (verses 16–17).

Tha language of 'going up' and 'coming down' need not trouble us. Any talk of God's coming near to us or of our going to be with him is almost bound to use such language. And clouds in the Bible regularly represent the revealed presence of God. The final coming of Christ marks the boundary between the present course of history and God's eternal kingdom. In life and death, there is encouragement in Christ, the goal of our existence and the one sure ground of hope (verse 18).

So Paul has offered assurance that because Christ has been raised from death, his people will be raised too. Whether they have died or are still alive when he comes, they will share in his glory. But by suggesting that this resurrection happens at Christ's final coming, Paul has left us wondering what happens in the meantime to those who die. We shall come back to that in passage 119. But for now, Paul wants to talk about how this hope affects life in the present.

Future hope transforms present life (5:1–11). Christ's coming will be sudden and unexpected, just when the unwary have been lulled into a false sense of security (verse 1–3).

But Christ's people are not to be caught unawares like that. We live already as 'children of the day' (verse 5). We act in a Christian way not because we are frightened of being caught off guard. Our Christian living flows out of what we already are because of God's work in us. The 'day of the Lord' (that is, the day of Christ's second coming, verse 2) has already shed its light on us and determines the quality of our living (verse 5).

Paul links assurance—'you are all children of light'—with exhortation—'so let us keep awake and be sober' (verse 5–7). Christian living means working out in practice what God's grace has made us in principle. If Christ is our Lord and Saviour, we are to abandon ill-discipline and cosy mediocrity, and to give ourselves singlemindedly to God's purpose.

What this implies in practice will vary from person to person and from time to time. But faith, hope and love are the constant marks of true Christianity, the armour which protects us against spiritual attack (verse 8).

To think about

A church in Holland has a stained glass window depicting faith, hope and love. That is the sequence which you see from the inside. But from the outside the order is reversed. People who are at present outside the Church must see the love of Christ's people if they are to discover hope and find faith for themselves.

113

God's Spirit within us

Before Paul ever visited Rome he wrote to the church there setting out his understanding of the Christian gospel. From this letter we choose two readings about the character of the Christian life.

Read Romans 8:1–17

'In Christ Jesus' (verses 1–4). Verse 1 uses Paul's favourite way of describing Christians. We are 'in Christ'—'united with Christ' (REB). Paul would say that in our ordinary human lives we are 'in Adam', subject to sin and death. But through faith and baptism we have become united with the living Christ, set free to live a new life.

We are released from the condemnation which our wrongdoing would bring down on us (verse 1). We can face God with a confidence which we had no right to expect. Why? Because God himself has acted. Left to ourselves, we cannot live up to God's standards, God's law. The law only shows up our failures. It has no power to give us life. But Christ himself entered into our human experience of temptation and overcame it. He confronted sin and defeated it (verse 3).

So now those who are united with him share in his victory over sin. We can do God's will because 'the life-giving law of the Spirit has set me free from the law of sin and death' (verse 2). To be 'in Christ' means to have the life and power of God within me, the power of the Holy Spirit.

Two kinds of existence (verses 5–11). To explain what this means, Paul sketches two kinds of people. The first kind are driven by the 'sinful nature' (REB, 'the old nature'; older translations have 'flesh', but this by no means implies that the physical body itself is sinful). The second kind are controlled by God's Spirit.

The first group are those who live without reference to God, people for whom their own desires are all that matters. That outlook leads only to death. The second group are enabled by the Spirit to be in tune with God (verse 5), to experience the life and peace which only God can give (verse 6). The Spirit guarantees their future resurrection in God's presence, because the life that he gives cannot be stopped by death (verse 11).

Paul does not imagine that human beings divide themselves so neatly between two different kinds of people. He knows that within ourselves we experience a conflict between our 'sinful nature' and our desire to please God. The temptation to sin didn't disappear the moment we committed ourselves to Christ. But he knows too that the power of God is infinitely greater than the power of temptation, and that God's Spirit is always working to transform us.

So basic is this experience of the Spirit living in us that it is impossible for Paul to think of a Christian without the Spirit (verse 9). And notice here that he speaks of 'the Spirit of Christ'. This implies that the Spirit's purpose is to make our lives Christ-like. He wants to develop in us the pattern of relating to God which we see in Jesus' relationship with his Father.

Children of God (verses 12–17). If God has given his Spirit to do all this in us, he calls us to resist what is evil and to open ourselves to the influence of the Spirit (verses 12–13). But that does not mean we are locked into a narrow, restrictive obedience. Quite the opposite! The role of God's Spirit is to enable us to relate to God not like slaves under orders, but like children enjoying the freedom of their Father's care and generosity (verses 14–15).

Paul's picture is of adopted children, welcomed into God's family and given all the privileges of a natural child. God accepts us as his children and invites us to call him 'Abba', Father, just as Jesus did. (On *Abba*, see passage 88.)

It is the Spirit who makes this relationship real to us. He creates within us the conviction that God has forgiven and accepted us, and cares for us as his children (verse 16). To have this 'Christian assurance' does not mean that we never have 'wilderness experiences' when our faith is thrown into turmoil. Nor does it mean that we claim certainty about every aspect of Christian belief. I may not always be sure what I believe, but 'I know *whom* I have believed' (Paul in 2 Timothy 1:12). I know that I am loved and held by God.

To think about

He owns me for his child,
His pardoning voice I hear;
In Jesus reconciled
I can no longer fear.
With confidence I now draw nigh,
And 'Father, Abba, Father!' cry.

Charles Wesley

114
Present strain, future glory

Romans 8:18–39

Christ died for us, God welcomes us as his children, the Spirit lives within us. But we don't possess everything God intends to give. The present life is often marked by pain, distress, conflict. But it will not always be so. In verse 17 Paul's mind was already turning towards the future: though God's children may suffer now, they await the inheritance which will be theirs in the future.

God's Spirit points us to God's future (verses 18–27). Paul knows that the destiny of God's children is to be raised to eternal life in God's presence. He now pictures the whole created world waiting with eager anticipation for that moment of transformation to take place at Christ's final coming (verse 19). For the creation itself is marked by disorder, death and uncertainty and longs to share in the perfection which will come in the end (verses 20–22). Earthquake, famine, disease are signs of a universe which is not yet what God intends it to be.

In verse 23 Paul says our adoption as children still lies in the future, though in verses 15–17 it is a present experience. That is typical of his understanding of Christian experience. We *already* have so much that God longs to give us. But we do *not yet* have it all.

The Spirit himself is the clue to this. He is 'the firstfruits'. We already met this picture when Paul described Christ's resurrection as the firstfruits of our resurrection (1 Corinthians 15:20, passage 111). Here he means that our experience of the Holy Spirit is a foretaste of the life of the world to come. A real taste, but only a partial taste of what we shall then receive in its fulness.

Because the Spirit is the guarantee of our future he keeps us going when we find life difficult here and now (verses 26–27). There are times when we feel our prayers are getting nowhere. We can't find the words. Or we have prayed and prayed about some problem and nothing seems to change. That is the very time when we can say simply, 'Spirit of God, I'm stuck. I'm puzzled and frustrated. I hand the whole thing over to you. Will you carry my questions and my longings to the Father, because you know his mind perfectly?'

And so through our 'sighs too deep for words' (verse 26, RSV) he prays in us and through us, and transfers the weight of our concerns to God.

God's eternal purpose (verses 28–30). In all our experiences, good and bad, God is at work for our good (verse 28). Paul is not saying that God causes bad things to happen to us. He is not pretending that the tragedies which come to us are really blessings in disguise. He does not deny the pain, the anger, the puzzlement. But he believes that the God who brought Easter Sunday out of Good Friday can bring blessing out of tragedy, growth out of weakness, life out of death.

The basis of his confidence is the purpose which God has always had for his people (verses 28–30). When he uses the word 'predestined' or 'foreordained' he doesn't mean that God has randomly selected some individuals for salvation and rejected others. He is stressing that our relationship to God depends on his grace from start to finish.

So confident is he in God (not in himself or in us) that he speaks of the whole sweep of what God does for us as though it had already happened. Even being 'glorified', which will be our destiny at the end of time, is as if it had already happened (verse 30)!

Praise for God's faithfulness (verses 31–39). If God has committed himself to us so totally, what have we to fear? If through Christ he has done everything to bring us close to him, who can possibly thwart his purpose? Though we experience persecution, rejection, tragedy or death, nothing can come between us and his love.

In that knowledge we may face the present, and look forward to the future.

A prayer

Father, you have promised
that nothing in all creation can separate me from your love.
Put your love between me and all those things which trouble me,
so that I may see them in their true perspective.
I entrust my present and my future
to your faithful and unending care.

115

Paul to his friends at Philippi

We have read selections from three of Paul's letters. But it is more satisfying to read a letter right through. Here is the short letter he wrote to the Philippians, a church with which he had warm relations over a number of years.

He founded the church there in about AD50 on his first visit to Greece. Now we find him in prison—probably in Rome about AD62, the period we read about in Acts 28:11–31 (passage 106). He is writing to thank them for a gift of money, and takes the opportunity to say other things as well.

Read Philippians 1:1–11

Greeting (verses 1–2). People often think of Paul as a loner. Maybe we imagine he was so single-minded, even fanatical, in his ministry that no one could work with him. That is a false picture. This letter, like several others, includes the name of one of his co-workers right at the beginning. No doubt Paul was the leader, but he always worked with a team. Missionary work is a team business, with different people contributing their gifts to the enterprise.

All Christians, not just a few special people, are 'saints'. The word means 'set apart, dedicated to God'. And it is used of Christians *together*. Paul never refers to an individual as a 'saint'. Modern Christians need to recapture this sense that we belong with one another as much as we belong to Christ.

As well as the Christians at Philippi as a whole, Paul mentions in particular the 'overseers (REB, bishops) and deacons'. We are apt—

wrongly—to read these terms as if they meant what they came to mean in later centuries.

The 'overseers' are the leaders, whose role is to guide the church's overall life. There are several of them at Philippi. There is no church in the New Testament which has one man (or one woman) as leader. The variety of God's gifts is reflected in those who lead. Deacons offered service such as visiting the sick and seeing that the practical needs of widows were met.

The greeting (verse 2) wishes for the church two great gifts of God. Grace is his loving favour. Peace is the positive relationship with him enjoyed by forgiven people.

Thanksgiving and prayer (verses 3–11). It is a great encouragement to know that someone is praying for you—especially when those prayers are not a vague 'God bless so-and-so', but actually talk to God about specific needs. So here Paul tells his friends what he has been praying for them.

Verses 3–8 deal with *thanksgiving*. Paul's prayer begins there because prayer is a response to what God has already done. Before we ever ask God to act or to meet particular needs, he has been at work making his grace known to us and to others.

Paul's thanks have a note of *joy* (verse 4) because of the evident signs of God's presence in the church at Philippi. He is *confident* that what God has begun he will see through to the end (verse 6). And there is a deep bond of *affection* between him and them (verse 8). Our commitment to pray for people is a measure of our love for them. And as that prayer draws those who pray and those who are prayed for closer to God, it draws them also closer to each other.

The particular reason for thanksgiving is their '*partnership in the gospel*' (verse 5). They have stood by Paul in his ministry, praying for him and now sending him the gift of which he will say more in chapter 4.

Again he is underlining the fact that the Church's mission isn't merely for 'specialists'. God equips particular people with special gifts as evangelists. But he asks of them no deeper commitment than he asks of all of us. We may contribute through prayer, through gifts of money, through helping others to share their faith, inviting friends to church or in a hundred other ways. But we're all in the same team aiming at the same goal.

In verses 9–11 Paul mentions his *specific requests* to God on behalf of the Philippians. It is thought-provoking to compare with them the kind of things which are the focus of our prayers.

Do we pray that people will grow in love, in understanding and spiritual insight (verse 9)? Do we pray that they will have a sure grasp of God's will, and God's power to enable them to live Christ-like lives (verses 10–11)?

116

A man in chains

Philippians 1:12–26

If you haven't seen people for a while, you write to update them on your situation. That is what is happening here.

The positive effects of Paul's imprisonment (verses 12–14). Paul the evangelist is held in chains. That sounds like bad news for his mission. But he is able to report an example in his own experience of how 'in all things God works for the good of those who love him' (Romans 8:28).

The whole imperial guard—a thousand or more soldiers, some of whom were assigned to guard him—and many other people too have learnt the reason for his imprisonment. And this witness of Paul's has spurred other Christians to share their faith boldly.

It is an encouragement to us to know that first-century Christians could be timid, as we often are, about letting their Christian commitment be known. They were spurred on by Paul's imprisonment. What does it take to make us less timid?

Preachers' motives (verses 15–18). The situation isn't quite so positive as Paul at first suggested. Some of those inspired to preach by Paul's example are true partners with him. But others are envious of his success and are preaching more in a spirit of competition than of love. Yet Paul will not let this squash his joy. Such rivalry is destructive, but maybe it is better that people preach with impure motives than not at all.

It may puzzle us that people behaved like this. Yet it happens more often than we like to think. At a recent city-wide mission where many churches were cooperating to bring the Christian message to the city, a few churches arranged rival events because they were only interested in trying to increase *their* membership. And we are sometimes tempted to idolize one preacher or leader and to ignore another, because the one is more interesting or entertaining than the other.

Confidence for the future (verses 19–26). There is a toughness about Paul which challenges today's Church. In so many Christians there is a softness at the centre which makes us cave in when things get difficult. But Paul's joy can't be crushed. He refuses to be defeated by circumstances or by opposition.

But that is not simply because of his own strength of character. He depends on the prayers of his friends and the power of the Holy Spirit (verse 19). Confident that he is supported in this way, he can face the future whatever happens. His chief hope is that he will be given the courage to bear a true Christian witness, whether during continued imprisonment or by speaking at his trial or by the way he faces death (verse 20).

He expects 'deliverance' (verse 19). The word might mean 'acquittal at my trial' or 'being brought safely through death to the presence of Christ'. He clearly has both possibilities in mind when he speaks of 'Christ being exalted in me, whether by life or by death' (verse 20).

What matters most to Paul is his relationship to Christ. From that everything else gains perspective. Life means to know, to love and to serve him. Death means to be welcomed with joy into his presence. He can muse on the pros and cons of both possibilities, because his confidence in Christ has enabled him to be relaxed about either outcome (verses 23–24).

A friend of mine actively served Christ long into his retirement. But after a heart attack he knew that death could not be long delayed. He called his family around him and asked his daughter to read from the twenty-third Psalm, which he and his wife had read together on their wedding night:

> The Lord is my shepherd, I shall not be in want . . .
> Even though I walk through the valley of the shadow of death,
> I will fear no evil, for you are with me . . .

He prayed for each member of the family. Shortly afterwards he died. He had lived life to the full, but he was ready for death because he shared Paul's conviction that death for the Christian means moving into the immediate presence of Christ.

Yet Paul refuses to put his own future or his own spiritual progress before his responsibility to others (verses 23–26). Heaven can wait. It will come in God's good time. While there's work to be done, let's get on with it!

To think about

Do you agree that Christians today tend to be timid about sharing their faith? If so, what might be done about it? Do we need a better understanding of our faith? More training? Encouragement from someone else's example? Or what?

117

A life worthy of the gospel   *Philippians 1:27—2:11*

'Stand together' (1:27–30). Whatever happens—to Paul or to his friends in Philippi—their calling is to live in a way which honours Christ (verse 27). The person who brought their gift to him must also have brought news of certain problems in the church at Philippi. To judge from what Paul now says to them, there is a tendency towards disunity and competitiveness.

Like him, they are facing opposition from those around them. They must stand together, face their opponents without fear, and be united in mind and spirit (verses 27–28). Tiny threads, when joined together, make a rope which can bear great strains. So it is when Christians are bound together in love and shared purpose. A church is made up of people with different gifts, different backgrounds and—on some matters—different opinions. But if there are no common goals, no real commitment to each other's welfare, disaster lurks just round the corner.

They may be tempted by suffering to think that God has forgotten them. But no—those for whom Christ suffered may themselves be called to suffer for him (verse 29).

'Have the same love for one another' (2:1–4). Paul begins this section with four reasons for Christian love. 'If' at the beginning doesn't imply doubt. It means 'if it is true—and of course it is!—then...'. So verses 1–2 mean something like this:

'Since your union with Christ stirs you to Christian action, since God's love for you is a great incentive, since you share in the power of the Spirit, since you know the tenderness and compassion of Christ, then crown my happiness by being of one mind, loving one another and being one in spirit and purpose.'

Nothing provokes loving behaviour more than the knowledge that we are loved. But then Paul spells out what loving one another means in the present situation (verses 3–4). No selfish ambition, no inflated egos, no concentrating on our own interests to the exclusion of others. In humility we are to reckon others better than ourselves.

This isn't telling us to pretend that someone else is a better preacher, a better musician, a more effective youth worker than we are, when any independent judge would say the opposite. But it is urging us to put ourselves in other people's shoes, to take other people's interests seriously, to rejoice rather than to be envious when other people do well. That is difficult—and Christ-like.

'Follow the attitude of Christ' (2:5–11). An even more compelling reason for behaving in this way lies in the example of Jesus himself. To make his point, Paul quotes what is probably a hymn about Christ, written earlier by himself or by someone else. The basic argument is this: 'Christ humbled himself and gave himself to death for you, and now lives as Lord of all. What stronger reason than this could there be for you to live in commitment to each other and humility before each other?'

At the same time, the hymn shows us what early Christian worshippers liked to sing about their Lord.

Verses 6–8 describe what Christ did. He shared equality with God. But, rather than cling to power, he gave it up in becoming human. He adopted the obedience of a slave as he surrendered himself to death on a cross. That's humility!

Verses 9–11 describe what God did. God put his stamp of approval on what Jesus did by raising him to the highest possible status. And he has given him the highest possible name—the name 'Lord', which is the name of God himself. So now the honour previously reserved for God is given also to Jesus Christ. That's why following his example is so important!

Many of the church's great hymns are hymns which describe and celebrate the life, death and resurrection of Jesus. From the 'Te Deum' ('We praise you, O God...') to Graham Kendrick's 'Servant King', they focus our minds and our worship on Christ and what he has done for us. Perhaps too many modern songs focus on our feelings, our intentions—songs which can do nothing for us when we're not feeling the emotions they express. Songs which point us to

Christ lift us out of ourselves and renew in us a sense of wonder and thanksgiving.

For prayer

If you have a hymn book or service book handy, use one of the hymns about Jesus as an expression of praise and worship. Or read slowly through Philippians 2:6–11 once again.

118

'Work out your salvation'

Philippians 2:12–30

Paul continues to explain what Christ's example implies. Just as he was obedient to the Father, so his followers are to continue in obedience (verse 12). This phrase 'work out your own salvation' (REB and other, older translations) has caused people a lot of trouble. Does it mean that our salvation, our getting closer to God, depends after all on our own efforts?

No. The meaning is that we are to express the results, the fruits of our salvation in our lives. Paul expresses the same message elsewhere in other words. 'If the Spirit is the source of our life, let the Spirit also direct our steps' (Galatians 5:25).

It is clear from verse 13 that Paul isn't suggesting that it all depends on us. God is at work in us, inspiring us to seek his will and giving us the strength to do it. Our responsibility is to be open to his influence upon us. A yachtsman is powerless to drive his boat, but he must set the sail to catch the wind.

Paul follows this general encouragement with specific instruction. If we follow in Christ's footsteps, grumbling and destructive argument must play no part in our lives (verse 14). Only then can we stand out as different in a self-centred and competitive world. Only then can our lives shine as lights in the darkness, as our lips 'offer the word of life' (verses 15–16).

Paul has a personal reason for longing that they should continue to grow in their Christian lives (verse 16). The 'boasting' of which he speaks (REB, 'pride') doesn't mean 'showing off'. Paul has a special way of using this word which we met already in 1 Corinthians 1:31 (passage 107): 'Let those who boast, boast in the Lord'. He knows that any pride which he can take in his churches is due not to his achievement but to God's work among them.

Paul is taking the long view when he thinks about his missionary task. Quick results and spectacular conversions may hit the headlines. But what matters is whether the results of our work *last*.

Verse 17 alludes to the fact that in the ancient world, when an animal was sacrificed, wine or oil was sometimes poured over it as an extra offering. Paul here sees the obedient service of the Philippian Christians as a 'sacrifice' dedicated to God, and his own death—if that is imminent—as accompanying it. Unwelcome such a death may be, but it won't stop Paul rejoicing, and encouraging them to rejoice also. If dedicated service brings joy to God, why should his servants be disheartened?

Co-workers (verses 19–30). Why should reading Paul's travel arrangements be any more useful to our spiritual growth than reading someone else's holiday postcards? But there are things here worth thinking about:

The need to keep in touch. Through Timothy and Epaphroditus, Paul wants to cheer his friends at Philippi with his news and he wants to be reassured about them. These are human needs which we easily forget in the busyness of getting on with our own tasks. Perhaps your church has a missionary working overseas. Or you know a student who has just gone to a strange place. A letter from you will assure them that someone understands their human need.

Faithful cooperation. Paul distinguishes rather sharply between Christian workers like Timothy, and others who are concerned only for their own interests, not those of Christ (verse 21). This might make us think he is like an unsympathetic employer, demanding impossible standards from those who work with him.

But that isn't what we find. We know from other letters that Timothy was a rather timid young man who some people thought wasn't up to the job. And we see here that Epaphroditus is homesick, longing to be with his friends again. Paul understands them, sees their qualities and backs them totally. God looks for people who desire to serve Christ sensitively and wholeheartedly, not for gifted prima donnas who serve him when it suits them.

Common sense and God's guidance. We see Paul here making common sense plans for visits to Philippi, yet he knows that the timing is not in his control and expresses trust that God will work things out as he wills. This is a helpful corrective to the assumption of some Christians that God's guidance only ever comes through deep spiritual experiences or special gifts of the Spirit. God expects us to use our minds to make thoughtful decisions. But at the same time we must be open to unexpected guidance—through circumstances, through 'hunches' that persist when we pray, through the insights of other people.

119
Looking back and looking forward

Philippians 3:1—4:1

We saw in Acts how Jews who didn't accept Jesus as Messiah caused trouble for Paul's infant churches. He now expects Jews around Philippi to renew their attempts to undermine the church. 'Dogs' (3:2) was a label of contempt which Jews pinned on Gentiles, and Paul ironically throws it back at them. As 'mutilators of the flesh' they insist that circumcision is the only way to gain access to God.

True worship (3:3–4). In contrast, Jesus' followers are the 'true circumcision', the true people of God. Paul describes two essential marks of the Church. First, we 'worship by the Spirit'—an inward offering of our lives to God. 'Worship' doesn't mean only what we do in church. The Bible doesn't divide life into compartments. What we call 'worship' and 'service' and 'everyday life' are all part of the offering of ourselves to God.

Secondly, our pride and confidence are focussed on Christ, not on human achievement or on physical marks such as circumcision. This leads Paul to reflect on his own experience.

Looking back (3:4–11). Since he met Christ, Paul has a new perspective on his past. All the privileges of Judaism, all his passionate attempts to defend and promote it, are as nothing compared with knowing Christ as Lord.

Paul is not here expressing rejection and hatred of Jews and Judaism. But he is rejecting the self-confidence which made Jews trust in their traditions and blinded them to Jesus their Messiah.

Traditions are not worthless but, *compared with knowing Christ*, they pale into insignificance.

Our relationship with Christ is described in four ways (verses 9–11). Our 'righteousness'—that is, our being *accepted* by God—comes not from reliance on the Law, but is a gift received by faith. We are being transformed by God's power which raised Jesus from death. Our lives are marked by the kind of obedience which led Jesus to suffering and death. The ultimate goal of it all is life with Christ beyond death. 'Somehow' (verse 11) doesn't imply doubt *whether* Paul will experience resurrection, but uncertainty about *how* it may happen for him.

Looking forward (3:12–16). Christ has taken firm hold of us, but we need ever firmer to take hold of him (verse 12).

Some Christians at Philippi perhaps claimed to be 'perfect' or 'mature'. Paul is knocking them off their pedestals and deepening their vision of what God can do in them. His picture of runners straining for the finishing tape makes clear that the Christian life involves effort. Although we live by the power of God, his service demands all our energies.

Paul, by now a man of sixty, is confident that there is still more of Christ to discover. As we grow beyond youthful enthusiasm we are apt to settle down, to mark time, to look to the past rather than the future. But God isn't in the past. He is out there in front of us, calling us forward to discover more of him and to serve him in new ways. Claude Monet painted his greatest pictures when he was over eighty. If he continued to develop his gifts into old age, how much more may the Christian grow who is looking to the living God!

Citizens of heaven (3:17—4:1). Paul now contrasts 'enemies of the cross of Christ'—probably the Jewish opponents of 3:2—with Christ's people. *They* are bound up with earthly things. *We* are citizens of heaven. Philippi was a Roman 'colony'. That meant Paul's readers were Roman citizens charged with the task of spreading Roman civilization and upholding Roman customs. Every local church is a colony of heaven, responsible for upholding the values of the heavenly city and bringing the world to know the rule of Christ.

We await Christ's final coming from heaven to claim the world as his own. Then we shall receive resurrection bodies, like Christ's risen body (3:20–21). We saw this in 1 Corinthians 15 and 1 Thessalonians 4 (passages 111 and 112). But how do we relate it to Philippians 1:23, which says that a person who dies goes straight to be with Christ?

The difference arises because in 1:23 Paul writes from the viewpoint of the individual who dies, whereas here the perspective is that of God's purpose for all his people. For the individual believer what happens at death is resurrection into Christ's presence. There is no gap, no waiting, because at death we pass beyond time as we now know it.

But the picture of resurrection at Christ's second coming stresses that resurrection isn't a private experience but something shared with all God's people. For us who are now alive it remains a future event. It marks the triumphant completion of what God has planned for his people.

120
Instruction, thanks, greetings *Philippians 4:2–23*

Instruction (verses 2–9). Paul offers examples of what it means to live as a 'colony of heaven'. First comes a *plea for unity* (verses 2–3). Imagine the blushes on the two women's faces when their names are read out! Paul is blunt, but he obviously loves the church, respects these women's Christian service, and is concerned that others should help them to set aside their differences.

It takes only two people to be at odds with each other for the life of a whole church to be paralysed. That's why the issue can't be left to fester.

'Rejoice!' (verse 4). Can you order someone to rejoice? No. But 'Rejoice in the Lord' doesn't mean simply, 'Cheer up'. It means, 'Think of the Lord and what he means to you, and that will bring you joy.'

Prayer controls anxiety (verses 6–7). Not all anxiety is wrong. I may be anxious about a relative's illness, or why a friend hasn't arrived at the appointed time. But a lot of worry arises from lack of trust in God. Paul urges people to take the antidote—prayer, which entrusts the problem to God. Notice what he says about it.

'In everything'. No need, no situation is too trivial or too difficult to be a proper matter for talking to our Father.

'With thanksgiving'. Nothing spurs us on to pray about today's anxiety more than thanks for how God dealt with yesterday's. Nothing builds our confidence for the future more than our memory of what God has already done.

'Make your requests'. This doesn't mean telling God what to do, but it is an encouragement to be specific. A father likes to hear his children talking to him not just vaguely, but about particular concerns.

'The peace of God'. The promise to those who bring their anxieties to God is that his peace will guard them just as soldiers protect Philippi from attack.

'The Lord is near' (verse 5). Does Paul mean that the return of Christ may come at any time, or that God is close to his people? Perhaps both. All our prayer is grounded in the confidence that God is near to those who pray. All our anxieties are got into perspective by the thought that Christ is coming to put all things right.

Positive thinking, positive living (verses 8–9). What goes on in the mind will eventually affect our actions. So, after urging his readers to think positively (verse 8), Paul urges them to 'put into practice' all the guidance which he has tried to give them (verse 9).

Verse 8 comes like a breath of fresh air to a society where there is so much that hinders our being truly human. You see signs of this in the sales figures of popular newspapers, the items on display in the local video hire shop, the negative talk about colleagues in the office, the readiness to sneer at genuine goodness in a person.

Paul is not encouraging a sentimental attitude which simply ignores the darker sides of human life. His first instruction is to think about what is *true*, and we can't do that without facing the reality of human suffering and evil.

The inscription in the entrance to the BBC's Broadcasting House includes a quotation of verse 8. It is sobering to consider how far TV and radio, which mirror atttitudes in society, live up today to that goal.

Thanks for the gift (verses 10–20). Paul manages both to offer warm thanks for his friends' generosity (verse 10) and to say that he has learnt not to rely on a particular level of income (verses 11–13). Both 'being in need' and 'having plenty' bring their own temptations. When our income is low we may worry and be full of self-pity. When we have surplus income we are tempted to 'live up to our income' and think too little of others. Through hard experience Paul has learnt the freedom of not being enslaved to possessions and to particular financial expectations.

He also knows that generous giving brings spiritual dividends to the giver (verse 17). Those who give to God's work with open-hearted generosity are open to receive all the blessings of God's generosity. See verses 11 and 19.

Final greetings (verses 21–23). The greetings come from not only Paul, but also his missionary colleagues ('brothers'), such as Timothy. And they are from all the Roman church, but especially those of Caesar's household. These would include soldiers of the imperial guard and people working for the emperor's civil service. The gospel is reaching the heart of Roman society.

The letter began by wishing God's grace upon the Christians at Philippi. It ends with the same prayer.

To think about

What might verse 8 imply for you at home, at work and at leisure?

1 2 1

Our story—past, present and future

The 'Letter to the Ephesians' was probably a circular letter sent not only to the church at Ephesus but to several other churches in western Turkey. In some ways it reads like a summary of Paul's understanding of what Christ has done and what it means for us. So to take two passages from it is a good way to end our readings from Paul.

Read Ephesians 2:1–10

We read here a summary of our own story and how Christ has transformed it.

Our past (verses 1–3). The light of God's love to us in Christ shows up the darkness of life without Christ. It may seem odd to describe ordinary people as 'dead' (verse 1). But without the richness of life in Christ, that is what human existence adds up to. Paul describes life without Christ from two perspectives.

First, we were victims of external forces (verse 2). We were pressurized to conform to society's prevailing attitudes—attitudes, for instance, about money or sex, or about using people for our own ends. Behind all this is 'the ruler of the spiritual powers of the air'—the devil who seeks to draw people away from God and his will.

But, secondly, we were personally responsible for our own wrongdoing (verses 1, 3). Psychiatrist Karl Menninger wrote a book called *Whatever Became of Sin?*, in which he highlighted the fact that people are so reluctant these days to take responsibility for their own actions. If someone commits a crime it is the fault of his background or his genes, not his wickedness.

Now of course our background and upbringing do influence our attitudes and behaviour. But we too easily take half an explanation and make it the whole explanation. And in so doing we make ourselves less than human. For freedom and responsibility are essential parts of what it means to be human. Take them away, and you make us animals or robots.

The truth is *both* that we are influenced by external pressures *and* that we make our own choices. God holds us responsible for the choices we make. As sinful human beings, we are under the cloud of God's 'wrath', cut off from friendship with him (verse 3). But that is not the end of the story.

Our present (verses 4–6). If God had waited for us to make ourselves fit for his presence, he would have waited for ever. No one can bring themselves from death to life. But through Christ that is what God has done for us. That is the meaning of 'grace'—God doing for us what we cannot do for ourselves.

God has brought us into union with the risen Christ. So vividly does Paul think of this that he can speak of us already sitting with Christ in heaven. Whatever the circumstances of our present life, we can begin to view it from God's perspective.

Our future (verse 7). It is hard to tell whether 'in the coming ages' refers to our future experience in this life or to eternal life after death. Both ideas are true to the New Testament. And Paul's point here is to stress that our new life in Christ isn't a flash in the pan, a 'brief encounter'. God's plan is to keep on and on revealing the wealth of his love to us, and through us to others.

Sometimes when people become Christians they wonder, 'What have I let myself in for? How will I ever be able to keep it up? Will the novelty wear off?' The answer here is that God will never run out of strength to keep us going. He will never give up sharing with us his life and his love.

Verses 8–10 reinforce what has already been said. Our experience of the forgiveness and new life that comes from Christ is entirely a gift of God's grace. There is nothing for which we can claim credit. But it is a gift with a transforming effect. We are God's workmanship, God's work of art, designed to do good in the world.

To think about

Though you can't see it in modern translations, Paul's description of our experience has moved from 'we once walked in trangressions and sins' (verses 1–2) to 'we are to walk in good works' (verse 10). The difference has been made by God's 'grace' (verses 5, 7, 8), made real for us 'with Christ' or 'in Christ' (verses 5, 6, 7, 10).

1 2 2

One in Christ

Ephesians 2:11–22

The focus shifts now from God's work in individuals to what Christ's death means for relations between Jews and Gentiles. In today's world divided by racial violence, in a nation with no common sense of purpose, no New Testament passage is more relevant than this one.

Racial division (verses 11–13). In Paul's day Romans commonly despised Jews for their odd customs such as observing the sabbath and refusing pork. Jews tended to look down on all who didn't belong to the chosen people, and didn't share their commitment to one God. Paul acknowledges this deep division. Speaking from a Jewish point of view, he lists what the Gentiles were missing (verse 12).

But now Christ through his death has changed everything. Notice the contrast between 'but now' (verse 13) and 'at that time' (verse 12). Rabbis spoke of Jews as 'near' and non-Jews as 'far away'. Now that divsion is broken down.

'He has made the two one' (verses 14–18). Through his death, Christ has 'put to death' the hostility between Jews and Gentiles.

There are three aspects to this. Christ abolished the Law as a way of coming to God which in fact formed a barrier between Jew and Gentile (verses 14–15). Rabbis spoke of the law as a 'fence' which protected Jews from sin and kept them apart from other nations. Now both Jew and Gentile have access to God on the same basis—through the Holy Spirit (verses 17–18).

Secondly, behind this division between races lay a deeper division between human beings and God. In his death Christ took upon himself this hostility to God. He absorbed the poison of it, like a surgeon drawing the poison out of a wound, and so opened the way to a new friendship with God (verse 16).

Thirdly, 'Christ himself is our peace' (verse 14). Peace with God and with each other isn't a vague idea or a state of mind. It is focussed in a person. As we relate to him we find a new way of relating to people whom we have long hated or despised.

Paul's language is very strong. He isn't talking about a slight adjustment in human relations, but a fundamental shift brought about by Christ. He came 'to create out of the two a single new humanity in himself' (verse 15, REB).

If that is the purpose of Christ's coming, no Christian has a right to object to it. We are left with no choice as to whether we accept people of other races as brothers and sisters, children of the same Father. Elsewhere Paul makes clear that no divisions which seek to make one group more important than another have any place among Christians. 'There is neither Jew nor Greek, slave nor free, male nor female, for you are all one in Christ Jesus' (Galatians 3:28).

Of course Paul knows that God hasn't simply waved a magic wand and stopped all hostility between different races. What Christ has achieved in principle has to be worked out in practice. That is often painful and difficult.

But by the power of God miracles happen. In the first century, where racial and class divisions were huge, the way in which divergent groups of people came together in Christ was breathtaking.

And it goes on happening. David Hamilton belonged to the Ulster Volunteer Force, Liam McCloskey to the Provisional IRA. Each hated what the other stood for. They both became Christians whilst in prison for offences in connection with terrorism. Their hatred was taken away. They later became friends and began to work together for peace in Northern Ireland. 'Through being reconciled with God,' said David, 'I was reconciled with my fellow-man.'

How might this affect the wider conflicts between races and nations, and between rival groups within nations? The passage makes no promises for the healing of such hostility, since Paul is describing what is true for people in Christ. But it does make clear that God's *will* is for diverse people to live in mutual respect and harmony. Every church has an urgent responsibility to show within its own life the acceptance of people who are different, so that the world can catch a glimpse of what is possible for human beings in God's world.

One family, one building (verses 19–22). Paul enjoys moving from one picture to another, even when it is a bit illogical. So here he says that Jews and Gentiles together have equal citizenship, belong to one household or family, and are a building based on the apostles and Christian prophets. The 'cornerstone' is probably a big stone at the top corner of the building which binds two walls together. In Christ these two formerly incompatible building materials—Jews and Gentiles—are bound together.

The building then turns out to be still growing, and to be a temple (verse 21)! Just as Jews regarded the Jerusalem temple as God's dwelling-place, so the Church—Christ's people as a united body—is the home of the living God.

123
Chosen people

Several letters towards the end of the New Testament are known as 'General Letters' because they were not written to one particular church but sent round to a number of churches in a region. The apostle Peter wrote to Christians in northern Turkey, to encourage them as they faced the threat of persecution. He reminds them of the spiritual wealth which is theirs because of Christ, and gives guidance about Christian behaviour in a pagan world.

Read 1 *Peter* 2:4–12

The Church's inheritance. Peter uses Old Testament language to describe the Church of Jesus the Messiah. The Church, in which Jews and Gentiles are united, doesn't negate the promises which God made to Israel. But, because it is the people of God's Messiah, it inherits those promises.

When our faith is under pressure, we easily find ourselves wondering if the promises of God are all that we were led to believe. Peter's response to such wondering is to remind his readers of their privilege as Christians.

'People may be hostile to you,' he says, 'but you are precious to God. Rejection of you is not surprising from people who have rejected Christ himself.' Like Paul in Ephesians 2, he describes Christ as the cornerstone (verse 6—the picture comes from Isaiah 28). 'The miracle is,' he goes on, 'that the stone rejected as unsuitable by Israel's leaders has become the cornerstone which crowns the building!' (verse 7, quoting Psalm 118).

When people really have the chance to think about Jesus, he always has this effect. To some he is like a stone to trip over. To others he is the solid rock on which our lives are built. There is no comfortable fence to sit on.

The Church's purpose. Echoing the description of God's covenant people in Exodus 19 (passage 17), Peter offers a vision of what the Church is, and what it is for.

We are 'a holy priesthood' (verse 5). Israel of old had a special priesthood appointed to offer sacrifices. It had a special place where God's presence dwelt and sacrifices were offered—the temple. The people of the Messiah have no special priesthood. All have access to God. All have a part to play in bringing people into touch with God and bringing people's needs to God in prayer. We need no special place for worship, for God dwells in the people, not in a special building.

We 'offer spiritual sacrifices' (verse 5). Instead of animals offered up on the altar, our offering to God is the worship of hearts that love him and the obedient service of our lives.

Our role is to 'declare the glorious deeds of him who has called us out of darkness into his wonderful light' (verse 9). We do this in several ways.

When the Church gathers for worship, we are declaring God's acts through song and word. That is worth doing even if only God is listening. But at the same time we are making a statement to the world that God's activity in history and in the lives of people today *matters* to us. Shoddy notice boards and windows that can't be seen through do a lot to hide from people that this is what we are about!

We declare God's glorious deeds also in our daily lives—by the way we live, by the way we cope with the good things and the bad things that come our way and by testimony to God's goodness in our lives.

The Church must also declare God's deeds through the specific task of making Christ known to those who do not yet belong to God's people. Each local church has good news to share and a commission from God to share it with people in the locality. To fulfil its calling, the church cannot leave this task to chance. It must ask, How are we to fulfil our particular missionary task in this place?

The church's response to criticism. Verses 11–12 recognize that persecution of Christians is often fired by people who are misinformed and prejudiced about our true character. The right response to them is to live such flawless lives at all times that their prejudice may give way to praise of God. The word translated 'see' (verse 12, NIV; REB has 'reflection') means 'watch carefully'. If critics of my Christianity could observe me at close quarters for a period of time, would my behaviour soften their criticism and lead them to honour God?

To think about

What does your church notice board and its various activities suggest about its main purposes? How does this compare with the Church's purpose as outlined by Peter?

124
Christian citizens and slaves 1 Peter 2:13–25

Peter has said what the Church is for and has urged blameless behaviour in face of public hostility and prejudice. His instruction to 'submit' to various kinds of authority must be understood against that background.

This passage illustrates what sometimes needs to be done when we find biblical writers giving instructions. We can't always make a straightfoward application to our own lives of an instruction which they give. Different circumstances may require different kinds of action. The Bible is always to be taken seriously, but it isn't always to be taken at face value. If there are reasons for not applying an instruction *literally*, we will still be able to find *principles* which we can apply in our own lives.

The state (verses 13–17). Peter was writing during the time of the emperor Nero. The final years of his rule were increasingly cruel and erratic. But Peter's experience was still that he and his provincial governors administered justice with reasonable fairness (verse 14). And since Christians were a small minority often suspected of strange crimes, it was important for them to show they were good citizens of the empire.

But in other situations other things may need to be said. Peter himself had said to the authorities in Jerusalem, 'We must obey God rather than men!' (Acts 5:29). If the state requires people to disobey divine instructions, their Christian duty is to observe God's law and take the consequences which the state's law may impose.

And what of a modern democracy? This short passage won't guide us on many aspects of our involvement in society, but it can give us some principles to work from.

'Submit'—this word doesn't mean, 'obey under all circumstances'. It means something like 'respect the authority of'.

The reason given for submission is 'for the Lord's sake' (verse 13). Governments are part of God's arrangement for the good order of human society. Every association of human beings, whether a working men's club or a nation, needs a structure and leaders in order to function properly. Even comparatively unjust or incompetent governments are better than anarchy.

The function of government is to promote justice in society (verses 14–15). This gives a guideline as to what kind of leadership we should expect, what kind of laws we should argue for.

Our respect for government is all of a piece with our love of fellow-Christians and our worship of God (verse 17). This challenges us to rethink the cynicism which we often adopt towards politicians. We do not expect to be cynical about other Christians or about God. So are there ways of showing more care, more sensitivity and more honour to national leaders as we recognize the difficulties and pressures of their work? Suppose we were willing to be more involved in national or local politics, and less readily to gloat over the revelations of the Sunday newspapers. Might we then have a healthier nation with more politicians genuinely committed to serving the nation rather than the party?

Slaves and masters (verses 18–25). Again, it is understandable in Peter's time that he should advise slaves to submit even to harsh masters. There really was little alternative. And the positive hope was that such behaviour would encourage masters to think well of Christians and of Christ.

But Christians came eventually to realize that the whole system of slavery violates the will of God. No one has the right to own other people as though they were kitchen utensils or factory machinery.

And it would be immoral for oppressive employers to justify from this passage their attitude towards employees.

Yet Peter's words can still say something to employees. We have obligations to employers and managers. And even when there are injustices which need to be put right, the gospel is commended by our respecting those in authority. We will use the available channels to try to correct injustice. But if we have been treated in a less-than-human way, a Christian response will always continue to respect the humanity of those who have wronged us.

Peter encourages his readers by reminding them of the example of Jesus (verses 21–25). If ever there was a case of unjust treatment, it was what happened to him. But when wronged he did not do wrong in return, but 'entrusted himself to him who judges justly' (verse 23).

And it was his acceptance of suffering which brought forgiveness and life to us all (verses 24–25). In the end, it is not merely the example of Jesus' life which inspires Christian behaviour. It is the knowledge that through his death and resurrection he has brought us to God and given us a new outlook on life, a new power for living.

1 2 5
Faith and works

James was the brother of Jesus. We met him in Acts 15 (passage 104) as a leader in the church in Jerusalem. His letter is full of down-to-earth guidance about Christian behaviour. There is no difficult theology. It's a bit like a New Testament equivalent to the book of Proverbs, designed to ensure that God's people have their feet on the ground rather than their head in the clouds. The following passage highlights James' concern that Christian faith should be lived, not merely believed.

Read James 2:14–26

We have to imagine a situation where people have listened to Paul and have conveniently misunderstood him. Paul's great gospel was that we are accepted by God, or 'justified', only on the basis of what Christ has done for us through his death and resurrection. It is a gift, received by faith. We can't earn it by belonging to the right religious group or by trying to do the right things. God gives, and we receive as a child receives a present from a parent.

Now Paul also taught that faith in Christ, if it is real faith, will always lead to a Christ-like life. He talks of 'faith working through love'. But there have always been people who have ignored that. They have been so taken up with 'grace' and 'faith' that they have run away from anything that smacks of effort and hard work. They have failed to realize that if faith brings us into a real relationship with God, that relationship is bound to cause profound changes to our attitudes and way of living.

James has met people like that. Their 'faith' is not an active trust and commitment to a life-changing God. It is confined to the mind. They say, 'I believe in God', but there is little evidence of God in their life.

James has a tough response to people who say, 'I believe in God, but I don't see what that has to do with serving soup to drop-outs.' Or even those who say, 'I'd like to help you find shelter, but I mustn't be late for the prayer meeting' (see verse 16).

Such faith is 'dead' (verse 17). It is no better than the faith of the demons who have no doubt about God's existence but don't serve his will (verse 19). It is 'useless' (verse 20).

In verses 21–24 James uses the example of Abraham to make his point. He quotes a text from Genesis (verse 23, quoting Genesis 15:6) which Paul had used to support *his* argument that it is through *faith* rather than deeds that we are accepted by God. Perhaps James had heard people quoting Paul on this matter in defence of their belief that actions count for nothing. So he throws it back at them, stressing that Abraham's faith was *not* merely a belief in the mind. Because of his faith he sought to act in *obedience* to God, whatever the cost.

And Rahab sheltered two Israelite spies in Jericho when Joshua was about to begin the conquest of the Promised Land (verse 25). In this way she showed that she was *committed* to the faith of Israel. Faith led to action.

What James says isn't in conflict with what Paul says. They are looking at Christian experience from two different angles. But this gives us no right to say, 'James agrees with Paul, so there's nothing for us to worry about.'

James' stress on the absolute need for practical Christian living is an uncomfortable challenge to every kind of Christianity which sees faith mainly in terms of believing the right things or going through an approved set of spiritual experiences. Such faith is as dead as a corpse (verse 25).

Examples of practical Christianity in James' letter include standing firm when our faith is tested (1:12), keeping a tight rein on the tongue (1:26), looking after widows and orphans in distress (1:27), not showing favouritism to the rich (2:1–11), paying just wages (5:4). That's enough to keep anyone's faith down-to-earth!

To think about

Why do you call me, 'Lord, Lord', and do not do what I say?

Jesus, in Luke 6:46

Do not merely listen to the word, and so deceive yourselves. Do what it says.

James 1:22

8

THE LORD IS KING

126

The church under pressure and the Christ who reigns

The problem of understanding the New Testament's most difficult book has led some Christians to ignore it altogether. Others, making the most of its vivid picture-language, have claimed to find in it detailed descriptions of the progress of world history. Suspiciously, they always seem to conclude that the end of history lies just around the corner, within their own lifetime.

But this book has much to teach us, if we take seriously its own clues about its purpose and meaning.

Read Revelation 1

The real author of this book is Christ himself (verse 1). He speaks through 'his servant John'—probably not John the apostle, but another John otherwise unknown to us.

His book is a *'revelation'* or *'apocalypse'* (verse 1). It has a similar style to parts of Daniel in the Old Testament and other Jewish 'apocalyptic' books. They use picture-language to express their faith in God's final triumph over political empires and the forces of evil.

It is a *'prophecy'* (verse 3). Like Old Testament prophets, John speaks God's word to particular situations. He expresses God's warnings of judgment and promises of deliverance.

It is also a *letter*, sent to seven specific churches in western Turkey (verses 4, 11). So, like the letters of Paul, it speaks to the needs of particular Christians. But, like other New Testament letters, it can speak also to us who overhear what God says to them and apply it to our own situation.

The time of writing is probably about AD95. John has been exiled to the Aegean island of Patmos because of his Christian witness (verse 9). But there he receives a vision of Christ, telling him to write to these seven churches (verses 10–11).

They also are suffering or are expecting to suffer soon. He is their 'companion in the suffering' (verse 9), and his description of Christ speaks movingly to their anxiety.

Christ is 'the faithful witness' (verse 5). 'Remember,' John is saying, 'Christ himself faced extreme suffering, and remained faithful. Let him be your example and inspiration. He triumphed over death, and—because of him—so will you. He, despite every appearance to the contrary, is the ruler of the kings of the earth. They may vent their fury and abuse their power in threatening you with persecution. But their power will be short-lived. They cannot win against the Christ who will come in glory and victory' (verse 7).

God is 'the Alpha and Omega' (verse 8). These are the first and last letters of the Greek alphabet. God was there before the world began. He will be there when the world as we know it is no more. He rules over all of human history.

John's vision (verses 12–20). If you tried to draw what John says about Christ here the combination of images would look bizarre. But each aspect of the vision is drawn from the Old Testament and speaks vividly of the significance of the risen Lord.

In verse 13 he is the 'man-like figure' who in Daniel 7 (passage 77) received from God a kingdom which can never be destroyed. The robe and sash, which were worn by high priests, suggest that Christ is the Great High Priest who wins for us access to God's presence. But he also has the 'hair like wool' which in Daniel 7 belongs to God himself (verse 14). By using such imagery John declares that Jesus is one with God the Father. The sword (verse 16) speaks of his power to bring judgment—not only on a godless world but on the Church itself, as we shall see.

Confronted by such holy majesty, John falls to the ground (verse 17). But he receives gentle reassurance from the one who through his resurrection holds power over death (verse 18). His followers can remain faithful in his service, confident that their ultimate future is secure in him.

This is the Christ whom John sees 'among the lampstands' (verse

12). The lampstands represent the seven churches (verses 12, 20). Each church has an 'angel', a heavenly counterpart of the church (verse 20). In saying that Christ is among the lampstands and he holds the seven stars (the angels of the churches—see verses 16, 20) in his hand, John is telling us that Christ is present with his people.

I think of that when I see an inner city church surrounded by enormous social questions, or a struggling village church. However weak it may be, however insignificant in the eyes of the world, each church is held and watched over by Christ. He knows our weakness, our difficulties and anxieties. He holds on to us. But he also asks questions about our faithfulness.

127

The church which has everything— and nothing

Chapters 2 and 3 contain a special message from the risen Christ for each of the seven churches. Each message shows intimate knowledge of the church's situation. Here is the last of the seven. Laodicea was a prosperous city. It stood at an important junction where roads from the coast of western Turkey met before continuing east to Syria and beyond.

Read Revelation 3:14–22

The character of Christ (verse 14). He is 'the Amen'—one whose witness is utterly reliable. He has all the firmness which the church lacks. As the ruler (or 'source', REB) of all creation he is Lord over all he has made, superior to all other spiritual forces in the universe.

The lukewarm church (verses 15–16). From Laodicea you could look across the valley to Hierapolis where there were hot springs with healing properties. A few miles up the valley was Colossae, famous for its cool, refreshing drinking water. Laodicea itself had to get water via an aqueduct from springs several miles away. By the time it reached the city it was warmed by the sun, and was full of mineral deposits which made it unpleasant for drinking.

The church's deeds are like the city. Just as the city has no cold water to refresh people and no hot water to heal them, the Christians are behaving in a way which serves no useful purpose. The effect of their conduct on Christ is like the effect of the city's water: it makes him sick.

The church which deceives itself (verse 17). The reason why Christ is so critical of the church is that it has taken on the character of the city in which it is placed. There were three things of which the city was especially proud.

It was a wealthy banking centre. When an earthquake devastated Laodicea in AD60, its citizens were able to rebuild it from their own resources, proudly declining financial help from Rome.

It was a centre of medical excellence, and had developed an eye ointment which was much sought after.

It was famous for its woollen products, and especially for glossy black garments made from the wool of local black sheep.

The church in this city of wealth has no spiritual riches to share. The church in this city which claims to heal the blindness of others is blind to its own poverty. The church in this city of fine clothes is naked. In proud and affluent Laodicea, the church is as self-satisfied as its pagan neighbours.

Laodicea's smugness has a remarkably modern ring. When Christians become 'poor, blind and naked' it isn't usually because someone has attacked their faith. It is because relative prosperity has as numbing effect on us as on anyone else. Without noticing, we take on the assumptions and attitudes of the surrounding society.

Churches can become so concerned with their own prosperity and success that they have no heart for the struggling inner-city church three miles away. This church at Laodicea must have known that many other churches in western Turkey were suffering. But they showed no sign of sympathizing with them. Maybe they even took their own affluence as a sign of God's favour, and suspected that if other Christians suffered it must be their own fault.

A church is naked when it fails to wear the character of Christ. Jesus' character is marked by self-giving. Churches are sometimes marked by self-preservation. Jesus reflects the character of God. Churches often reflect simply the character of the society where they are placed.

The invitation of love (verse 18–20). The very harshness of Christ's criticism is a mark of the persistent love which longs for the best and is satisfied with nothing less.

264

'Buy from me'. Christ can make the church truly rich. He can open its eyes to see its own need and renew its vision of his purpose. He can clothe it with his own outgoing love.

But only if it will repent and 'open the door'. The allusion here is probably to the city gates, recently rebuilt after the earthquake. 'Now at last,' people might say, 'we can decide who comes in and who is kept out.' Christ knocks at the church's gate. He doesn't force an entry. His coming isn't a threat, but a precious promise to those who will invite him in.

Surprisingly, after so far addressing the whole Laodicean chuch, Christ begins here to speak of 'anyone'. The invitation to open the door is addressed to each church member individually. Each one's name is on an invitation to the dinner which will mark the beginning of a new relationship with Christ.

To think about

Read verse 22. What particular message may God be speaking to me through this passage?

1 2 8
The fall of 'Babylon'

The main part of Revelation is about God's activity in history and the way in which his rule is established over the world. In the experience of his readers, the forces of evil are at work through the power of an oppressive state. But those forces will destroy themselves and give way to the eternal and perfect rule of God. In chapter 18 John's vision moves towards its climax as the collapse of Rome's power is foreseen. But he calls the city 'Babylon', which since Old Testament times had symbolized political systems which defy God.

We shall not comment in detail on this severe and vivid poetry. That would be like trying to analyse every note in a piece of music: we wouldn't hear the tune. It is best simply to read it—perhaps aloud— and sense how tragic, how poignant, how catastrophic and inevitable is the collapse of a world power which overreaches itself.

Read Revelation 18

Though we won't survey the details, we can stand back from them and notice some features which will help us appreciate what is happening here.

The Old Testament's influence. Although John never actually quotes the Old Testament, his mind is full of its language and pictures. Much of his description of the fall of 'Babylon' echoes passages in Old Testament prophets which speak of the fall of the real Babylon or of other great cities of that period. Isaiah 13, for example, prophesied the end of Babylon's empire. And we read Ezekiel's prophecy against Tyre (Ezekiel 28, passage 48)—though verses 9–20 here in fact contain many echoes of the 'lament for Tyre' in Ezekiel 27.

This repetition of themes illustrates something important about how biblical writers understand God's activity in the world. Just as there are similarities between the ways in which various political powers assert their oppressive force in the world, so there there are similarities in the fate they experience as God works out his purpose in history.

Every great act of judgment on political and military arrogance is a sign of his final judgment on human sinfulness. The fall of Rome envisaged by John was not the final example in history of God bringing empires to an end. But it serves as a dramatic example of the fate of all empires which in their greed for power defy the will of God.

The basis of Rome's evil power. John's description exposes the source of Rome's strength. It is an empire built on economic strength. The merchants and their exotic wares are paraded before us (especially in verses 11–13). But their trade isn't only in luxury goods but in human lives: 'bodies and souls of men' in verse 13 means 'slaves'. Rome's prosperity depended on the labour of human beings who were traded like merchandize and used like disposable tools. By seductive deceit and at enormous human cost it has made itself great (verses 23–24). On the surface Rome's empire is luxurious, enterprising, creative. Underneath it is morally rotten.

Our prosperity today is not built on slavery. But it is built in part on the low wages of the tea-picker and the the tin-miner, on the exploitation of the rainforests, on the pollution of the seas which leaves for future generations problems which we aren't prepared to pay for ourselves.

John doesn't mince words. To compromise with the prevailing culture, to accept the politicians' promises of ever-increasing

266

standards of living, is 'adultery' or 'fornication' (verse 3). God's people are called to stand out against the economics of oppression, to reject the prosperity which comes from the exploitation of the poor (verse 4).

Practical ways of doing this might be withdrawing my account from a bank which is known to make big profits from third world debt. It might mean buying tea and coffee from trading organizations (such as Tearcraft or Traidcraft) which have been set up to give the producer a fair deal. It might mean not buying hardwoods which have come from a rainforest where trees are being felled quicker than new ones are growing. Such actions may seem small and insignificant, like trying to dig the Channel Tunnel with a pen-knife. But they are practical, personal things which we *can do*.

As you read John's words you can sense a genuine appreciation of the God-given creativity which has brought these cultural riches to Rome. But you see also the human cost—the oppression of the many so that the few may enjoy comparative luxury. The God of justice cannot leave such injustice untouched. Political and economic empires rise, but they also fall. And the individuals who profit from them have to answer to God for their deeds.

129

New heavens and a new earth   *Revelation 21*

The message of judgment on oppressive empires (chapter 18) and on individuals (which comes in 20:11–15) is not God's final word. The story of Revelation has been the story of conflict between heaven—where God's will is done—and an earth where God's will is resisted by a hostile world and imperfectly done in the Church.

But the day is coming when that conflict will end. Heaven and earth will be at one, because God will renew his creation. His people will enjoy eternal life and he will dwell among them for ever. In a number of pictures John describes what God's new world will be like.

Nothing more to fear. The Jews never felt at home on the sea. They saw it as a threat, a symbol of chaos and danger. So the promise of 'no longer any sea' (verse 1) is a promise that God will remove all that threatens our well-being.

God is in the midst of humankind. The picture of a new heaven and new earth (verse 1) quickly gives way to the picture of the new Jerusalem (verse 2). The city which was a symbol of God's presence in Israel becomes a way of describing God's new creation, for he is now among his people.

The Old Testament promised that God would live among humankind, and they would be his people and he would be their God (Ezekiel 37:27, passage 49). The significance of Jesus is that he was 'Immanuel, which means "God with us"' (Matthew 1:23). Now that promise is fully and permanently made real.

No more pain, no more death. When God's kingdom comes, everything which has caused pain and sadness will be gone for ever. It is a new world, fitted for God's people to live for ever in his presence (verse 4–5).

Life from God. The life of God's people will be sustained by God himself (verse 6).

The sense of *space* and *safety* in the new Jerusalem is in complete contrast with the constant danger and uncertainty to which John's contemporaries were exposed. Shining with splendour, it is a huge city with protective walls and gates (verses 10–21). Its shape (verse 16) is a perfect cube. That of course is impossible for a real city. But it was the shape of the 'most holy place', the central shrine of the temple. Once again, John's imagery underlines that the dwelling of God is with men and women.

No temple, no sun, no moon, no night (verses 22–25). Because God is fully present with his people there is no need of a temple to represent his presence to them. Because he is the source of all light, there is no need of created lights. There is no darkness to bring fear and uncertainty.

The glory and honour of the nations. It is easy to get the impression from John's book that earthly rulers are always destined to suppress the truth and oppress God's people. But we find him offering a vision of the nations coming to God's city in worship and bringing their splendour into it (verses 24, 26). Despite the warnings in chapter 18 about culture built on human exploitation, John here sees all that truly enriches human experience as being carried over into God's coming kingdom.

Whenever we are tempted to dismiss the wealth of human culture and to think of the whole world as hopelessly embroiled in evil, we need this reminder that God has other plans.

The inhabitants of the new Jerusalem will see God face to face and will share his character ('bear his name', 22:4). We cannot say how, but John's vision encourages us to believe that the perfection of God's future kingdom involves the perfection of all that truly enriches human life and expresses the generous creativity of God.

If that is so, it means that longing for God's kingdom to come isn't simply a matter of waiting for God to act. It means that every act of real goodness, every work of art which reflects God's own creative purpose, contributes to the building of God's eternal city.

Nothing impure. A wholly positive vision of the future excludes the negative. There is no room in God's kingdom for all that is impure, all that is destructive of human well-being and hostile to God (21:8, 27). There is a division, ultimately, between 'those whose names are written in the Lamb's book of life' and those who aren't.

John doesn't mean that there can be no forgiveness for anyone who has ever committed the kind of sins mentioned in 21:8. He knows too well the life-giving power of the crucified and risen Christ. But he does mean that those who commit such sins persistently and without repentance shut themselves out from God's holy presence.

John's vision is a vision of a city. The city for him doesn't evoke thoughts of crime and deprivation as it does for so many people today. It speaks of life and activity and above all of community. Christian hope is never hope merely for the individual. It is always hope for relationship with God and with one another.

130

The goal of all things

Revelation 22:7–21

The final section of the book draws together some key themes.

The importance of the message. John is reminded by his heavenly messenger of the vital nature of the vision which has been revealed to him (verses 6, 18–19). Its words are to be 'kept' or 'taken to heart' (verse 7). This means not only that the message is to be preserved but that it is to be put into practice.

Biblical prophecy is never given to satisfy curiosity about the future. It is given to create a new perspective on life, to challenge people to live in the light of God's promises and warnings. Having read the message to Laodicea and the warning of the fall of 'Babylon' (passages 127 and 128), we are called to seek Christ's remedy for blindness, poverty and nakedness, and to stand out against the seductions of an affluent society. If we read other parts of the book we would find much else to challenge and guide our Christian living in a secular atmosphere.

John's vision is that God, not secular values, will have the last word on the human story. It is a vision of a new world in which everything will be set right, and the God revealed to us in Jesus will be the focus of true love and worship. Seriously to live in the light of such promises is truly hopeful, truly revolutionary.

The coming of Christ. Three times the risen Christ says, 'I am coming soon' (verses 7, 12, 20). This, as we saw when we looked at the message of Jesus (passage 92), is not the 'soon' of clock-time. It indicates not the timetable but the certainty of his coming.

We believe that Christ *came*, to live and die and be raised from death, to bring us to God. We believe that he *comes* to us in our present experience, to comfort and to challenge. He comes in the ups and downs of history, revealing the justice and the saving power of God.

We believe he *will come* finally, to bring history to an end and to set up his eternal kingdom of justice and love. The promise of that kingdom draws from us the echoing desire for his coming (verses 17, 20). We long for it, not because we want the world or our own earthly lives to come to an end, but because we long for a world ruled by God's love and justice.

From this viewpoint the last book of the Bible is the book which makes sense of all the rest. We have seen how, from Abraham's time onwards, the story of Israel and of Jesus' followers has been a story of people moving forward towards a better world. Now, with clearer vision, we see how Christ's final coming marks the goal of that story.

The nature of Christ. In Revelation 1:8 God the Father was 'Alpha and Omega', the one on whom the universe depends from start to finish. In 22:13 the same title is given to Jesus. Jesus is nothing less than God—God made known in human flesh.

He is also 'the Root and Offspring of David'—the Messiah who brings the story of God's work among men and women to its goal (verse 16). And he is 'the bright Morning Star'. This also was a title which Jews sometimes used for the Messiah.

But for John's readers there was another meaning too. The morning star was the planet Venus. And the goddess Venus was a symbol of authority for the Roman emperors, who claimed to trace their ancestry to her. In AD95—probably very close to the time when Revelation was written—a Roman poet anxious to flatter the current emperor compared him to the morning star. So to call Christ 'the Morning Star' is to say that he, not the emperor, is the one who really holds authority over the nations. There is a ruler in Rome—and others, perhaps, in London and Moscow, Beijing and Washington—who thinks he rules the world. But his position is merely temporary.

Invitation and demand. To those who stick close to Christ there are promises in abundance (verses 14, 17, 21). But to those who resist him the time is fast approaching when it will be too late to change (verses 11, 15). So the book's mingling of reassurance and challenge is maintained to the end.

Sometimes Christ confronts us with insistent urgency, perhaps through a preacher or through a situation crying out for action. Sometimes he creeps up on us like a lover surprising his beloved, warming our hearts with his presence. However he comes, the question is the same: what will we do with the invitation and the demand which he holds out to us? Do we have 'ears to hear' what he is saying to us today?

A prayer

Lord, you are the Alpha and the Omega, the Beginning and the End.
You are the Ruler of the nations.
When will your kingdom come?
When will you dwell with us?
When will you wipe away every tear?
When will all people walk by your light?

Amen. Come, Lord Jesus.

Bible Reference Index

Time Charts
and Maps

▌ Old Testament time chart

The following chart gives approximate dates of the main events referred to in the book

BC

1900	Abraham
1700	Joseph
1270	Exodus from Egypt
1230	Settlement in Canaan under Joshua
1220–1050	Period of the judges
1050–1010	Saul
1010–970	David
970–930	Solomon
930–722	The land divided into two kingdoms, Judah and Israel
930–913	Rehoboam king of Judah
930–909	Jeroboam I king of Israel
873–853	Ahab king of Israel
	Elijah prophet in Israel
850–800	Elisha prophet in Israel
760	Amos prophet in Israel
750–722	Hosea prophet in Israel
740–700	Isaiah prophet in Judah
722	Samaria falls to Assyrians; end of the kingdom of Israel
639–609	Josiah king of Judah
621–580	Jeremiah prophet in Judah and Egypt
605–562	Nebuchadnezzar II ruler of Babylon
587	Fall of Jerusalem; thousands of Jews exiled to Babylon
593–570	Ezekiel prophet in Babylon
539	Cyrus of Persia conquers Babylon; Jews allowed to return to Judah
539–331	Palestine under Persian rule
520	Zechariah prophet in Judah
516	The temple rebuilt
458	Ezra returns to Jerusalem
445	Nehemiah returns to Jerusalem
331	Alexander the Great defeats the Persians; Palestine comes under Greek rule
167	Maccabean revolt

▌New Testament time chart

The following chart gives approximate dates of the main events referred to in the book

BC

63	Palestine comes under Roman influence
37–4	Herod the Great king of Judea
6	Birth of Jesus

AD

27–30	Public ministry of Jesus
30	The beginnings of the church
34	Paul's conversion
46–47	Paul's missionary journey to Cyprus and beyond
49	The Council at Jerusalem
50–52	Paul at Philippi, Thessalonica, Athens, Corinth
50	Paul writes 1 Thessalonians
54	Paul writes 1 Corinthians
55	Paul writes Romans
59	Paul arrested in Jerusalem, imprisoned in Caesarea
62–64	Paul in Rome; writes Ephesians, Philippians?
63	Peter writes 1 Peter
66–70	Jewish revolt, Jerusalem destroyed by the Romans
80	Luke writes his Gospel and Acts?
95	John writes the Revelation?

Roman emperors in the New Testament period

27BC–AD14	Augustus
AD14–37	Tiberius
37–41	Gaius Caligula
41–54	Claudius
54–68	Nero
68–69	Galba, Otho, Vitellius
69–79	Vespasian
79–81	Titus
81–96	Domitian

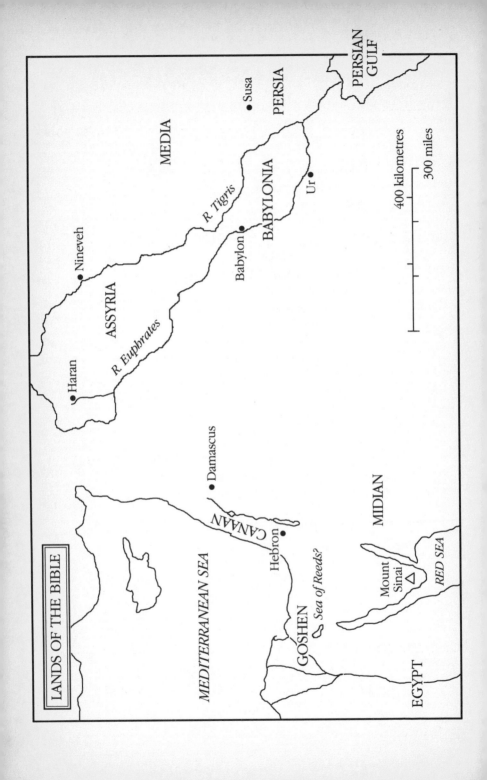

LANDS OF THE BIBLE

MEDITERRANEAN SEA

CANAAN

Damascus

Hebron

GOSHEN

Sea of Reeds?

EGYPT

MIDIAN

Mount Sinai

RED SEA

Haran

ASSYRIA

R Euphrates

R Tigris

Nineveh

MEDIA

Babylon

BABYLONIA

Ur

Susa

PERSIA

PERSIAN GULF

400 kilometres

300 miles

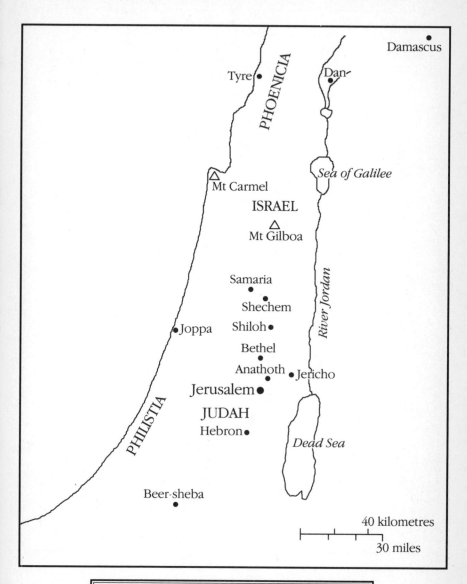

PALESTINE IN OLD TESTAMENT TIMES

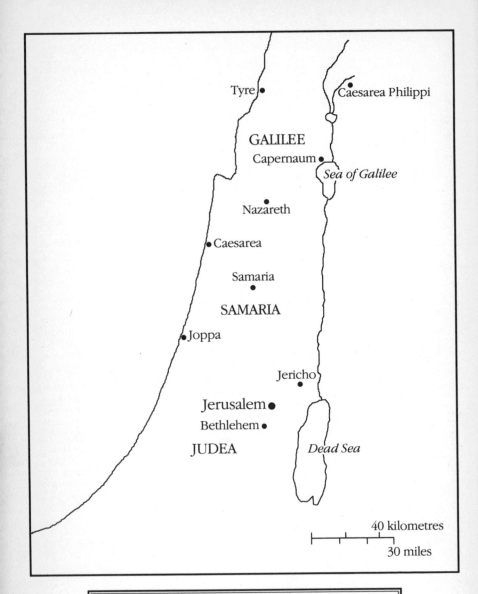

Tyre •

• Caesarea Philippi

GALILEE

Capernaum •

Sea of Galilee

Nazareth •

• Caesarea

Samaria
•

SAMARIA

• Joppa

Jericho)

Jerusalem •

Bethlehem •

JUDEA

Dead Sea

40 kilometres

30 miles

PALESTINE IN NEW TESTAMENT TIMES

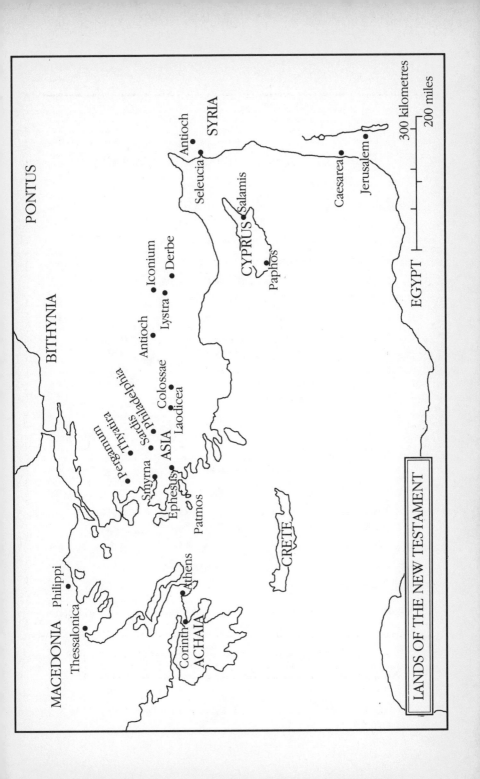

PONTUS

BITHYNIA

MACEDONIA Philippi

Thessalonica

Pergamum

Thyatira

Smyrna Sardis Philadelphia

Ephesus

ASIA

Patmos

Antioch

Colossae

Laodicea

Iconium

Lystra

Derbe

Athens

Corinth

ACHAIA

CRETE

CYPRUS Salamis

Paphos

Antioch

SYRIA

Seleucia

Caesarea

Jerusalem

EGYPT

300 kilometres

200 miles

LANDS OF THE NEW TESTAMENT

Bible reading notes from BRF

BRF publishes two regular series of Bible reading notes—
New Daylight and *Guidelines*. These are published three
times a year (in January, May and September).

New Daylight provides a pattern for daily Bible reading.
Each day's reading contains a Bible passage (printed out
in full, from the version chosen by the contributor), along
with a brief commentary and explanation, and a suggestion for prayer, meditation or reflection. The sections of
commentary often draw on and reflect the experiences of
the contributors themselves and thus offer contemporary
and personal insights into the readings. Sunday readings
focus on the themes of prayer and Holy Communion.

Guidelines contains running commentary, with introduc-
tions and background information, arranged in weekly
units. Each week's material is usually broken up into at
least six sections. Readers can take as much or as little at a
time as they wish. The whole 'week' can be used at a
sitting, or split up into convenient parts: this flexible
arrangement allows for one section to be used each
weekday. A Bible will be needed. The last section of each
week is usually called 'Guidelines' and has points for
thought, meditation and prayer. A short list of books, to
help with further reading, appears at the end of some
contributions.

Both *New Daylight* and *Guidelines* may be obtained from
your local Christian bookshop or by subscription direct
from BRF.

For more information about the notes and the full range
of BRF publications, write to: BRF, Peter's Way, Sandy
Lane West, OXFORD, OX4 5HG (Tel: 01865 748227)